Shall We Wake the President?

SHALL WE WAKE THE PRESIDENT?

Two Centuries of Disaster Management
from the Oval Office

TEVI TROY

Guilford, Connecticut

An imprint of The Rowman & Littlefield Publishing Group, Inc.
4501 Forbes Blvd., Ste. 200
Lanham, MD 20706
www.rowman.com

Distributed by NATIONAL BOOK NETWORK

British Library Cataloguing in Publication Information Available
Library of Congress Cataloging-in-Publication Data Available

ISBN 978-1-4930-4873-1 (paperback)
ISBN 978-1-4930-2465-0 (e-book)

♾™ The paper used in this publication meets the minimum requirements of American National Standard for Information Sciences—Permanence of Paper for Printed Library Materials, ANSI/NISO Z39.48-1992.

A friend loves at all times, and a brother is born for adversity.
—PROVERBS 17:17

*To my brothers, Dan and Gil Troy, role models of excellence,
each of whom "is important in his own right."*

CONTENTS

Foreword

Presidents and Disasters
by the Honorable Joseph Lieberman, former US Senator for Connecticut

AMERICA CANNOT CHOOSE THE DISASTERS THAT CONFRONT US, BUT WE can prepare for them. That was a critical lesson of the Blue Ribbon Study Panel on Biodefense, which I had the privilege of co-chairing with former Department of Homeland Security secretary Tom Ridge. The panel found that America does face a range of grave threats on the biodefense front—and, unfortunately, we are unprepared for many of them.

Our report said, "The United States is underprepared for biological threats. Nation states and unaffiliated terrorists (via biological terrorism) and nature itself (via emerging and reemerging infectious diseases) threaten us. While biological events may be inevitable, their level of impact on our country is not."

The panel identified a particular weakness where the United States is falling short in the effort to prepare for biological attacks and emerging and reemerging infectious diseases. That weakness is the lack of strong centralized leadership at the highest level of government.

To that end, our panel recommended steps that the president could take to shore up our biodefense capabilities. "The insufficiency of our fragmented biodefense activities persists because biodefense lacks focused leadership. Capable individuals oversee elements at the department and agency levels, but no steward guides them collectively," our report concluded. We need strong presidential leadership to get us where we need to go on the preparedness front.

When disaster strikes, citizens look to the president. This means that regardless of the type of disaster, the president needs to be prepared. The need for presidential leadership in preparing for and responding to disasters is no strange topic to my good friend Dr. Tevi Troy, an *ex officio* member of the panel and trusted colleague in our preparedness endeavor. As a former deputy secretary of the Department of Health and Human Services (HHS), Tevi understands the nature of the threats we face in the areas of bioterror and infectious diseases. While at HHS, Tevi worked on preparing the US government's plan for avian flu, a plan that the Obama administration later put to good use in the Swine flu outbreak of 2009.

As a presidential historian and former White House aide, Tevi also understands that to address potential threats most effectively will require leadership in Washington that not only recognizes the magnitude of various biohazards but also the limits of presidential power and the need for coordination by federal, state, and local governments.

This book—*Shall We Wake the President?*—will help future US presidents as well as policymakers of all levels prepare for the disasters that will inevitably come. It goes beyond bioterror attacks and infectious disease outbreaks. Tevi looks at a wide range of potential threats that a president may face. He talks about how state and local governments can do their part. And he even gives practical advice for how individuals can—and should—prepare for the disasters that may strike our nation.

Fifteen years after the terror attacks of 9/11, it is clear that our nation has done much to make ourselves better defended and better prepared. But it is also clear that we still have more work to do. Reading this book will give insights from history, illuminate the role of past presidents in meeting challenges, and point us all in the direction to make more progress together in securing our homeland.

I urge our presidential candidates, one of whom will be our next president, to read this book, and I urge you to read it as well.

Joseph I. Lieberman
US Senator, 1989–2013
Co-Chair, Blue Ribbon Study Panel on Biodefense

INTRODUCTION

I SPENT MOST OF THE FIRST DECADE OF THE TWENTY-FIRST CENTURY working in the executive branch of the US government. My experiences there were framed and shaped by the challenge of effectively dealing with disasters. Just eight months before the attacks on 9/11, I began working at the Department of Labor, and gained enough perspective to appreciate how a catastrophe can expose and reshape government, culture, and history. From that fateful day on, my time at the Department of Labor was focused on response—from how to get federal resources to Ground Zero to the longer-term effort of emergency preparedness and federal reorganization. The 9/11 attacks brought home the important lesson that every branch of the federal government and every level of government has a role to play in disaster recovery efforts, no matter how seemingly remote its responsibilities.

Within six months of the 9/11 attacks, President George W. Bush initiated a White House staff shake-up to cope with the post-9/11 realities. This reorganization led to my first position at the White House, on the Domestic Policy Council. While serving at the DPC, I saw and worked with colleagues to bring together agencies and resources to anticipate post-9/11 needs. For example, Project Bioshield was designed to prepare for the possibility of biological warfare. And then there was the merging of the bulk of US security programs into the newly formed Department of Homeland Security (DHS).

After President Bush was reelected—in a campaign shaped by his strong 9/11 response—I was promoted to a more senior position at the DPC. While I was there, President Bush reported to his senior advisers that he had read John Barry's *The Great Influenza*, about the Spanish Flu that killed tens of millions of people in the period between 1918 and

1920. The book had a powerful impact on him, and he wanted the United States to develop a robust plan for flu pandemic prevention and response. I spent much of my time in that job working with the Departments of Health and Human Services (HHS) and Homeland Security to develop such a plan for dealing with a possible viral outbreak.

Within six months of my starting this new White House position, though, another disaster struck: Hurricane Katrina. This disaster, and the response of government at all levels, would shape Bush's second term, just as 9/11 shaped his first term. Katrina exposed the importance of communication, coordination, and accountability. As America would soon learn, Katrina was not the end of the challenges faced by Bush in his second term—as the subprime financial crises of 2007 and 2008 soon led to the Great Recession, the most severe banking crisis and economic dislocation since the Great Depression.

Even after I left government service, the prospect of additional disasters continued to resonate. Within months of the Obama administration taking office, and before any of its senior HHS appointees were even confirmed by the Senate, a swine flu, or H1N1, outbreak emerged in Mexico and threatened to spread to the United States. The death toll from this outbreak was minor, in part because of the deployment of the flu plan developed by the Bush administration in its second term, a plan that I had worked on at the White House and helped implement while serving as deputy secretary of HHS. The swine flu was only the beginning of the challenges that President Obama would face. In the years that followed, the Obama administration saw shipping threatened by Somali pirates, stood helpless as a massive oil spill in the Gulf of Mexico spewed forth billions of gallons of oil, and tried to cope with a new terrorist threat that arose in the form of ISIS. They sought solutions to calm public concern as a large-scale Ebola outbreak in West Africa reached American soil. And they were forced to monitor civil unrest and rioting following controversial deaths involving the police and African Americans in places like Ferguson, Missouri, and Baltimore, Maryland. This is only a partial list of a twenty-first century already filled with disaster and tragedy. I was not alone in sensing that something seemed to be amiss in this new millennium. As Nate Silver, one of America's most prominent prognosticators, observed in his book *The Signal and the Noise*, "the first twelve years of the new millennium have been rough, with one unpredicted disaster after another."[1]

Many of these incidents—9/11, Katrina, the economic collapse, a widespread flu outbreak—fit in the category of disasters that presidents must face. A disaster is worse than a plane crash or a forest fire. To qualify as a true disaster, an incident must have scale and ripple effects. A car crash, even one that kills dozens of people, is not a national disaster. A crash involving a truck containing a virulent and deadly pathogen that escapes into the atmosphere is. To qualify as a disaster, an incident must have an impact beyond one local area and have at least the potential to cause some kind of systemic breakdown.

As bad as the first decade and a half of the twenty-first century have been, there are troubling indications that things are on track to be even worse in the years ahead. The *Wall Street Journal*'s "Numbers Guy," Carl Bialik, wrote, referring to events such as Hurricane Sandy and the 2012 "derecho" thunderstorm, among others, that "the current decade is on pace to outrank the prior three in cost from inflation-adjusted climate catastrophes costing at least $1 billion in 2013 dollars."[2] What's worse, emergencies related to severe weather events are just one of the many types of crises we could face.

For a variety of reasons, America has become a powerful magnet for a disproportionate share of these kinds of incidents. Dr. Erwann Michel-Kerjan, managing director of the Wharton Risk Management and Decision Processes Center, looked at the twenty biggest disasters since 1987 and found that half took place in the years since 2001, and nine of them took place in the United States.[3] He also found a significant spike in the number of presidential disaster declarations over time and across decades.

It is not fully clear why these problems appear to be worse recently, or why they are more likely to happen here, but there are a number of possibilities. The world is more complex and interwoven than ever before. We are more dependent on technologies for our daily living than ever before, and system failures can have disastrous consequences. This is particularly so in the technology-dependent and -driven United States. Technology, for all of its beneficences, also provides humanity with increasingly powerful ways to wreak destruction, including nuclear explosions, bioterror attacks, and cyberattacks. As a nation that has benefited disproportionately from technology, we are also more vulnerable to threats to those technologies. In addition, instantaneous and constant communications technologies send us word of disasters taking place anywhere in the world far more rapidly, giving disasters an immediacy to plugged-in Americans that was absent in the past.

With disasters more imminent, immense, and intense, we must be ready to respond, as a nation and as individuals. In doing so, the American people look to the person in charge of the federal government, the US president, to lead the way. Localized accidents can and should be handled by state and local officials, but large-scale disasters merit a federal and even a presidential response. Yet presidents, for all the expectations foisted upon them, are often inexperienced and too often unprepared. As the journalists Mark Halperin and John Heilemann noted in their book *Double Down*, President Obama and his team were taken aback by the "staggering" number of crises that a president needed to deal with, including swine flu, BP's Macondo oil spill, and the Somali pirates who attacked an American ship. Many of these did not quite reach disaster status, but Obama's reaction to the constant stream of crises was unnerving: "Who thought we were going to have to deal with pirates?"[4]

In addition to the proliferation of disasters, there is also the issue of the politicization of disasters. The presidency is an inherently political job, and presidential actions are increasingly viewed through a partisan lens. This is unfortunate. Crisis management and response should be nonpartisan. The insertion of partisanship in disaster response—or just the perception of such—could lead to its own deleterious consequences for democracy, with liberals ignoring the instructions of a Republican administration or conservatives rejecting the advice of Democratic officials.

Furthermore, it is not just the people who take partisan perspectives in disasters, but the presidents as well. Strikingly, even FEMA declarations are sensitive to the political cycle, suggesting a political element to the response to disasters. Bill Clinton issued fifty-eight FEMA declarations in 1993, his first year in office, close to the all-time previous high at the time. In 1996, the year he ran for reelection, he issued 158 declarations, breaking the previous record by almost 100.[5]

Unexpected and difficult as facing crises may be, it is part of the job of our commander-in-chief. For the president, and for the rest of us, to deal with potential problems of the future, including man-made as well as natural disasters, we need to do four key things:

First, we must do all we can to prevent the disasters of the future from taking place. From putting in place tough anti-terror policies and upholding border security to monitoring possible disease outbreaks and restoring fiscal sanity, the next president is going to have his or her hands full grappling with a host of possible and yet preventable problems. Presidents must work hard at the ultimately thankless but necessary mission of avoiding potential yet preventable problems.

Second, the president must take positive steps to ensure that the federal government is ready in case some kind of disaster does take place. This means that the president needs to hold the government accountable for maintaining a robust toolkit of available countermeasures to deal with a variety of possible emergencies. Having a toolkit is not enough, though. The president should also oversee the development of federal government plans to use those tools and have his team practice those plans so that they can be deployed effectively.

Third, the president must display strong leadership in the face of a crisis. He or she must present accurate and actionable information to the American people, and do so in such a way that does not induce panic in the populace, but does produce cooperative, constructive behavior, leveraging the power and initiative of a free people to work together. During a crisis the American people need clear information based on the best intelligence and data at the time, presented by officials with a reputation for integrity who are in command of the government and of their emotions. This will empower the American people to fulfill their own responsibilities and respond to the directives and suggestions of government officials. It is only then that government officials can fully leverage the resources of every level of government, the power of every institution, and the initiative of free citizens.

Fourth, the president must learn from previous responses, both his own and those of his predecessors, about how to handle the disasters of the future. The lessons that presidents learn should not be strictly in the realm of how to respond. Presidential wisdom must include determining whether to do so. The federal government cannot prevent every disaster, nor can it solve every problem; presidents need to decide when and whether the federal government should intervene, and when it should not. In fact, the more that the federal government takes on, the less capable it appears to be at handling its core functions.

All of these needs fall on the president, and on the enormous government over which he presides. The US government is a mammoth four-million-person operation, counting the military but not including the countless government contractors. Most of these individuals do not participate in crisis response (we are still trying to figure out what it is many of them do), but the president has both many people and many tools at his disposal. As individual Americans, we hope that the president makes wise decisions. At the same time, we share considerable responsibility for ourselves and our families. As we have seen too many times in the recent past, individuals cannot—and should not—count solely on their government in times of crisis. Sobering and yet inspiring examples of citizens taking charge in response to disaster, or to government failure in the wake of disaster, include Korean shopkeepers during the LA riots, civil patrol boats evacuating Manhattan on 9/11, Todd Beamer's insurrection on Flight 93 that same day, the passengers who quickly responded to restrain the shoe bomber in December of 2001, and the compassionate citizens who stopped arterial bleeds and worked to save the wounded at the Boston Marathon bombing of 2013. These are just a few front-page examples. They don't include the thousands of stories of neighbors banding together to help one another after tornados, hurricanes, earthquakes, and blizzards.

These tales remind us of America's great republican asset of "the local." Long ago, Edmund Burke praised the "little platoon," and Alexis de Tocqueville spoke of the American propensity for "voluntary associations." Americans can and should return to these visions, both in our daily lives but especially in coping with disasters.

A little more than fifty years ago, John Kennedy said in his inaugural address, "Ask not what your country can do for you, ask what you can do for your country." Kennedy's message was never fully absorbed by the people, as what we have seen throughout the twentieth century has been a rising set of expectations of what the federal government can do for individuals, on a regular basis and especially in times of disaster. Unfortunately, the modern American response to disaster has included the expected government handout—a ritualized response that complicates the federal role and distracts government officials from their primary mission of prevention and, failing that, immediate recovery and response.[6] Unfortunately, these expectations exist regardless of one's philosophy or political ideology. As Obama aide David Axelrod observed, "It is a fact of modern political life that when such disasters strike, even those Americans who say they believe in smaller government, or no government at all, quickly break glass and call the government, demanding relief."[7]

Despite these rising and often unrealistic expectations on government, though, in times of crisis, there is often little our country can do for us, and not much we can do for our country. This book will help answer the question of what we can do for ourselves. Smart policies and wise presidential leadership can help us avoid some, but not all, crises of the future. If presidents follow the advice laid out in these pages, the federal government will be more prepared and more capable in dealing with disaster. If, however, our presidents fail us, you can and must prepare yourself and your family in case disaster does strike.

The chapters of this book depict a variety of disasters—both natural and man-made—that we have faced in the past. The disasters our presidents have addressed in the past—including terror attacks, economic collapse, bioterror attacks, and hurricanes—provide lessons for how our leaders can address them in the future. This exercise could have life-saving potential, even at the individual level. While focusing on presidential successes and failures in the past, and dos and don'ts in the future, all of us can benefit by thinking about how the government responds to disaster.

This effort at the individual level begins with recognizing that the government is not always the best first responder. Therefore, you need to think about how you can protect yourself and your family. You may never have the opportunity to direct disaster management at the federal, state, or local level—although this book will help advise those who do— but reading this book will leave you far more aware of what you can do should disaster strike and the government lets you down.

Section One:
Acts of God

CHAPTER ONE

The Pandemic Threat

THE GREAT, OR SPANISH, INFLUENZA OF 1918–19 KILLED APPROXI-
mately fifty million people worldwide. Although there are no exact
numbers, it is estimated that as many as 675,000 Americans died as well.
There is no way around the fact that this extraordinary loss of life was
tragic. But only through foresight and preparation can we avoid, or at
least minimize, the impact of this kind of wave of death and destruction
in the future. Understanding and preparing for such a challenge must
begin with learning the lessons of the past, and looking at how weak
presidential leadership at the time cost lives.

The Spanish Flu devastated both Americans and the world. The virus
infected more than a quarter of the US population. The enormous number of casualties reduced the national average for life expectancy by an
entire decade. It struck and killed rapidly. In contrast to most flu viruses,
it was particularly deadly among young adults. The disease was so pervasive it even inspired a little ditty about the disease that schoolchildren
would sing:

> I had a little bird,
> Its name was Enza.
> I opened the window,
> And in-flu-enza.[1]

The Great Influenza occurred while Americans were fighting what
they called the Great War—later labeled World War I. Our twenty-eighth

president, Woodrow Wilson, had committed America to total war. The nation was fully mobilized in pursuit of this aim.[2] Such a wholehearted commitment unleashed unintended consequences, as the interpersonal contact on military bases and troop movements helped spread the flu virus. According to author John Barry, the outbreak likely began in late February 1918 in Haskell County, Kansas, when someone brought the virus to Kansas's Camp Funston. Within three weeks, 1,100 troops were hospitalized with the disease.[3] The tight quarters in army camps and troop transports would spread the disease throughout the country and across the ocean. Consequently, the disease was particularly deadly to members of the military: Approximately 43,000 US servicemen fell from the disease. Of the American soldiers who died in Europe, half died from the flu.[4]

Eventually, Dr. Cary Grayson, Wilson's own doctor, as well as a US Navy admiral, brought the issue to the president's attention. In October 1918—a month in which the disease killed 200,000 people—Wilson met with General Peyton March, the army's chief of staff, to discuss the matter. Wilson raised the possibility of stopping the transports across the Atlantic while the disease raged, but March resisted. March argued that the army was examining and culling sick soldiers before sending the transports, and that the war effort required the transports to continue. In sum, the general argued, "The shipment of troops should not be stopped for any cause." He may have been right regarding military need, but his approach showed little concern for the victims of the disease. General March observed to Wilson, somewhat callously, that each soldier who died in transit "has just as surely played his part as his comrade who died in France."[5]

Wilson quickly caved in to March. He nodded, then looked out the window and asked, "General, I wonder if you have heard this limerick?

I had a little bird
And its name was Enza . . ."[6]

In agreeing to continue the transports, Wilson unnecessarily sentenced a great many Americans to death. According to author Pete Davies, Wilson's decision sentenced US troops to what he called a "viral lottery," in which "six in every 100 men who fell ill aboard the ship would die."[7]

Perhaps the saddest part of the story is that the war was effectively over at the time. Wilson allowed the war effort to trump public health just two months before the war would end, giving in to March's demand that "the shipment of troops should not be stopped for any cause." By this point the Kaiser no longer ran Germany, and Germany's allies were rapidly leaving the field of war. Yet, in Barry's judgment, "Wilson did nothing about influenza other than express concerns about shipping troops to Europe." Besides this one meeting with March, Wilson does not appear to have said anything else about the disease, publicly or privately, and he did not try to mobilize the nonmilitary components of the US government to alleviate its impact on the civilian population.[8]

This incident is far from the only one in history in which military bullheadedness likely contributed to the spread of a deadly disease. Over two thousand years earlier, during the Peloponnesian War (431–404 BCE), Athens was devastated by a series of plagues that may have killed more than one-third of its population. The spread of the mysterious plague—it may have been typhus, although no one is sure—was exacerbated in part by Pericles's strategy of abandoning the countryside and consolidating those under Athens's protection inside the crowded city. In addition to a large number of deaths, the plague also contributed to a breakdown in the social order. Thucydides, the great historian of the war, lamented the "lawless extravagance which owed its origin to the plague."[9]

Wilson fell short in other ways as well. He had been reelected, in part, because of his promise to keep the nation out of the war. In his second term, once the war began, it became his top priority. In his attempt to sell a reluctant public on the war, Wilson created an enormous propaganda machine to promote the conflict and to root out sedition. The Sedition Act of 1918, which forbade "disloyal, profane, scurrilous, or abusive language about the form of government of the United States," was indicative of the rise of the coercive power of the federal government during the Wilson administration.[10]

The Sedition Act also established an unspoken contempt for the needs of the individual within the context of the conflict. This disregard extended from individual liberty to individual lives.[11] As John C. Wise wrote in *Military Surgeon*—the army publication for army doctors—in 1918, when it comes to winning the war, "the consideration of human life also becomes quite secondary." The same journal editorialized, also in the summer of 1918, that "every single activity of this country is directed toward one single object, the winning of the war; nothing else counts now."[12] As Wilson biographer A. Scott Berg pointed out, the government's departure from constitutional protections was not accidental. Berg further noted that no president "had ever suppressed free speech to so great an extent in order to realize his principles."[13]

A second consequence of the propaganda mentality was that it kept the government from providing citizens with information about the scope and developments of the influenza outbreak. The government dismissed the illness as some type of ordinary "grippe." The false reassurance was eventually exposed and contributed to a collapse of trust in the government. Barry has a stark assessment regarding the government officials at all levels who failed to level with the people: "They lost trust because they lied." In telling those lies, he argued, "at least some people must have exposed themselves to the virus in ways they would not have otherwise, at least some of those people must've died who would otherwise have lived."[14]

This betrayal of the government's first responsibility—the self-defense of its citizenry—is an object lesson in setting and keeping the right priorities whatever your leadership position. For presidents it is especially critical, because even if the government wants to address an urgent public problem, mistrust by the citizenry can make it harder for society to respond effectively and for the government to provide guidance or even assistance.

With the surrender of Germany, President Wilson left the country to attend the Versailles negotiations, which would shape the postwar world. These negotiations began with great promise but ended up imposing extraordinary, even impossible, burdens on Germany, which many historians blame for helping initiate World War II. Indeed, even at the time, John Maynard Keynes, who had been present at the negotiations, famously warned that as a result of the Versailles Treaty, "Germany has in effect engaged herself to hand over to the Allies the whole of her surplus production in perpetuity." He further noted that there could be dire consequences to the treaty's shortsightedness: "Who can say how much is endurable, or in what direction men will seek at last to escape from their misfortunes?"[15]

Ironically, while in Europe, Wilson himself may have become one of the victims of his own inattentiveness to the flu threat. While he was on his overseas mission—Wilson made history as the first president to cross the Atlantic as president—he became terribly ill. Historians differ about the cause of his illness, although the consensus is that he was significantly impaired by whatever struck him. Although historians like H. W. Brands and John Milton Cooper believe the illness was a stroke,[16] John Barry and Alfred Crosby insist it was the Spanish Flu. As Barry put it, "There was no stroke. There was only influenza."[17] A. Scott Berg provides a more measured judgment, but one that helps support Barry and Crosby when he wrote, "Whatever the case, in April 1919, at a moment of physical and nervous exhaustion, Woodrow Wilson was struck by a viral infection that had neurological ramifications."[18]

A physically impaired Wilson at Versailles agreed to things that a pre-illness Wilson had decried, and that a healthy Wilson would have almost certainly rejected. The punitive reparations imposed on Germany created a bitter nation that was later ripe for takeover by Adolf Hitler and the totalitarian Nazi state. It is impossible to say if this would have happened regardless of the Versailles Treaty, or regardless of Wilson's impairment. However, one thing is certain: Hitler's rise did lead directly to World War II, a conflict that took an additional sixty million lives. If you add the fifty million lives lost to the flu pandemic to the lives lost as a result of World War II, we are looking at truly civilization-altering numbers. One can always take these things too far, but if you believe that World War II was caused in part by the failures of the Versailles Treaty, which may in turn have been caused in part by Wilson falling victim to the Great Influenza at Versailles, then that disease's death toll would now exceed one hundred million lives.

FLU IN THE MODERN ERA

America was not ready for a flu outbreak in 1918. The flu exposed this lack of readiness at both the governmental and the individual level. But there is one major difference between the situations we face today and the flu of 1918: We were far less knowledgeable about viruses in 1918 than we are today. Since 1918 we have learned a great deal about what causes viruses, how they spread, and how to stop them. Yet despite the great advances in knowledge about flu since 1918, there is still much that we do not know, which underscores the potential for a new and deadly outbreak.

The specter of the 1918 flu continues to inform much of our thinking on pandemic preparedness. For years public health officials have warned that the world is overdue for an outbreak of a new global flu infection. Pandemics are cyclical, the argument goes, and over the last dozen decades, the world experienced not only the Great Influenza, but also the Russian Flu of 1889–90, the Asian Flu of 1957–58, and the Hong Kong Flu of 1968–69. While the pattern lacks the reliable punctuality of Halley's Comet or recurring cicada broods, some observers believe that there is a cyclical nature to flu pandemics, and that mankind may somehow be "due" for another one. As science journalist Gaia Vince wrote in 2013, "We know a pandemic has occurred every 10–50 years for the past few centuries, and the last one was in 1968, so we're overdue one."[19]

Pandemic	Date	Estimated Worldwide Deaths	Estimated US Deaths
Russian Flu	1889–90	1 million	250,000
Great Influenza	1918–20	50 million	500,000 to 675,000
Asian Flu	1957–58	1.5 to 2 million	70,000
Hong Kong Flu	1968–69	1 million	34,000
Swine Flu	2009–10	18,500	8,870 to 18,300[20]

Even in popular culture there is a niggling fear that we are overdue for an outbreak. In books and movies, we often see manifestations of this dread. In 2011, for example, *Contagion*, starring Matt Damon, told of a frightening fictional international flu pandemic. The film showed how a pandemic could relatively easily travel from China to America, and then quickly spread around the rest of the world before the authorities could do much to respond to it. On the tenth anniversary of September 11, *Contagion* terrified enough Americans to become the No. 1 box-office movie in America. The *New York Post*'s Lou Lumenick declared it "easily the scariest of the disaster films" since September 11.[21] Other examples of this fear have included the vampire/virus mashup *The Strain*, the survivor drama *The Last Ship*, and the zombie apocalypse hit show *The Walking Dead*.

But the fears also had some (emphasis on *some*) basis in reality. In the spring of 2009, swine flu—officially known as H1N1—broke out in Mexico, and many were convinced that this was the long-feared overdue pandemic. The hype was unwarranted, and neither a pandemic nor a widespread panic took place, thankfully. The death toll for the swine flu outbreak was far lower than the others mentioned above, all of which claimed more than a million victims. Compared to the fifty million killed by the 1918 virus, swine flu was relatively minor, killing perhaps fewer than nineteen thousand people (see table). This figure was lower than the typical annual total of seasonal flu deaths throughout the 1990s, which was around thirty-six thousand. The H1N1 virus as it played out clearly did not fit with the "pattern" set by previous pandemics. In the end, its overall future effects were generally comparable to seasonal flu rather than some of the killer outbreaks of the past.

So what happened? Was H1N1 part of the series of cyclical outbreaks we had been warned about? Contrary to claims from flu experts, is there actually no cycle to these things? Or was the appearance of H1N1 in fact the expected outbreak, but effectively countered by our new technological ability to attenuate a pandemic's worst effects? The truth is that we do not know. As US Centers for Disease Control and Prevention (CDC) director Dr. Thomas Frieden said on the day before the twelfth anniversary of September 11: "The only thing protecting us from a global pandemic right now is the fact that it doesn't yet spread from person to person. I can't predict if that's going to happen tomorrow, in 10 years or never."[22] Somewhat more sharply, the epidemiologist Marc Lipsitch told prognosticator extraordinaire Nate Silver that "it's stupid to predict based on three data points. . . . All you can do is plan for different scenarios."[23]

Much about influenza remains mysterious. In the last half century, though, scientists have learned much about its pathology. We now know, for example, that so-called seasonal flu epidemics spread around the world from person to person. More importantly, we have also gained new tools to help with influenza prevention, detection, and treatment. Influenza is fast mutating, but we now have the ability to develop new vaccines each year to anticipate and counter the new strains. Meanwhile, animals harbor countless constantly evolving strains of influenza viruses—with birds being particularly susceptible to incubating the viruses and spreading them around the world. Bird-borne flu viruses sometimes mutate into strains that can infect and spread among mammals, including pigs (hence the informal name swine flu), cats, and humans, where they can further mutate and swap genetic material with other flu viruses. Any place where people interact regularly with sick birds—industrial chicken operations, small-time poultry flocks, town markets with live birds for sale, backyard coops, and even underground cockfighting rings—holds the potential to become a launching point for human infection.

In recent years Asia has for various reasons been the focus of much epidemiological concern. These concerns stem from the cross proximity of cities to farms and the frequency of human to animal contact. Even though Asia is now a locus for the origination of new virus strains, the ease of international travel and trade means that a small number of human infections anywhere could, if not effectively countered, begin a global pandemic.

There is, however, another answer to the question: Smart policy at the presidential level helped a great deal in staving off the swine flu's effects. In January 2005, as a result of President Bush's reading John Barry's history of the 1918 influenza, the US government launched an initiative to prepare for a possible outbreak of avian flu (H5N1). There had been a number of worrisome events in the early 2000s, including the 2002 outbreak of SARS (Severe Acute Respiratory Syndrome), the anthrax mailings that came on the heels of the 9/11 attacks, and increasing reports of avian influenza devastating poultry flocks beginning in 2004. These developments heightened policymakers' awareness of the potential impact of a viral outbreak and/or a biological attack, and for a corresponding need to be prepared.

In November 2005 President Bush announced a $7 billion strategy to combat an influenza pandemic, which included investments in vaccines, antivirals, domestic preparedness, and international cooperation. The plan highlighted four key aspects of preparedness: first, rapid diagnosis of the phenomenon, at both the individual and the societal level; second, antimicrobial treatments to address the condition; third, making the vaccine available to promote prophylaxis; and fourth, the ability for public health officials to quarantine carriers.[24]

As the 2014 Ebola outbreak showed, the quarantine element is extremely difficult to manage in a free society. A workable approach to quarantine requires a long-term commitment by the government to inform citizens, which in turn requires maintaining the trust of the citizenry. To do this, it is important for presidents, their appointees, and civil servants to point to past successes as much as to lay the groundwork for the future. That is the democratic way. There have been many successful instances of semi-voluntary quarantine in the guise of "social distancing"—the agreement within a community to refrain from large-scale interactions such as parties, community events, and even school—in order to reduce the spread of an infection. According to medical historian Howard Markel, these types of non-pharmaceutical interventions have been remarkably effective at controlling disease outbreaks. In the 1918 epidemic, for example, St. Louis employed social distancing while Philadelphia did not; Philadelphia consequently suffered three times as many deaths per capita as St. Louis.[25]

For good and for ill, our legal system makes staving off pandemic by government fiat difficult. This difficulty makes communication and voluntary action more critical. In addition, it puts pressure on the other priorities delineated above. Recognizing the potential for legal conflict and challenges, President Bush sought "to remove one of the greatest obstacles to domestic vaccine production: the growing burden of litigation."[26] Under the Public Readiness and Emergency Preparedness (PREP) Act of 2006, the government gained the authority to issue "PREP Act Declarations" granting liability protection to manufacturers whose products were used in public health emergencies.

When I served at the Department of Health and Human Services in 2007 and 2008, the government issued a series of such declarations for the manufacture of influenza vaccines and pandemic antivirals, as well as anthrax, smallpox, and botulism products. These declarations, however, took place only after significant effort from the political leadership (this author included), and in the face of much quiet, but persistent, bureaucratic opposition.

In more recent years the Obama administration has issued PREP Act declarations to widen liability protections to some H1N1-related products, but this remains a tool that could and should be used more expansively.

There is a tremendous lesson here that should not be missed: The fact that two administrations headed by two presidents of such differing ideological positions could advance these commonsense policies is a reason for optimism and reflection. They should also be celebrated as the foundation for bipartisan progress in an age characterized by often bitter, paralyzing progress.

Although the Bush administration was most concerned with H5N1, the administration's "all-hazards approach" was intended to strengthen the United States' ability to respond to a range of exigencies. This approach paid off in 2009 when, in the Obama administration's early days—at a time when not one of its top twenty HHS appointees had yet been confirmed by the Senate—it dusted off the Bush flu plan to address the swine flu outbreak. This plan, which included a robust communications strategy to hold off panic, a stockpiling of fifty million courses of antiviral drugs, and a mechanism for accelerated vaccine production, helped keep the H1N1 outbreak under control.

Still, the event exposed some serious gaps in preparedness, as well. For starters, public health officials were somewhat slow to identify the threat. Veratect, a now-defunct Seattle-based company with an early detection system, identified a problem in Mexico as early as April 6, 2009. More than two weeks passed before the Pan American Health Organization

(PAHO) and the CDC issued public alerts. Earlier identification of the threat by the Mexican government, PAHO, and US agencies could have lessened the spread of the disease.

Another problem arose on the public relations front. Vice President Joe Biden said on the *Today* show that he "would tell members of my family, and I have, I wouldn't go anywhere in confined places now." This statement, which was made worse by Biden's making it about his own family than about the country, threatened to drive people away from air travel and public transportation. White House press secretary Robert Gibbs had to walk back the remarks by claiming that Biden meant to tell already sick people to avoid confined places. As Gibbs put it, "Obviously, if anybody was unduly alarmed for whatever reason, we would apologize for that. And I hope that my remarks and remarks of people at CDC and Secretary Napolitano have appropriately cleared up what he meant to say." Although this explanation was not supported by the video of Biden's remarks, Biden's notoriety for misspeaking helped mitigate the political fallout of his error, as apparently few people took him seriously as a spokesman for administration policy on the issue.[27]

The need for public officials to issue accurate, timely, and calming statements in these cases is essential. The government should even have quotes prepared for each level of intensity. Wilson said nothing in 1918, and Biden said the wrong thing in 2009. When discussing viral outbreaks, public officials need to walk a fine line between the need to promote calm and the need to get the American people to act in a recommended manner. It is essential to avoid panic, and not to give people incorrect information, as Biden did in 2009. At the same time, Wilson's refusal to address the Great Influenza of 1918 meant that the government lost an opportunity to inform the American public of steps they could take to protect themselves. Wilson's silence cost lives. In contrast to both of these approaches, a good example of walking this line took place during the 2009 swine flu, in which acting CDC head Dr. Rich Besser was so soothing, effective, and ubiquitous that he parlayed his newfound fame into a position as senior health and medical editor at *ABC News*.

Another key to effective pandemic response is delivering on promises. To some degree the Obama administration over-promised and under-delivered when it came to vaccine availability during the H1N1 outbreak. In July 2009 the government projected having 160 million doses of H1N1 vaccine available by the fall. Yet those predictions did not come true, and HHS officials had to lower the estimates a number of times. When it became known that the vaccine was in short supply, it also emerged that the government had known for at least a month that the projections were wrong before notifying the public. This was a serious mistake, as governmental transparency is critical, and trust in government is essential in a public health crisis: It protects the health of markets and the rule of law, and increases the chances that the public will abide by the instructions of public health officials. Thinking back to Wilson and his propaganda machine, the trust of the people is a very valuable commodity. Failing to fulfill promises will erode that commodity.

This erosion took place in 2009. As the *New York Times*'s Andrew Pollack and Donald McNeil Jr. wrote in October 2009, the government found its credibility "undermined by overly rosy projections that did not take account of the vagaries of vaccine production." Government officials were aware in September 2009 that the vaccine amounts they were promising would not be available, yet waited until the next month, in the face of obvious shortages and people being turned away from clinics, to lower their estimates from forty million available doses to twenty-eight million.[28]

Unfortunately, when the vaccine did arrive, much of it came long after it could have been of any use: It arrived too late for some who needed it, and more generally, it arrived well after the projections of doom were clearly not materializing. In the end, the government had to discard millions of expiring doses of the vaccine. In policy, as in so much else, timing is everything. The government's timing was unfortunately terrible.[29] When it comes to sharing information regarding countermeasure availability, the best approach is to under-promise and over-deliver, which is the opposite of what the government did. More realistic projections could have diminished expectations on the front end and, at the same time, reduced pressure to come up with an artificial target figure of doses that ended up arriving after the threat had already waned.

As the H1N1 incident shows, well thought out policies are essential to defeating a pandemic. Smart policies are not the result of instantaneous judgments, but of advance thought and preparation. Government cannot control nature, but it can control how it reacts to what nature brings. This is not only true of the virus and its potency, but also of the way the media responds. In recent years some media reports have created a credibility problem for the government with respect to the question of vaccine safety. Dr. Andrew Wakefield's now-discredited claims linking the MMR (measles, mumps, and rubella) vaccine to autism awakened a wider public discomfort regarding vaccine safety. Anti-vaccine sentiment grew in the aftermath of the Wakefield study, and to such a degree that public health officials studied the demographics of vaccine resisters and developed outreach strategies for working among those groups. One surprising result from their studies was the degree to which anti-vaccine parents were more likely to be prevalent in liberal college towns like Ann Arbor, Michigan, and Boulder, Colorado, than in conservative states such as Wyoming or Idaho. Another analysis, by *Real Clear Science*'s Alex Berezow, found that "4 of the 5 most anti-vaccine states are solid blue," meaning states that consistently vote for Democratic presidential candidates.[30] The anti-vaccine sentiments among liberals even prompted a funny segment on *The Daily Show*, in which correspondent Samantha Bee had trouble resolving her belief that liberals were pro-science with the anti-vaccine beliefs of the leftist blogger she interviewed.

Vaccine anxiety affected the public perception of the H1N1 vaccine, even though the seasonal flu vaccine was widely considered to be safe, and the swine flu vaccine only differed from the seasonal flu vaccine in that it included the H1N1 strain. Furthermore, the benefits to immunizations as a whole are overwhelming and difficult to deny. According to a CDC report, vaccination of children in the United States over a two-decade period led to the prevention of 322 million illnesses, twenty-one million hospitalizations, and 732,000 deaths over the course of those children's lifetimes. These health gains brought about significant financial benefits as well, to the tune of $295 billion in direct costs and an eye-popping $1.38 trillion for society overall.[31]

Despite the enormous benefits to immunizations, vaccine hesitancy has remained a persistent problem. In the case of H1N1, the problem was exacerbated by media figures from both the left and the right who recklessly told their audiences not to get vaccines. One of the worst offenders in this regard was liberal talk-show host Bill Maher, who called people who get flu shots "idiots." On the right, Glenn Beck, then of *Fox News*, directed listeners to his talk-radio show to ignore the Department of Homeland Security's recommendations on the pandemic, saying, "If somebody had the swine flu right now, I would have them cough on me. I'd do the exact opposite of what the Homeland Security says."[32]

Another irresponsible critique, leveled by journalist Michael Fumento, was that swine flu was all a "hoax." Fumento claimed that concerns about H1N1 were overstated and that public health officials, especially at the World Health Organization (WHO), used the swine flu outbreak to maintain their credibility in the face of repeated predictions of an avian flu outbreak that did not arrive, and to justify previous high-cost investments in pandemic preparedness.[33]

This topic brings to bear an issue that is both a challenge for government officials and for democratic citizens. There is a balance to be maintained by both groups to understand the vast Spanish Flu–like casualties that are possible while not endangering the ability to understand when science-backed preparation may be mitigating damage—or even when the crisis has passed. Fumento was correct that the swine flu pandemic of 2009–10 turned out to be milder than expected, but he was wrong in ascribing nefarious motives to public health officials in this instance. It is not in their interest to overhype disease scares that turn out to be wrong, as they know that their voices will be ignored if they are seen as having cried wolf too often. In my experience both in the White House and at HHS, US health officials, regardless of party, are concerned with protecting the populace and making sure that we are ready should we face a biological threat, be it natural or man-made. While the H1N1 outbreak was limited, a more serious one could have significant consequences.

The CDC has long projected that a medium-level outbreak in the United States could cause 89,000 to 207,000 deaths, with the cost ranging from $71 billion to $167 billion. Some economic estimates are even higher, such as one from WBB Securities predicting a one-year loss to the US economy of $488 billion. Given this deadly and costly potential, the government will need to address the lingering perception problems—about overhyping, about the safety of vaccines, and about matching vaccine availability with public need—if we are to be ready for the next event.[34]

Fumento may be unfair, but the government's actions and levels of preparation remain far from perfect. Overall, the federal government handled the swine flu crisis fairly well, following the proper procedures given the potential for pandemic. Mature leadership must always recognize that we can only control our preparation, not the actual outcome.

Nevertheless, the next president should look to a number of specific areas for improvement. One of those areas is in refining communication and outreach to the public in the "age of social media." The government must be forthright and detailed about its projections, the seriousness of potential threats, as well as the limitations of government capabilities and the concomitant responsibility of the citizenry. The miscommunication regarding vaccine availability led to consternation among those who wanted the vaccine in the fall of 2009 and to unwarranted waste of vaccine doses in the spring of 2010. Such blunders would have been more costly had the outbreak been more severe.

The H7N9 and the Flus of the Future

In 2013 a new flu emerged, the H7N9 variety, in China. H7N9 killed about forty-five people in 2013, but had a high mortality rate, worrying many public health officials. H7N9 did not, and may not ever, emerge as a global health threat, but the H7N9 episode showed both encouraging and worrisome aspects of our ability to prepare for potential pandemic outbreaks.

From a positive perspective, China showed itself to be more cooperative than previously in trying to get H7N9 under control. In response to H7N9, China shared information with the World Health Organization, closely monitored the disease itself, and aggressively culled flocks of chickens that could be infected.

These steps represented a significant improvement from the way China had dealt with the SARS virus a decade earlier. During the 2002

SARS outbreak, Beijing took a secretive and closed approach, keeping outside organizations such as WHO in the dark about the outbreak, which ultimately infected eight thousand people and killed about eight hundred, and cost the global economy as much as $50 billion.[35] In addition, SARS, like MERS, a coronavirus, spread across the Pacific Ocean to Canada, although not to the United States. It seems clear that a quicker and more open Chinese response could have limited the outbreak and prevented its transoceanic spread.

Over the course of a decade, China appeared to have learned its lesson regarding how to handle a dangerous viral outbreak. Despite the improvements, however, the West cannot yet rest easy when it comes to the issue of Chinese cooperation. This is a place where a president's prioritization and outreach could help bring two powerful nations together for global leadership and cooperation.

The H7N9 outbreak began in Shanghai, which is a relatively open part of China. It's not clear that this level of transparency about public health emergencies would exist in every region of China. In addition, the director-general of the World Health Organization at the time of the outbreak was China's own Margaret Chan. Her term ends in 2017, and Beijing may not wish to be as cooperative with her successors. Still, the improved Chinese response to H7N9 was a most favorable sign, especially as China has a significant share of the world population, is steadily becoming more important economically, and tends to serve as the origination point for many deadly pathogens.

Another positive sign with H7N9 was in vaccine development and production. Thanks in large part to the push for greater vaccine capacity during the Bush administration, discussed above, the United States now has a more reliable annual supply of the regular flu vaccine. Researchers in the United States have also seen improvements in cell-based vaccine technology that can supplement and perhaps even supplant traditional egg-based vaccines—meaning that vaccine quantity wouldn't be limited by the supply of eggs and wouldn't risk harming people with food allergies.

Chinese authorities shared the H7N9 virus samples with international flu labs, which let US health officials develop lab strains to allow American manufacturers to produce large amounts of a vaccine if needed. The Biomedical Advanced Research and Development Authority (BARDA) and Novartis have a partnership that enabled them to start creating a vaccine before H7N9 even left China, based on the posted genetic sequence.

At the same time, there were a number of worrisome aspects about the H7N9 episode, interestingly on the US front. First, the appearance of the virus did not seem to cause much, if any, stir in the United States. While absence of panic is certainly a good thing, an overly blasé attitude to potential health crises is worrisome as well.

More importantly, a number of critics raised the point that even though BARDA had matched the virus strain and that the H7 strain was hard for vaccine makers to match, HHS held back for a long period on giving the go ahead to begin making the vaccine. It is unclear why this was the case, although it could have stemmed in part from the uninterested public reaction to the seemingly remote outbreak. Former Food and Drug Administration (FDA) official Peter Pitts blamed the delay on HHS's "slogging bureaucracy" and warned that the delay could be costly if the virus mutated so that it began to spread faster.[36] As someone who has worked at HHS, I suspect that cost did have something to do with the delay, namely that waiting to produce the vaccine until absolutely necessary could save scarce dollars if the virus did not become a problem. The problem with this theory is that profligate spending has not held HHS back in the past, and if H7N9 had reached our shores, the decision to hold back would have appeared penny wise, but pound foolish.

Another concern about the episode is that only conservative media organizations seemed to cover the story. Conservative sources like the *Daily Caller*, *Breitbart*, and the *Washington Examiner* ran articles on the subject. In addition, the delay was also covered by nonconservative sources like the *Huffington Post* and *The Hill*, but in articles written by conservative authors. The conservatives were only too glad to criticize the Obama administration for the delay in proceeding with the purchase of the vaccine, while liberals seemed loathe to call attention to something that might be damaging to the Obama administration.

This suggests, but does not prove, that if the roles had been reversed, and a Republican administration had not proceeded with a vaccine purchase, the liberals might have been more vocal while the conservatives would have overlooked the lack of action. If so, this is a disconcerting development. Crisis management and response need to be nonpartisan in order to be effective. Anti-vaccine hard-liners may be in the minority, but if they gain a certain percentage of objectors from each administration for political reasons, they could end up with more sway than their small numbers would suggest.

EBOLA AND OTHER THREATS ABROAD

The swine flu outbreak of 2009 showed that the United States has made real progress in its ability to deal with viral outbreaks in the United States. Unfortunately, most diseases will emerge outside the United States. Notwithstanding the progress made with China in dealing with H7N9, overall the United States has far fewer levers for combating diseases outside our borders. One troubling non-flu outbreak was MERS—Middle East Respiratory Syndrome—which emerged in 2012 and infected more than 1,100 people. Over a third of those infections were fatal.

MERS, a coronavirus, emerged in Saudi Arabia. The Saudis initially resisted the notion that MERS might be zoonotic, or animal based, even though camels were eventually identified as the likely culprit for transmitting MERS to humans. This resistance, which stemmed in part from the cultural and economic importance of camels in Saudi Arabia, had practical effects. Saudi officials were reluctant to test to see if camel milk could spread the disease, one of many important facts health officials need to know. They did, however, eventually issue warnings against drinking raw, unpasteurized camel milk. The warnings, however, have not eliminated the disease. In June 2015 just one person who had visited Saudi Arabia brought the disease to South Korea, killing at least four people and creating a mini-panic there.

MERS was also worrisome because of the Hajj. This annual pilgrimage of two million Muslim worshippers to the holy city of Mecca threatened to carry MERS to all corners of the globe. As long as MERS remains a problem, the onset of the Hajj will continue to highlight the danger of diseases developing and spreading around the world from a convergence point, be it a world war, a holy city, or a sporting event like the Olympics or the World Cup.

The Ebola outbreak that emerged in West Africa in 2014 killed over eleven thousand people, almost half of those who came down with it. Ebola was particularly worrisome because, in addition to a high mortality rate, it had neither a vaccine nor a cure, so no countermeasures could be stockpiled. On the positive side, and in contrast to the flu or a coronavirus, which are airborne, Ebola is only transmitted via bodily fluids. This means that Ebola, while deadly, is relatively difficult to transmit.

Before 2014 public health officials thought, and asserted, that a nation with a modern medical system like the United States could and would limit the spread of a disease like Ebola with proper infection controls, including isolation, rubber gloves, masks, and proper disposal of the virus's victims and their contaminated possessions. All of these measures were in short supply in West Africa, and the 2014 outbreak infected more people than any previous Ebola outbreak. At one point health experts suggested that the disease might infect 1.4 million people.[37] The outbreak also raised worrisome questions about societal breakdown in the wake of a pandemic, and Liberia's defense minister even called the disease "a serious threat to its national existence."[38]

The United States, however, was supposedly safe, or so the public health officials said. The 2014 Ebola outbreak brought a handful of Ebola-infected individuals into the country, and the United States also experienced some secondary spread once the patients were identified, in contrast to the repeated assurances of public health experts and government officials. US outbreaks, even the smallest ones, led to school shutdowns, isolation and quarantine of those who interacted with the victims, high costs to local hospitals and first responders, and more than a fair degree of panic in numerous American cities.

The 2014 Ebola pandemic brought with it a number of lessons for the United States and international preparedness officials. First, there was no doubt that our detection capabilities were found wanting, as the United States and the World Health Organization were slow to detect and respond to the initial outbreaks in West Africa. In addition, when it was clear that public health measures alone could not stem the virus's spread, our capabilities to develop new medical countermeasures also came up short. Despite the existence of BARDA, the development of new vaccines or medications to counter high-risk, deadly diseases was too slow and unfocused to come up with an Ebola countermeasure in advance of the 2014 outbreak. Third, our communication efforts were inadequate, as bland reassurances from public officials that would quickly be proven wrong by fast-breaking events led to a loss of credibility in official statements. Finally, the disease revealed that CDC protocols regarding screening, decontamination, and isolation of potentially exposed individuals were out of date, insufficient, or not user friendly. CDC adapted to its problems and changed its protocols, but doing so after the fact caused unnecessary turmoil during a difficult time.

West Africa bore the brunt of the Ebola costs. But because we live in a global world, with borders easily traversed (legally and illegally), the United States was unable to sit out the Ebola crisis. Air travel meant that Ebola patients inevitably ended up inside the United States. As a result of the damage Ebola caused in West Africa, President Obama needed to direct additional US resources to address the pandemic. The US government sent supplies and personnel to the region, and also worked to accelerate the development of an Ebola vaccine. While the fact that Ebola was not an airborne disease made it somewhat easier to control, the incident was a frightening preview of what could happen with a more contagious, yet equally deadly, disease.

POLICY RESPONSES

Viruses present policymakers with a panoply of challenges. Pandemic preparation and response are especially difficult given the fact that sources of disease often lie outside our borders. Fortunately, there are tools presidents can use to improve US response to unanticipated and deadly outbreaks of contagious diseases. To be successful responding to a serious disease outbreak, presidents must be skilled at handling multiple aspects of the crisis at once. With respect to the communications challenge, the president and top White House aides need to engage in media training for crisis management. This should include real-time exercises in which government officials simulate and practice crisis response. One of the reasons that Biden stumbled while Besser was sure-footed was that Biden was new to the executive branch in the spring of 2009. Besser had been a long-serving career official in the federal government, and had been through his share of training exercises during which top officials game out scenarios and practice initiating preplanned responses and communicating with the public.

The exercises usually include wrinkles on widely anticipated scenarios to test officials' abilities to improvise. For example, officials might be told to react to a mysterious viral outbreak coinciding with a nuclear explosion. Exercises not only train officials how to react, but they also introduce high-level officials in our heavily siloed government to each other so that they can establish relationships and build trust before an emergency takes place. For all of these reasons, a top priority for incoming administrations needs to be preparing top political officials to handle crisis management. The H1N1 virus did not ask if the Obama administration was new to the job, or if it had managed to get top officials confirmed yet, before striking. The virus showed up at the door unannounced, and the government was left to deal with it.

In addition, the president needs to recognize public concerns about overhype and not dismiss critics out of hand, but rather attempt to address complaints with a serious communications plan. As we saw under Wilson, government too often wants to control the flow of information or present only positive information to the public. For this reason the presentation of any sobering information needs to be carefully calibrated, lest the public, assuming the government is underselling matters, falls into a panic. In the Ebola outbreak, for example, public opinion and the judgment of public health officials diverged on certain issues. The public overwhelmingly wanted a travel ban put in place, but the best recommendation of public health officials was that a travel ban was unnecessary and would be counterproductive. In circumstances such as these, presidents must not only resist the temptation to succumb to the public will, but also must be willing and able to persuade the public why they are following the correct path.

The kind of trust that presidents and government health spokespeople need to have in emergencies cannot be built overnight. It must be developed over time. Furthermore, there are a host of circumstances in which just hearing from a health spokesperson will not do. For a variety of reasons, the nation looks to the president in times of crisis. For this reason it is the president who must reassure an anxious nation. This role cannot be outsourced.

The president is also important in promoting international cooperation. Given the likelihood that a pandemic will start outside of our borders, the president will have to work with other nations on fighting off flu. As we saw in the contrast between the Chinese handling of SARS versus H7N9, it makes a big difference if nations are willing to be open and transparent about diseases that are raging within their borders. For example, the sharing of virus samples could allow other nations to get a jump on a cure that could help every nation in the case of a wider outbreak. In addition, the Ebola crisis showed that while the United States may be able to handle a viral outbreak domestically, less developed nations have more difficulty in maintaining basic infection controls. But the United States cannot rest easy and rely on its technological superiority for protection. After all, nations may establish borders, but pathogens are not going to respect them. For this reason international cooperation, among rival or even feuding nations, is essential. In many cases the president may have to step in to ensure that cooperation.

The government must also continue to encourage new technologies and countermeasures—such as improved detection systems, diagnostics, antivirals, and vaccines—via strategic investments, accelerated approvals when appropriate, and liability protection for essential products. The private sector is a powerful tool for helping government develop and stockpile the countermeasures needed to combat deadly outbreaks.

Government can harm, as well as help, technological development. At the same time that the government is working to develop new technologies, the president needs to keep careful watch to ensure that other arms of the government are not getting in the way of technological progress. The president should have an office under his own purview tasked with removing bureaucratic barriers and identifying liability concerns that threaten effective preparation. The office must also leverage our federal system to pull the best ideas from every part of the nation to ensure our government is equipped and equipping every part of society to anticipate and respond to potential health issues. This office could be in the White House, or in the Office of Management and Budget, but should be within the domain of the executive office of the president. It does our nation little good to have BARDA work with industry to create a new cure, only to have the FDA unnecessarily delay its approval. Too often, different arms of the government work at cross-purposes with one another, creating what could be termed the "pushmi-pullyu" effect, after the Dr. Doolittle creature with two heads going off in different directions. Once government bureaucracies are at war with each other, it's very hard to stop them from feuding. In circumstances where thousands of lives could be on the line, the president cannot just shrug his shoulders and grumble about bureaucratic infighting. Presidential leadership is required to make sure that internal policy disagreements do not get in the way of life-saving technological advancements.

One specific area that could stand improvement is the development of coronavirus countermeasures. Both MERS and SARS were worrisome pathogens, and the world lacked the countermeasures to combat them. Fortunately, science has advanced to the point where effective vaccine platforms will typically allow us to develop vaccines for new strains of an existing disease. With respect to flu, for example, we have the ability to develop new vaccines to inoculate against rapidly evolving new strains. With coronaviruses, we do not yet have those platforms. National Institutes of Health (NIH) has started down this path, but we also need HHS's BARDA to spur private-sector development of a MERS countermeasure. The next president should put this effort on his or her to-do list.

Developing countermeasures is important, but so is taking care of them. A recent Department of Homeland Security Inspector General's report was headlined, "DHS Has Not Effectively Managed Pandemic Personal Protective Equipment and Antiviral Medical Countermeasures." Somewhat disturbingly, the report found that even though Congress had appropriated funds for DHS to "plan, train, and prepare for a potential pandemic," the department was not ready to respond appropriately if a pandemic took place. According to the report, DHS had not sufficiently assessed its needs or managed the countermeasures in its own stockpile. The report included eleven specific recommendations that DHS needed to follow. DHS agreed with all eleven recommendations, which indicated there was internal knowledge of the agency's failings on this front. While presidents do not personally manage stockpiled countermeasures, they do need to make sure that these internal failings are addressed and taken care of.[39]

Finally, the president can help sort out sticky issues of command and control. In 2006 White House chief of staff Andrew Card asked Homeland Security adviser Fran Townsend who would be in charge if a flu pandemic broke out. Townsend, who was at the time flanked by HHS secretary Michael Leavitt and DHS secretary Michael Chertoff, answered "Mike." Although it was good for a laugh at the time, there was a serious and understandable disagreement about the right answer. Similarly, during the Ebola outbreak in Africa, veteran GOP congressman Frank Wolf complained to CDC director Thomas Frieden that "no one could tell me who was in charge on the issue." Wolf told Frieden that the lack of coordination among federal agencies "should be a very top priority of the White House." The government could have all the countermeasures and disaster plans in the world, but lack of a clearly delineated command-and-control structure could paralyze effective execution of carefully preplanned efforts.[40]

All of these recommendations put a lot on the president's plate. Perhaps more than any crisis, a pandemic requires the need for the president—and the government as a whole—to multitask, to focus on more than one thing. Assuming a president can manage all of these strategies, they, combined with our existing plans, should put us on a better footing in the future. The government needs to maintain its preparedness efforts as if the threat remains, while doing its best to use limited resources efficiently and to avoid losing credibility in case of future emergencies.

Conclusion

We cannot know if or when a new pandemic might strike. If it happens, it is only small comfort that we are now more knowledgeable and better prepared for facing such a disaster. Modern travel and evolving superbugs—

infections resistant to antibiotics because of antibiotic overuse—mean that we are still quite vulnerable to a devastating and deadly pandemic.

At the same time, we now have many more tools, at the national and individual level, for coping with such an incident. Should the next superbug come to our shores, we need to use those tools wisely, and keep our heads, to deal with it. At the presidential level, presidents must be able to deal with multiple challenges at once, something Woodrow Wilson—consumed with World War I—was unable to do. Should the time come, we now know that the government will be much more likely to help than it was under Wilson. At the same time, we also know that the government is far from infallible, and that smart individual action will also be necessary to protect ourselves and our families.

CHAPTER TWO

Food and Water Crisis

As the year 2014 began, Americans took for granted that they had a clean, safe, and abundant water supply. Unfortunately, within ten days of the beginning of the New Year, this comfort would be severely tested for 300,000 residents of West Virginia, living not that far from the nation's capital of Washington, DC. This crisis, affecting 1 percent of the US population, all began because of a one-inch hole.[1]

On January 9, 2014, an obscure chemical called 4-methylcyclohexane methanol (MCHM) began leaking into West Virginia's Elk River. The chemical seeped out of a small hole in a decades-old steel storage tank at "tank farm"—a chemical storage facility.[2] Out of that small hole came 7,500 gallons of MCHM.[3] It did not take long for residents to notice that there was a problem with their water supply.

The tainted water smelled like licorice. It caused a variety of symptoms, including "nausea, vomiting, dizziness, diarrhea, rashes and reddened skin," according to Ian Simpson, a reporter for *Reuters*.[4] It also closed schools and restaurants, sent dozens of people to area hospitals, and led to official warnings not to use the water for anything besides flushing toilets. Unsurprisingly, these announcements led to a run on bottled water, and stores quickly ran out of supplies.

Although water is generally a local issue, the magnitude of the crisis led to federal intervention. By January 10 President Barack Obama had declared a state of emergency in West Virginia, ordering "federal aid to supplement state and local response efforts." As a result of this order, FEMA, the Federal Emergency Management Agency, deployed to Boone, Clay, Jackson, Kanawha, Lincoln, Logan, Putnam, and Roane Counties in West Virginia, and the federal government pledged to pay for 75 percent of the costs of combating the chemical spill.[5] In addition, FEMA sent in forty additional trucks full of bottled water to supplement state and local efforts. FEMA pledged to continue sending in the water as long as it was needed. The agency had the capacity to do this since the disaster was a localized problem. A larger, multistate spill might have prevented FEMA from making such an expansive promise.[6]

President Obama's response to the crisis was relatively muted. The White House said in a statement on the issue that "the president was briefed this morning during the Presidential Daily Briefing and will continue to be updated." Obama also "directed his team to stay in close touch with our partners at the federal, state and local level and keep him apprised of the situation." Overall, though, according to *Politico*, the White House "said little about the emergency."[7]

To be fair, it is not clear how much the federal government could or should do in such a situation. The problem was a local one, and local officials appropriately have point on dealing with these sorts of crises. Still, Obama's relatively quiet response did attract some criticism, even from generally friendly quarters. The *Washington Post*'s Eugene Robinson complained that the incident generated "little outrage from officials in Washington, who seem to expect West Virginians to take the whole thing in stride." Robinson also wondered if there was a geographic bias on the part of the media covering the story, and from politicians in reacting to it: "I can't help but wonder what the reaction would be if this had happened on the Upper East Side of Manhattan or in one of the wealthier zip codes of Southern California." In addition, Robinson, who is usually an Obama defender, did not spare the president from criticism in this case, writing that "from the president and the leadership in Congress, we've heard not a peep" about the incident. Robinson even ended by asking, "How do the EPA and the White House respond? Please speak up. We can't hear you."[8]

Robinson acknowledged his interest in the subject was personal. His son's family lived in the affected area. But his column suggests that it does not take long for critics to emerge in times of crisis. Even in a situation like this one, which was largely out of the president's control, and in which he pressed the relatively few levers he had available, there is a very narrow window for presidents before their actions come under harsh scrutiny and review.

Fortunately, the worst part of the contamination ended rather quickly. Although Centers for Disease Control (CDC) had one false start when it prematurely declared the water safe to drink, most residents were given the all clear sign within about ten days.

Unfortunately, it was not the only threat to a local water system that year. In August 2014 local officials told 500,000 residents of Toledo, Ohio, that their water was undrinkable due to toxic algae in the water supply. The irony of this is palpable, given Toledo's presence among the Great Lakes, which collectively contain 20 percent of the entire world's freshwater supply. The *Toledo Blade*'s Tom Henry called the situation a "once-unthinkable crisis in the world's greatest freshwater region."[9]

As with West Virginia, the situation was resolved fairly quickly. After a stressful weekend, and a lot of noise about the situation on cable news, Toledo mayor Michael Collins announced, "Our water is safe. Families can return to normal life." The White House and President Obama did not get involved, although both the state and federal Environmental Protection Agencies did. Neighboring states like Michigan pitched in by setting up water stations for Toledo residents, and stores for hundreds of miles around reported runs on bottled water. The Ohio National Guard also pitched in with water purification assistance. For the most part the private sector and local officials handled the crisis.[10]

In 2016 an even worse crisis emerged with respect to the water supply of Flint, Michigan. After the city decided to stop purchasing costly water from Detroit in 2013, it began bringing in water via the murky Flint River while preparing to use Lake Huron as its water source. This led to disastrous results, as the city's population was stuck with dangerously unclean water, leading to a host of health hazards. When the extent of the crisis became clear, President Obama declared a state of emergency, which was the extent of what he could do at that point. In the buildup to the crisis, however, there was evidence of widespread governmental failure at the local, state, and federal level.[11]

The first two of these water-tainting incidents passed with no casualties and in relatively short order. The Flint situation was more complicated, and may even have contributed to some deaths related to a Legionnaires' Disease outbreak. In all three the aftereffects of these incidents would linger, however, in the form of lawsuits, recriminations, and continued concerns about the water supply. And even in areas where the incident was not heavily covered in the media, these water taintings provided a stark reminder of the vulnerability and precariousness of essential products we often take for granted. While presidents—and the rest of us—don't typically worry about this issue, safe and abundant food and water are essential to our security as a nation.

OUR FOOD AND WATER SYSTEM

For most of human history, the story of man has been one of a constant search for the food and water needed to survive. Reading the Bible, or ancient history, a modern reader is quickly reminded that droughts were all too common, and cities were often just one war or one siege away from facing thirst and starvation. Even in the New World, the first struggles for survival were not always successful. The Puritans of Massachusetts Bay and the earliest Virginians of Roanoke and Jamestown grappled with death by starvation. In the 1840s the nation was reshaped by hundreds of thousands of Irish immigrants who came to its shores after the potato blight that devastated Ireland.

This quest for food is not limited to ancient history books. It is not that long ago that millions of people faced starvation in European wars, be it in Nazi concentration camps or in sieges of places like Stalingrad. And within many of our own lifetimes, horrific droughts in Africa or cruel government policies in Maoist China and the Soviet Union have led to mass starvations.

Here in America the people of plenty often take for granted how easy it is to obtain food. Americans spend only about 10 percent of their annual after-tax budgets on food.[12] In doing so, they consume about 2,250 calories daily. In fact, Americans face the problem of consuming too many, not too few, calories. Such is our situation that a study finding that Americans are consuming 78 calories fewer than in earlier studies is touted as good news, not as evidence that food is somehow harder to come by.[13]

In addition to the general stores of abundance, Americans are also blessed with great variety. American cooking is often derided, with some justification, as a mix of fast foods such as pizza, hot dogs, hamburgers, and french fries. And yet, in the past few decades, there has been a food revolution in America, and those who are interested now have access to the widest variety of high-quality and exotic foods. Sushi, kimchi, and pho are no longer foreign words in America, even if they may have been unheard of just a few short decades ago. Other, more exotic, foods continue to come in, as Americans now expect that they can eat what they want, when they want, and in whatever quantity they want it.

This combination of abundance and variety comes with risks. Our nation's food and water supplies face a number of vulnerabilities. Some, like the chemical spill, are mainly threats to water. Others, as we shall see, are mainly threats to the food system. And still other threats could affect both. But it is crucial from a national survival perspective that we maintain access to sufficient food and water. If either were threatened in a serious way, it would create a national crisis, one that would land squarely on the president's desk.

Food and Water Threats

Food and water are different, of course, but understanding that difference helps shape the most appropriate responses at all levels—from the federal government to the emergency preparedness of individual citizens. Put simply, the greatest threats to water are local, and the most common threats to food come from abroad. Beyond that, threats to our food and water system fall into a variety of categories, some overlapping and some unique to each source of sustenance. Overall, the threats fall into three main categories: accidental contamination, external threat, and drought or famine.

The most frequent threat is one that comes from a food-borne illness or water contamination. We already saw examples of water contamination with the West Virginia and Toledo situations, but the truth is that food-borne illnesses are already an all-too-common occurrence. They are also increasing in frequency. According to the CDC, imported food caused 39 food-borne outbreaks between the years 2005 and 2010—averaging about 6.5 a year. That is more than double the 2.7 a year from 1998 to 2004. Almost half of the 39 outbreaks in the later period took place in 2009 and 2010 alone. One of the most frequent causes of outbreaks is from fish, and about 85 percent of fish is imported. Such outbreaks have the potential to affect thousands of individual victims. A 2008 salmonella incident sickened as many as 1,400 individuals, with more than 280 of them hospitalized.[14]

These import-based illnesses constitute only a fraction of the overall number of annual incidents. Food-borne illnesses kill about three thousand Americans annually, in addition to causing forty-eight million sicknesses and about 128,000 hospitalizations.[15] In fact, the number of illnesses may be even higher, as many minor stomach ailments go unreported. (To be clear, they are not minor to the people suffering from them.) These incidents of dyspepsia or worse, while disturbing, are generally viewed as the cost of doing business. The victims of these illnesses, however, do not take such an insouciant view of things. Furthermore, as with the West Virginia water incident, these incidents tend to be localized, either geographically or based on ingestion of a particular food, wherever it might be distributed. The most challenging outbreaks, however, are when a source ingredient is tainted, thereby contaminating multiple food products. If there were ever a widespread outbreak of such a source ingredient, the level of concern, not to mention the potential for serious illness, would be much higher.

One difficulty with our food system is the variety of points of origin. According to CDC epidemiologist Hannah Gould, "We don't always know where food comes from."[16] American ports are busy twenty-four hours a day bringing in all kinds of foods from all kinds of places. While the Food and Drug Administration (FDA) has strict regulations about food safety in the United States, other nations are not always so careful, and government officials cannot inspect every item without bringing the entire system to a halt. Americans import more than $100 billion worth of food annually, including $17 billion worth of fish, $12 billion worth of fruit, and $11 billion worth of vegetables. All this food comes from more than 275,000 registered foreign food facilities. Before 2011 the FDA was inspecting facilities at a rate of about two hundred a year, which meant that it would cover every foreign facility over the course of about 1,391 years. In recent years, following the 2011 Food Safety Modernization Act, the FDA has increased its pace of inspections, and is now moving toward a pace of 9,600 inspections a year, which will allow them to inspect every foreign locale over a twenty-eight-year cycle.[17] Obviously, the safety of our food system does not and cannot rely on regular inspections of every facility, or even every port.

Domestic food facilities may be inspected somewhat more regularly, but this does not mean that they are safe. Imports make up only a fraction of our food supply—about 16 percent, and rising. Most of our food still comes from domestic sources. There are more than 170,000 domestic food facilities, and the FDA does not have the capacity to inspect all of them either. Nor should they.

The most frequent forms of food- and water-based contamination are natural or accidental. But there also remains the possibility of nefarious action tainting some part of the food or water supply. The Department of Homeland Security and the FDA have looked into the prospect of terrorist attacks on food sources, and FDA added additional authorities after 9/11, enabling it to do more to prevent intentional tampering with the food supply. Even if such an incident took place, it would likely be a localized incident. Still, tampering could come from anywhere and take place anywhere, giving our homeland security and food safety officials one more thing to worry about when it comes to protecting our food supply.

The magnitude of the potential problem, be it natural or man-made, does not mean we lack ways to address it. As mentioned, inspections of every facility are not only unrealistic but also unnecessary. The FDA correctly takes a risk-based approach to facility inspections. There are, of course, disagreements about some of the parameters of the risk-based approach. It is often a euphemism for increased regulation. But it does not have to be so. According to Dr. David Acheson, who used to head food safety for the FDA, "There's a tendency from the regulator side to want it all wrapped up in a nice little bow, and then take it to the food industry and say, 'We've got you.'" According to Acheson, though, this method is ineffectual, as the FDA needs force-multipliers. Acheson believes we need the collective insights and vigilance of private-sector actors to make up for deficiencies in government manpower and financial resources. Acheson's preferred approach is for the regulators and the regulated community to collaborate more, and develop more trust between and among those two disparate groups to combat the problem of food-borne illnesses.[18]

The good news is that the FDA is already relying on the private sector in some meaningful ways. In June 2013 the FDA called for greater reliance in food inspections on private companies, with the companies being held accountable for the results. According to FDA deputy commissioner Michael Taylor, "We will continue to check food at our borders." However, Taylor added, "Rather than relying almost entirely on FDA's investigators at the ports to detect and respond to food safety problems, importers would—for the first time—be held accountable for verifying, in a manner transparent to FDA, that the food they import is safe."[19]

This private-sector certification approach has two key advantages. First, it allows the FDA to leverage its own limited resources. At the same time, it also recognizes that private companies have an enormous incentive to keep food safe—their own good names. According to Marianne Rowden, president and chief executive of the American Association of Exporters & Importers, "The food companies are very conscious about their brands." As Rowden put it, companies look at the opportunity to certify the safety of imported food "as brand protection, rather than just new regulation."[20]

Prevention of food- or water-based contamination is a necessary and ongoing government activity. A second aspect is in how to react when a widespread incident takes place. As we saw in West Virginia, FEMA has the capability to bring necessities to a localized area. In such a case, the president and indeed the upper echelons of the US government need to step back and let the machinery of government do its work: FEMA is designed for these kinds of short-term interventions, and typically can do its job without White House interference.

This applies to detecting the source of the problem as well. When I served in government, I witnessed the tendency of Congress to want to investigate outbreaks while they were taking place. Such an approach does not employ limited resources in the most efficient way. The legislative branch needs to monitor and propose legislative improvements to agency capabilities, but the executive branch needs to have the flexibility and authority to deploy those resources in times of crisis. Congressional investigations that take place during crises put agencies like the FDA and CDC in a difficult position. Preparing an FDA commissioner or CDC director for a congressional hearing can take hundreds of man-hours and demand the focus of senior career officials at those agencies. The people who are most knowledgeable about the incident, who need to prepare the principal for the hearing, are the very people who need to be investigating the source of the problem, mitigating further risk, and responding to the needs of citizens. During one salmonella incident during the 2000s, the FDA commissioner even called a senior senator to ask him to postpone a hearing until after the source of the contamination was discovered, so as not to take officials off the investigation team to join the hearing-preparation squad. The senator replied that the very fact the commissioner was making the request was suspicious and insisted that the hearing take place. These types of senior official interventions make it harder, not easier, to solve the problem.

This type of interaction was not atypical, unfortunately. During one seventeen-month stretch in 2007 and 2008, Democrats in the House of Representatives held fourteen separate hearings on perceived shortfalls in FDA funding and activities. At some point the motivation behind the hearings appears to be more about political theater than about improving agency operations. Worse, excessive numbers of hearings can get in the way of an agency's ability to prevent or address disasters. Partisan politics are admittedly a tricky business at times, but an important reality of modern presidential leadership is the necessity to find ways to work with Congress so that vital executive functions can continue to operate in a crisis.

Of course, the problem of food-borne illnesses needs to be taken in context. The overwhelming majority of foods we eat, and water we drink, are perfectly safe. But therein lies the issue. Americans are so used to safe and abundant food and water that any deviation from this norm would be so disturbing and unexpected that it could quickly reach crisis mode. Such breakdowns in order would clearly make governmental responses to the crisis that much more difficult. They would also create greater dangers for citizens in the affected areas. (For a fuller description of the challenges created by social breakdown, see chapter 9, "Civil Unrest.")

FOOD OR WATER COLLAPSE

Thus far we have looked at localized problems of food or water safety. For the most part, the president has little involvement in these kinds of issues, other than directing resources toward investigating and alleviating a problem. Still, for a president faced with such a crisis at the local level, the president or senior official briefing on the problem will need to be able to articulate risks within the bands of probability in such a way that can convey the reality of the situation without inciting panic. A far bigger problem, one requiring significant presidential involvement, would be if the entire country were to experience a massive food and/or water shortage.

A massive food or water shortage is not and has not been a problem in modern America. Though there are certainly pockets of hunger in the United States, most Americans have access to an affordable and abundant food supply. Food costs take up a relatively small part of the average American's budget. In addition, even the poorest Americans have government assistance in the form of programs such as food stamps that help them purchase food. But this does not mean that food crises do not take place in the modern world.

In 2008 the world experienced a severe shortage in key commodities. This shortage, which also stirred up domestic tensions in dozens of countries, was the result of monetary policies as well as continued ethanol policies creating upward price pressures. The price of wheat and corn skyrocketed, and many countries in Africa, Latin America, and the Middle East experienced significant food deprivation. At the time, thirty countries had food riots, something unheard of in the twenty-first-century United States. A number of countries, including Russia, Ukraine, India, and Argentina, were worried about their own food supplies and cut off grain exports, exacerbating the crisis.

The fact that the food shortage did not take place in the United States does not mean that future crises will leave America unscathed. A number of analysts have warned that a future famine could impact the United States as well. Most of them tend to be on the left, but some conservatives have worried about this as well. In late 2012, for example, former White House speechwriter David Frum warned that 2013 would be a "year of crisis" because of the drought taking place in a number of farm-producing states. Fortunately, it did not happen.

———

But California has been experiencing a severe drought in recent years. Despite some improvement in 2016, the drought has been one of the worst in California's history. The year 2013 saw less rain than in any year since California entered the Union in 1850.[21] In addition, 2014 was also the third consecutive year in which California experienced a dry rainy season, which greatly exacerbated the situation. According to a report by the University of California's Center for Watershed Sciences, the drought cost California $2.2 billion in 2014 in agricultural losses and additional expenses, as well as 17,100 jobs.[22] The year 2015 was somewhat better from the rain perspective, but it was also the second warmest year in California's history.[23]

The governmental response to the crisis was mainly state based, and President Obama had little part to play. Even in a drought as severe as the one in California, the role of the nation's chief executive in dealing with droughts is a minor one. Obama did declare California to be a disaster area in 2014, and allowed for federal disaster aid to be directed to drought-stricken areas. He also used the drought to his rhetorical advantage, citing it in making his case for action on climate change. He called for the creation of a $1 billion climate resiliency fund as well. Overall, though, dealing with the drought was mainly in the hands of state and local officials.

At the state level, California governor Jerry Brown declared a drought emergency and called on Californians to reduce water consumption by 20 percent. The state declaration gave California agencies additional flexibilities and powers to deal with the problem, but it was unclear what they could realistically accomplish. Residents of harder-hit areas were required to reduce water usage by 30 percent, a difficult-to-attain goal. Many farmers considered improving or digging more wells, which is costly and time-consuming, while others chose to farm less land, which entails additional opportunity costs.[24] As for the government, possible solutions included trucking in more water, connecting impacted areas to other water systems, and desalinization. All were costly, and none was perfect.

Dealing with droughts after they take place is obviously worse than preventing them in the first place. As the California Farm Bureau Federation's Paul Wenger observed, "One of the saddest things about the losses caused by the drought is that they could have been prevented."[25] While the government cannot control the weather, there are a number of steps that California could have taken in the preceding decades that would have alleviated the effects of the recent dryness. According to historian (and California farmer) Victor Davis Hanson, never before has "farming been so central to a state suffering from the aftershocks of a housing collapse, chronic high unemployment, overregulation, and the nation's highest sales, income, and gas taxes." Despite this centrality of California agriculture, Hanson argued, the California drought had a significant component that was man-made, meaning it could have been prevented. As Hanson put it, the affluence of California in the 1980s led "Pacific-corridor residents from San Diego to Berkeley . . . not to worry so much about the old Neanderthal concerns like keeping up freeways and airports." Hanson classified these Pacific Coasters as living "dreamy existences without any clue how to supply their own daily necessities." As for the policies that led to the drought danger, Hanson noted that California added twenty million people over the last three decades, but had not added any major reservoirs in that time. In addition, he blamed environmentalists for suing to divert millions of acre-feet of water to the ocean to help endangered fish. As a result of these short-sighted policies, he argued, the drought had the potential to bring about "surreal things in

California—towns without water, farms reverting to scrub, majestic parks with dead landscaping—fit for Hollywood's disaster movies."[26]

Stanford economist Edward Lazear made a similar claim, arguing that governmental misallocation of water resources had led to the crisis. Lazear, a former head of the White House Council of Economic Advisers, compared California's drought to the 1970s oil shortages and said, "Rather than praying for rain, we should get the government out of the water-allocation business." According to Lazear, there were three ways to alleviate California's water woes: by allowing water owners to sell their water rights without government interference; by making environmental agencies with water demands pay for their water use and in the process budget for the cost of their water diversions; and by allowing farmers who received water discounts a transition period as compensation before having to pay market prices for water use. This free market approach to water distribution would have placed limitations on the government's ability to redirect water supplies while at the same time ensuring that market mechanisms would best sort out the sticky question of highest value water uses. Given current political realities, these reforms were unlikely to take place, but they did highlight the distortionary impact of government policies on water prices and availability.[27]

The California drought was especially problematic because of California's agricultural importance to America, and to the world. California is America's largest producer of agriculture, with 80,500 farms and ranches. In 2012 the state produced $44.7 billion worth of livestock. Key California crops, areas in which California dominates US production, include almonds, dates, figs, kiwis, pistachios, prunes, strawberries, and walnuts, among many others. Making matters worse is the fact that 80 percent of California's developed water supply is devoted to its agricultural production. Loss of California's agricultural sector, due to drought or anything else, would be disastrous to both the United States' and the world's food supply. It might not lead to starvation or famine by itself, but it would certainly lead to significantly higher food prices, in this country and around the world.[28] Just to take one example, the drought led to a 25 percent drop in production of the California-produced rice used in sushi. This kind of rapid production decline would almost certainly lead to higher prices for sushi nationwide.[29]

In addition, the increasingly integrated world makes it more likely that a severe food crisis could have worldwide implications. According to the World Food Program's Richard Leach, smartphones can change the way farmers behave all over the world. As Leach explained, "Someone with a cell phone in Uganda can access the commodity exchange in Chicago and figure out what the price is for maize." For the most part, this has positive implications. That farmer can use technology to both hedge his risks and get the best possible price for his product. At the same time, it can also accelerate panic over lack of supply and drive up prices in problematic times.[30]

Real-time resupply also creates another challenge. Real-time resupply increases efficiency by using technology to let retailers tell suppliers what and how much they need of various products. It has been a boon for much of the economy, but it also means that our supply chain is vulnerable to unexpected disruptions. Furthermore, there are precious few reserves available. Unlike petroleum or biological countermeasures, the United States does not have its own strategic food reserve, and for good reason. We have been blessed by bounty and have not needed it in recent decades.

This bounty is a good thing. It is also one of the reasons that a severe food shortage should be lower on the president's worry list than most of the scenarios laid out in this book. When prioritizing, presidents need to balance the risk that something might happen against the potential impact of it taking place. Furthermore, food and water availability are issues that are best taken care of at the local or state rather than the national level. At the same time, a nation that has as high an expectation of cheap and abundant food as the United States does faces a particular vulnerability. While other nations in the developed world have some experience with food insecurity, it is rare in this country. In fact, among the poorest Americans, obesity is a bigger problem than deprivation. What this means, however, is that a severe food shortage in the United States could shatter Americans' high expectations, leading to significant social instability. Americans unaccustomed to going without could be particularly querulous when faced with such a new and uncertain reality. For this reason presidents should classify a massive food or water shortage as a low-probability event, but one with the direst of consequences.

Conclusion

Presidents need to be able to prioritize the dangers our nation faces. Prioritization requires analyzing the level of risk as well as the potential level of harm. As this chapter makes clear, widespread food or water collapse is a low-probability event, but one with potentially devastating consequences. For the most part, then, food and water dangers should be seen as local or state concerns. A food or water problem could arise in a specific area of the country. Another possibility is the tainting of a specific type of food, such as an E. coli outbreak on a certain type of meat or vegetable. This kind of tainting might be narrow in terms of only affecting a specific food, but could have wider geographic consequences.

Given that nationwide food or water shortages are a low-probability risk, they will most likely be handled at the state or local level. Low probability, however, is not zero probability, and a food or water disaster remains one that both presidents and individual Americans need to think about. Most food- or water-crisis scenarios will not call for significant presidential involvement. If, however, a crisis arose in this area of such magnitude that it did require presidential attention, every American would be relieved that both they and their government had made contingency plans for addressing the problem.

CHAPTER THREE

Weather: A Growing Federal Role

PRESIDENTS ENTER OFFICE UNSURE OF WHAT TRIALS THEY WILL FACE. Presidents cannot predict what disasters might befall the nation during their tenure, which is why they must be prepared for every contingency. Despite this unpredictability, there is one thing we can guarantee about every presidential tenure: Somewhere in this vast nation, there will be weather-based disasters.

FEMA, the Federal Emergency Management Agency, tracks major disaster declarations going back to 1953. Most of these declarations stem from weather-related events, be they drought, extreme weather, hurricanes, mudslides, storms, or tornadoes, just to name a selection. In no year since that time have there been fewer than seven major disasters declared in any one year. Furthermore, the frequency of these declarations has been increasing over time. In most decades since the 1950s, the average number of declarations per decade has grown, and declarations have been on a steady upward trajectory (see chart below). Overall, the average number of annual declarations in the 2010s so far is almost ten times higher than it was in the 1950s.[1]

Decade	Average Declarations per Year
1950s (from 1953)	13
1960s	19
1970s	45
1980s	29
1990s	74
2000s	127
2010–2015	120

Of course, there are many reasons these increases could be taking place. Politics may play a role. In nine of the last fifteen presidential election years, the number of disaster declarations increased from the year before, and on a number of occasions by more than double. This suggests, but does not prove, that notwithstanding formal criteria for such declarations, presidential administrations may be more inclined to issue declarations during presidential election years. Second, there is the possibility that climate change is leading to more weather anomalies. In May 2014 President Obama told weatherman Al Roker that "whether it means increased flooding, greater vulnerability to drought, more severe wildfires—all these things are having an impact on Americans as we speak."[2] There remains disagreement on this issue, but it is telling that the president of the United States was making this case.

Third and most compelling is the fact that the scope of disasters covered by the government keeps increasing, and has steadily done so over the last century. Whereas weather disasters were once local or regional problems handled mainly by local first responders and the private sector, they are now national issues, and the federal government is increasingly expected to prevent them from happening, rescue people while they are happening, and make people whole after they happen. This expectation did not exist in previous eras.

Along with this increased scope of disasters covered by the government is an increase in the level of presidential involvement. We can see this progression by looking at how presidents have dealt with a variety of weather-based crises over the last 125 years. A review of five major weather-based disasters during this period—the 1889 Johnstown Flood, the 1927 Mississippi floods, 1969's Hurricane Camille, 1992's Hurricane Andrew, and 2005's Hurricane Katrina—illustrates the evolution of both presidential and governmental involvement in these disasters.

Before the development of rapid communications mechanisms such as the telegraph and later the telephone, the president would not have even been aware of a natural disaster for some time. Those on the East Coast of the United States were not even notified of the 1811 Missouri earthquakes until six weeks after they took place. Given this time lag, disaster expert Patrick Roberts has observed that "there was hardly an expectation that the federal government would take direct action in response to a storm or fire in any one of the states."[3]

Even in the case of the Johnstown Flood of 1889, which occurred after the invention of the telephone and telegraph, presidential involvement, even in a disaster of epic proportions, was relatively minimal. In May 1889 the area around Johnstown, Pennsylvania, was hit with extremely heavy rains. When the nearby South Fork dam broke, much of the town of Johnstown was washed away. Over 2,200 people died, and bodies were discovered as far away as Cincinnati—some 350 miles away.[4]

Today the Johnstown Flood is remembered for a number of things. First, it was the largest loss of life on American soil in a single day until the events of September 11, 2001. In addition, it was the event that established the reputation of the American Red Cross, and particularly Clara Barton, who worked tirelessly to help the victims of the catastrophe. It is also remembered for the way in which new communications technologies such as the telegraph, railroad, and power printing press helped spread news of the disaster around the United States, and around the world.

One of the things for which the flood is not remembered is the role played by President Benjamin Harrison. There is a reason for this: Despite his lofty position, Harrison, the only grandson of a president to become president, had only a minor role in the entire affair. His involvement, small as it was, stemmed from his being directly contacted by the leaders of the Johnstown community. On June 3, a few days after the flood, a group called the "Masonic Committee" telegraphed "His Excellency, Benjamin Harrison," at the White House. The committee notified the president, "Situation at Johnstown appalling in extreme," and added that "unless immediate steps are taken to remove the dead from water, every river affected by waters of Conemaugh will carry pestilence in its course." Their specific request was worded in a strangely deferential way, given the urgency of the situation: "Can you not send a government sanitary corps to the scene without a moment's delay?" Finally, to press the seriousness of the crisis, they concluded with: "Every hours delay serious. . . . Death and devastation incomprehensible."[5]

The request put Harrison in a bind. Of course, he wanted to help. Every compassionate being, not to mention every election-minded politician, would have wanted to help. But he was limited both in terms of his powers and his resources, points he made in his reply of the same day. First, he made the limited resources point: "Our only sanitary corps consists of a few medical officers." Then he expressed the state-based mindset that predominated at the time, explaining that Pennsylvania residents had "a State Board of Health, and unless the governor should request it, Surgeon-General Hamilton could not interfere." It was only after he made these two points that he stressed his eagerness to assist, saying, "We are anxious to extend every possible help." Even here, though, Harrison felt it necessary to explain that "what you need is systematic work under proper authority." Finally, he closed with: "If the governor and your State Board of Health make any call upon me in any matter in my discretion I will gladly respond, and will direct Dr. Carrington to report the situation, and Dr. Hamilton will communicate at once with your State Board of Health."[6]

Harrison's message was remarkable. The United States had just suffered one of the worst days of devastation in its entire history, and the president responded to a request for help with a litany of the ways in which he was curtailed from doing so. Harrison told them that he had few medical officers, couldn't do anything unless the governor asked (twice), and noted that he could only act on matters in his discretion. Modern spinmeisters would never allow a president or senior politician to issue such an excuse-laden statement today. If they did, opprobrium and ridicule would likely follow.

Harrison's view of federal distance from local disasters was not just a Republican perspective. Just two years earlier, in February 1887, Democratic president Grover Cleveland vetoed a bill to appropriate money to provide seeds to drought-stricken counties of Texas. Cleveland's justification for this veto was that he could "find no warrant for such an appropriation in the Constitution." Furthermore, he did "not believe that the power and duty of the general government ought to be extended to the relief of individual suffering which is in no manner properly related to the public service or benefit." Cleveland clearly understood the way that such appropriations would increase expectations in the instance of further disasters, saying that "federal aid in such cases encourages the expectation of paternal care on the part of the government and weakens the sturdiness of our national character, while it prevents the indulgence among our people of that kindly sentiment and conduct which strengthens the bonds of a common brotherhood."[7] The history of federal involvement in disaster relief over the next century would prove Cleveland right.

Given this bipartisan approach to federal disaster involvement, the Masonic Committee seemed pleased with Harrison's response to their telegram. In reply to Harrison, the group wrote, "Your very satisfactory telegram received. We thought it proper to communicate with you in view of national government relation to water highways. We thank you." Not only did presidents of the time have a better sense of the limits of their own powers, but the citizenry did as well. Today it is more likely that the Masonic Committee would have responded with a negative press release, hired a lobbyist, and initiated a lawsuit.[8]

None of this is to suggest that Harrison was unsympathetic or uncompassionate in any way. At the request of Pennsylvania's governor, he sent the US Army Corps of Engineers to help with bridge construction and the removal of debris, steps he understood as within his purview.[9] He presided over a fund-raiser in Washington to raise money for the victims. The event raised $10,000, the equivalent of over $250,000 in today's dollars. Harrison even contributed $300 of his own. Furthermore, he would later recognize the efforts of Clara Barton and the Red Cross, attending a dinner at the Willard Hotel honoring her after her five months of tireless effort helping the victims at Johnstown. As David McCullough noted about the significance of Barton's attendance at the dinner, "The Red Cross had clearly arrived."[10]

Four decades later, during the great Mississippi floods of 1927, the rise of radio and widespread daily newspapers made the plight of the victims even better known. On April 16 the collapse of a levee in Illinois brought enormous flooding along areas near the Mississippi River. Five days later another levee, in Mississippi, burst, exacerbating matters further. The effects of the flooding were devastating: 16.5 million acres flooded, 637,000 persons dislocated, forty-one thousand destroyed buildings, and an unknown number of deaths, usually estimated to be in the range of 250 to 1,000.[11]

The flood became national news. Of course, having electronic forms of media during a disaster and getting their attention focused on the disaster were two different things. Outside of the areas directly impacted by the flood, more coverage went to the notorious "dumb-bell" murderers: Ruth Snyder and Judd Gray, who conspired to kill Snyder's husband in Queens Village, New York. The case, which inspired the book *Double Indemnity*, did more to grab the public's attention at the time than the floods did.[12]

Still, the flood demanded enough attention to spur federal action. President Calvin Coolidge, famous for his taciturnity and his noninterventionist approach to governing, convened his cabinet on April 22 to discuss the situation. At that meeting he put Herbert Hoover in charge of relief efforts, making him the first disaster czar in this nation's history.[13]

Hoover was a good choice. He was far more energetic than Coolidge and eager to jump in and address a disaster. As will be discussed later (see chapter 4, "Economic Collapse"), Hoover was an engineer whose previous crisis management had earned him the moniker "the Master of Emergencies." He also liked to run things, even those not within his purview, which led his colleagues to call him "the secretary of commerce and undersecretary of everything else." Coolidge, for his part, said of Hoover, "That man has offered me unsolicited advice for six years, all of it bad!"[14]

Regardless of how his boss and colleagues viewed him, Hoover earned high marks for his work on the Mississippi floods. He spent much of the next two months in the area, and in the process made himself a household name. As John Barry wrote, "Hoover performed masterfully—organizing rescue fleets and displaced persons camps as well as the delivery of food and supplies—and he made sure everyone knew it."[15] President Coolidge, who seemed to have outsourced handling the disaster to Hoover, suffered by comparison. He even became the butt of jokes, such as Will Rogers's observation that Coolidge's dilatory approach stemmed from his "hope that those needing relief will perhaps have conveniently died in the meantime."[16]

Despite the mockery, Coolidge had a method to his approach. First, he was understandably reluctant to direct federal involvement because of the precedent it would set. As David Greenberg wrote, "Taking center stage, Coolidge feared, would feed demands for a greater federal role in dealing with the calamity." Predecessors from both parties, such as Grover Cleveland and the intervention-minded Theodore Roosevelt, had previously resisted greater federal involvement in what was supposed to be local issues. Even the *New York Times* had some sympathy with Hoover's approach here, writing at the time, "Fortunately, there are still some things that can be done, without the wisdom of Congress and the all-fathering federal government."[17]

Second, in selecting Hoover, Coolidge knew what he was getting. Putting Hoover in charge was a smart move, as he was the right man for the job. His strong suits included disaster response and logistics management. Third, according to historian Kevin Kosar, Coolidge intentionally sought to keep the federal response limited to the executive branch. He did not want Congress to step in and direct appropriations to the region. Instead, he wanted to use the executive branch to coordinate relief efforts. As Kosar wrote, "Coolidge's version of a disaster response and recovery czar enabled quick and apparently efficient utilization of governmental and private sector resources and personnel."[18]

The federal response to the flood was far from perfect. Furthermore, the response has come under criticism from contemporary historians such as John Barry, David Greenberg, and Steven Ambrose, among others. To be fair to Coolidge, though, his approach was rooted in a view of the federal government that predated the period and the attitudes of these later historians. Coolidge was trying to preserve a worldview and an approach to the Constitution that he inherited from those who came before him. This view did not survive the administration of Franklin Delano Roosevelt and the onset of the New Deal in the 1930s. Roosevelt's expansion of the role of the state in economic affairs also applied to the federal government's role in disaster response. In addition, the growth of the national security state after World War II led to the creation of a series of agencies with civil defense or disaster management capabilities. As a result of these developments, when future presidents faced natural disasters, they would take very different approaches. Coolidge's fears about setting precedents for the federal government to be in charge of local disasters came increasingly to fruition.

In 1969, for example, Hurricane Camille killed over 250 people and caused over $1.4 billion in damages. The worst of the damage took place off the Gulf Coast, especially in Mississippi, Alabama, and Louisiana. President Richard Nixon and his administration were heavily involved in disaster recovery in a number of areas. Nixon flew over the affected areas, in contrast to Coolidge, who stayed in Washington after the Mississippi floods. Nixon also spoke out forcefully on the issue, pledging "a continuation of the interest we have already shown" from "all the departments of Government, all the agencies in Government" and from the US Congress.[19] Clearly, the concept of a limited federal disaster response was no longer operable.

Nixon not only pledged to help, but he also provided support to the impacted areas. He sent over sixteen thousand military personnel to the affected areas.[20] The troops brought supplies, helped clear away debris, and worked to maintain order. In addition, Nixon sent his vice president, Spiro Agnew, to the area, in contrast to Coolidge's deployment of a mere commerce secretary in the form of Hoover.[21] In another contrast to Coolidge and Hoover, Nixon also wanted to hear what his emissary learned on his fact-finding mission. Agnew came back and reported to the president on the devastation and the relief efforts. Nixon was quite taken with Agnew's report and appeared to have absorbed Agnew's briefing. During a Red Cross telethon conversation with comedian Bob Hope, Nixon mentioned Agnew's observation that Camille was "probably the worst natural disaster we have had in this century."[22]

Nixon's willingness to learn from Agnew's visit led to the development of an important tool still with us today. In response to Agnew's report, Nixon commented on the inability of forecasters to predict dangerous weather patterns. Agnew said he would confer with the president's science adviser, Lee DuBridge, and come up with a recommendation. On August 25 Nixon ordered federal officials to improve their weather forecasting ability, a move that would have significant impact.[23]

In response to this request, National Hurricane Center director Robert Simpson worked with an outside consultant named Herbert Saffir on a way to categorize major storms. Saffir had already developed a five-category storm scale, but he and Simpson worked together on the five-tier category of hurricanes familiar to us today. The familiar storm rating system, which gives government officials, relief agencies, and ordinary citizens a sense of how to plan for a storm, is a direct outgrowth of this Camille-based presidential directive.[24]

Camille was influential in another way as well. According to Saffir, "Hurricane Camille was sort of a red light to the federal government to learn what can happen with a hurricane. Before Camille," he added, "I think most people were thinking of a hurricane as a sort of local event." After Camille the federal government would now be a major player in weather events.[25]

Overall, the response to Camille has to be considered a success. According to Hurricane Camille expert Philip Hearn, President Richard Nixon's prediction that "the Gulf Coast would rebuild better than ever was fundamentally fulfilled."[26] Local counties adopted and began to enforce stricter building codes. And yet the extent of the alphabet soup of agencies responding to the crisis would have terrified Coolidge. It also would have convinced him that he was right to try to resist greater federal involvement in these matters. In addition to the Department of Defense, other federal agencies that participated in Camille recovery efforts included the Departments of Agriculture; Commerce; Housing and Urban Development; Health, Education and Welfare (HEW); Justice; and Treasury.[27] No doubt many more departments would have gotten involved, such as Homeland Security and the Environmental Protection Agency, but they had yet to be created.

By 1969 Congress had become increasingly involved in disasters as well, especially on the appropriations front. It was in the realm of Congress's emergency appropriations powers that the heavy arm of the federal government intervened in ways that Coolidge would have found most disturbing. Officials at HEW, the precursor agency to both Health and Human Services (HHS) and the Department of Education, tried to tie funding for disaster relief to the issue of school desegregation. US Office of Education official Guy Clark told administrators of Mississippi schools affected by Camille that "they could expect no federal assistance for repair and replacement of buildings, supplies, and equipment if their schools were not in compliance with Title VI of the Civil Rights Act of

1964."[28] According to historian Mark Smith, the move "showed a great deal of imagination for federal bureaucrats."[29]

HEW's effort to tie disaster relief to the administration's policy preferences reflected a new view of federalism that had been growing in prominence since the New Deal. The Roosevelt administration had pushed for greater federal involvement in interstate commerce to combat the Great Depression. In fits and starts, the Roosevelt team eventually got the Supreme Court to accede to their view that the Interstate Commerce Clause enabled all kinds of federal regulatory interventions that previously would not have been allowed. Federalism suffered a further blow in the 1950s and 1960s when Southern states tried to use states' rights to maintain their system of state-sanctioned bigotry and segregation. By the time the Nixon administration came round in 1969, the concept of states' rights had been greatly diminished, allowing for the expansive interpretation of federal powers that HEW attempted during Camille.

Despite the creative attempt, though, the storm relief leverage did not end up accelerating school desegregation. It turned out that the Nixon administration had a higher priority in the form of funding for a new antiballistic missile system. Mississippi senator John Stennis, a Democrat, threatened to withhold the missile funding if HEW maintained the threat, and Nixon forced HEW secretary Robert Finch to back down.[30]

The goal of school integration is of course a noble one. However, the creative method of tying federal disaster relief to state compliance with federal policy preferences pushed the bounds of federalism in a new and uncomfortable way. Four decades earlier Coolidge had been concerned about federal intervention imposing unrealistic expectations on the federal government. In the second half of the twentieth century, the expectation for federal disaster intervention increased enormously. In conjunction with those increased expectations, the levers of the federal government expanded as well, as did the federal use of those levers to advance the administration's political and policy goals.

As the federal government became more and more involved in disaster relief, disasters became more of an issue in elections as well. In August 1992 Hurricane Andrew devastated Florida and other parts of the

Southeast, directly causing twenty-six deaths (with another forty indirectly), $25 billion in damages, and destroying over twenty-five thousand homes.[31] Within days of Andrew making landfall on August 24, one local told a camera crew, "It's more like a third world country down here."[32]

What was remarkable about this storm was the immediate sense that it was the federal government that was now responsible for the recovery. FEMA had been created in 1979, and the government was expected not only to forecast the weather but also to lead recovery efforts. As a result, disaster recovery became a metric for judging the effectiveness of a president, a development with significant political implications.

By August 28, only four days after the storm made landfall, the *New York Times* ran a headline: "Bush Sending Army to Florida Amid Criticism of Relief Effort." The lede of the piece spoke of "angry local criticism of the Federal relief effort in South Florida."[33] The best-known piece of this "angry local criticism" came from Dade County's emergency operations director, Kate Hale, who plaintively and famously asked at an August 27 news conference, "Where in the hell is the cavalry on this one?" Hale was direct in her criticism of federal officials, saying, "They keep saying we're going to get supplies. For God's sake, where are they?"[34]

The Bush administration got the message. On August 28 Bush held a news conference in which he detailed federal efforts to address the situation. According to Bush, the resources being directed to the affected area included seven thousand troops, with another one thousand marines coming; two tent cities to accommodate five thousand people; 400,000 meals; and twenty mobile kitchen trailers. As the president said, in words that would have been shocking to Harrison and disturbing to Coolidge, "The Federal Government has a leading role in the humanitarian relief." Bush did, however, acknowledge that the federal government had a more limited role on the security side of things, adding that the federal government "does not have a role in the security right now."[35] This was due in large part to the 1878 Posse Comitatus Act, which limits the ability of the federal government to use federal troops in the states without the express permission of the governor of that state.

Of course, the primary motivation behind the recovery efforts was compassion for the thousands of people displaced or harmed by the massive storm. But the coverage of the situation had a heavy overlay of politics and of the political motivations behind Bush's actions. The *New York Times* reported that Bush cancelled both a weekend trip and a campaign swing to deal with Andrew. In detailing the administration's efforts, *Times* reporter Edmund Andrews felt the need to indicate that "Florida, the nation's fourth most populous state, is considered crucial to Mr. Bush's reelection." At the same time, Andrews noted that "the Bush Administration had confined its relief effort to the scale appropriate for past disasters and had refrained from taking extraordinary measures."[36]

The politics ended up being important. Bush won Florida (narrowly) but lost the election. There were a lot of factors contributing to Bush's loss in 1992, including a sluggish economy, a feisty third-party candidate in Ross Perot, and Bill Clinton's impressive ability to connect with the Baby Boom generation. But one factor that also contributed to Bush's surprising loss—he had an 89 percent approval rating in February/March 1991—was the nagging sense that the federal government had not adequately responded to Hurricane Andrew's impact three months before he faced the voters that November.

Bush had not just one but two sons who went on to become governors: Jeb in Florida and George W. in Texas. As governors, both had a healthy realization of the importance of disaster management to their political fortunes. As president, George W. Bush maintained this sense of prioritization when it came to disaster management. As late as 2004, articles were appearing praising Bush's handling of disasters, and recognizing that his emphasis on disaster management stemmed from his recognition that poor disaster management had hurt his father politically in the 1992 election.

The articles on Bush's disaster management may have questioned Bush's motivations, but they did not question his competence. NBC's Tom Curry, for example, wrote in 2004 that both "President Bush and his brother Jeb, Florida's governor, know the lessons of August 1992, when their father, President George H. W. Bush, reacted too slowly with federal aid to help speed recovery after Hurricane Andrew ravaged Florida." As proof, Curry cited the alacrity with which President Bush 43 showed up in Florida following August 2004's Hurricane Charley. Curry showed

Bush's awareness of the political aspect of disaster management, quoting Bush's statement: "Yeah, if I didn't come, they would've said we should have been here more rapidly." Curry also noted that Bush 43's chief of staff Andrew Card was Bush 41's point person on the Andrew situation, suggesting that the sensitivity to dealing with disasters extended to the staff level as well.[37]

Given the second Bush administration's focus on disaster response, it is ironic that one of the biggest black marks on George W. Bush's record is the federal response to Hurricane Katrina. That storm, in August 2005, killed over 1,800 people and caused over $148 billion in damages. It was particularly destructive not just because of the storm itself, but also because of the damage the storm wreaked on the levees, which caused massive flooding. The storm and attendant floods made 600,000 families homeless, left 3 million homes without power, and damaged or destroyed 1.2 million homes. It painted an indelible picture of government helplessness, as images of the suffering Gulf Staters went around the country and around the world.[38] Katrina also reshaped the landscape of New Orleans. Nine years after the storm, the city still had only 78 percent of its pre-storm population.[39]

Beyond all the devastation, Katrina is perhaps best remembered for the devastating impact it had on the Bush presidency. In his own memoir, Bush wrote regarding Katrina that "the legacy of fall 2005 lingered for the rest of my time in office."[40]

Bush was willing to admit mistakes on his part in the Katrina response. In his memoir he lists at least four of them, including the failure to urge an earlier evacuation, his failure to return to Washington sooner, his slowness in showing both sympathy and federal action, and his waiting too long to call in federal troops.[41]

Other critics were far harsher than this tough self-assessment. The entertainer Kanye West said that "George Bush doesn't care about black people." Singer Harry Belafonte said, "Clearly, Bush faltered deeply. His arrogance was really quite key to that." Professor Michael Eric Dyson wrote an entire book critical of Bush's handling of Katrina, saying things like "Bush's myopic attention to terror has also kept him from paying critical attention to natural disasters," and "Bush proved he couldn't balance domestic demands and foreign forays."[42] According to *New York Times* reporter Peter Baker, citing Bush White House aide Dan Bartlett, the TV coverage on the night that Bush flew over, but did not land in, a flooded New Orleans was "probably the worst of the entire presidency."[43]

Regardless, the Katrina response was a flawed one. But the Katrina response must be viewed in context. As Patrick Roberts noted, "Given the severity of both the hurricane and the flooding, casualties were relatively low, and hundreds of thousands of residents were evacuated by federal authorities from the city within six days."[44] Furthermore, while the federal government could and should have done more, the efforts by state and local officials, who had frontline responsibilities, were significantly worse. The delays in evacuating the city, and in deciding on whether to allow in federal troops, were costly. State and local officials lacked the means to communicate with one another in emergencies, and basic tasks typically assigned to state and local officials were left to federal responders. Both Governor Kathleen Blanco and New Orleans mayor Ray Nagin—later sentenced to ten years in prison for corruption while in office—were clearly out of their depth and exacerbated an already bad situation. As Bob Williams wrote in the *Wall Street Journal*, "The plain fact is, lives were needlessly lost in New Orleans due to the failure of Louisiana's governor, Kathleen Blanco, and the city's mayor, Ray Nagin."[45] The basic failures at the state and local level put additional responsibilities on the federal government.

The expectations game plays a role here as well. It is only in this era where expectations regarding federal response are so high that the inability of the federal government to mitigate the effects of a massive hurricane and flood striking a coastal region constitute an epic failure. For almost the first two centuries of our republic, the federal government was not seen as responsible, let alone equipped, to deal with massive disasters.[46] As this survey thus far has shown, the idea of federal involvement is something that has been increasing over the past five decades, with the expectations appearing to grow with each and every disaster.

From Harrison making a donation after Johnstown to criticisms that Bush failed to single-handedly hold back the floodwaters and personally rebuild New Orleans, American expectations regarding the federal role in disasters are ever growing. Presidential authority and levers of power have expanded tremendously as well, but it is not realistic to expect presidents to be able to prevent acts of God and undo them should they happen. During the Gulf Oil spill of 2010, President Obama shared that his daughter knocked on his door and asked him, "Did you plug the hole yet, Daddy?"[47] Some in the media may have visions of Obama as Superman, but mere mortals lack the ability to hold back nature, and disaster planning in the future will be better served by having expectations for disaster management better aligned with reality.[48]

IMPROVING OUR RESPONSE TO WEATHER CATASTROPHES

Despite all the technological progress humans have made over the last few centuries, Mother Nature remains largely beyond our control. In fact, when it comes to weather, many scientists believe that the offshoots of technological progress exacerbate weather-based disruptions. Regardless of where one stands on this debate, the fact remains that there is little that government officials can do in the short term, and probably even in the long term, to prevent catastrophic weather events from taking place. Government officials, up to and including the president, also cannot minimize the physical impact of a storm, earthquake, or flood, although government efforts can and do alleviate suffering and help rebuild in the wake of such an event.

In other words, presidents, for all their power, cannot control the weather. This section operates under the assumption that weather is out of presidential control, and also that presidents will have to react to multiple weather challenges during their tenure. Despite the fact that President Harrison had little role in the Johnstown Flood, presidents must also play according to the rules of the game for twenty-first-century disasters, not nineteenth-century ones.

One other rule for presidents is that they will be judged only as successfully as they handled their most recent disaster. President George W. Bush, as noted above, got high marks for his handling of disasters before Katrina, even if reporters were cynical about his motivations for the attention he gave to crisis management. As someone who worked in the Bush White House during Katrina, I heard the frustrations of both the president and members of his staff, who would claim that every disaster declaration prior to Katrina, of which there were over two dozen, had gone off without a hitch. Perhaps so, but the media only focused on the one that went poorly.

Presidents, therefore, are in a tough bind. They must be prepared for disasters and know that they will be judged on how they handle disasters, while at the same time know that they cannot prevent them. There are a number of implications to this realization. First, presidents and their teams must set realistic expectations. When George W. Bush said in 2003 that "we have a responsibility that when somebody hurts, Government has got to move,"[49] he set the bar too high not only for himself, but for any administration. "Somebody" always hurts, and government cannot realistically address the pain of every single one of its citizens. This sentiment alienated conservatives who felt that it was an improper and misleading depiction of governmental responsibilities in our constitutional system.

The "somebody hurts" line stuck to Bush, and not in a good way. Conservatives such as Jonah Goldberg, Bruce Bartlett, James Antle, and Jeremy Lott all used the line to criticize Bush's commitment to conservatism. Bartlett said of Bush's "somebody hurts" line, "A more succinct description of liberalism would be hard to find."[50] Goldberg used the line to issue his "silver-lining hope" that "George W. Bush's compassionate conservatism gets wiped out like a taco hut in the path of a Cat. 5 storm."[51] In addition to the assaults from the right, "somebody hurts" also left Bush vulnerable to critics on all sides of the aisle who could use the line to demonstrate that people were "hurt" in Katrina, and government was not moving nearly fast or far enough.

Beyond managing expectations, presidents must also make sure that their administrations meet the properly calibrated promises they issue. Even this is not easy. The federal government has evolved into a massive and behemoth bureaucracy with two million employees, a number impossible for anyone to control. President Obama once explained this point by recounting some advice he had received from Defense Secretary Robert Gates: "Somewhere, somehow, somebody in the federal government is screwing up."[52] The point is not to excuse incompetence. However, presidents know that they are held responsible for the actions of the government as a whole. This means that whatever disaster promises they make, they had better make sure their government is keeping them, regardless of the fact that somebody, somewhere, somehow is screwing up.

Nothing can ensure the complete absence of screw-ups. But smart leadership can make sure that key offices are prepared to deal with crises. Since weather is the one thing presidents know they are going to face, they should make sure that they and their top officials are ready when the bad weather hits. Senior officials tend not to like to drill or practice for potential crises. There always seem to be more pressing priorities. But given the certainty of weather-based events, presidents should make sure that they and their senior officials engage in preparation drills early on in their administrations, and that they continue to do so periodically.

Within the realm of realistic expectations, the president also needs to develop realistic budget numbers. The government spends a staggering amount of money on disasters, but it does not budget properly for that spending. According to the Center for American Progress's Daniel J. Weiss and Jackie Weidman, the US government spent $136 billion on disaster relief between 2011 and 2013, approximately $400 per US household. This spending takes place among nineteen different departments, expected agencies like the Department of Homeland Security, but also unexpected ones like the Smithsonian Institution and NASA. The Department of Agriculture alone has nineteen disaster-related programs.[53]

This spending exacerbates Washington's already difficult attempts to get the debt and deficit under control. The money the government spends in response to disasters typically comes in the form of what is known in Washington as a "supplemental," meaning the spending is a supplement to the normal budget process. This money is rarely budgeted for, and therefore adds to our deficit challenges. As Weiss and Weidman put it, "Since additional federal recovery assistance is rarely offset by budget cuts or revenue increases, this aid will likely add to the federal budget deficit."[54]

The impact that unplanned spending has on our budget is enormous. Nevertheless, it remains possible to draw certain conclusions to guide our future decision making. The most surprising aspect of the $136 billion in spending is the fact that it had to be estimated by an outside organization. The US government has little idea of how much it spends on disasters and does not budget for disasters as it does with other line items. Therefore, one needed reform a president could impose unilaterally is to order the Office of Management and Budget to prepare an annual accounting of federal spending on disasters. Developing this figure over time would make it easier for policymakers on both sides of Capitol Hill to budget for future years.

Another problem is the degree to which disaster funding is improvised. The government does have an annual disaster contingency fund of about $12 billion.[55] But this pales next to the $136 billion that the government actually spent from 2011 to 2013. This improvisational approach harms attempts at responsible budgeting, but it also harms the affected communities as well. As the Rockefeller Institute's James W. Fossett has argued, "The federal government has no single expedited process for allocating and spending relief money."[56] What this means is that emergency appropriations get directed to federal agencies, and localities must then petition the individual agencies to get specific types of assistance for their communities. This approach imposes additional burdens on the communities seeking relief. It is also inefficient. Each office, each agency, each bureaucracy through which disaster money is directed spends money in the process of directing said funds. At the end of the process, less money ends up in the hands of the victims than the taxpayers directed on their behalf.

Another problem with this cumbersome process is that it is inherently political. The appropriations must go through Congress, which takes time and also imposes additional costs on relief legislation. Hurricane Sandy in 2012, for example, caused over $70 billion in damages and killed two hundred people. It also caused three times as many power outages as Katrina had, with many of the outages continuing for months.[57] Overall, it seemed that the lessons of Katrina had not been learned, at the local or the federal level.

In the aftermath of the hurricane, many Republicans complained that the Sandy relief bill was larded up with additional spending unrelated to the disaster. This was inarguably true, as not all, and perhaps not even most,[58] of the $60 billion in emergency Sandy funding went to the victims. This is, sadly, typical of Congress. As New Hampshire senator Kelly Ayotte wrote on the subject, "The days of using a crisis to pass bloated bills stuffed with non-emergency spending further burying us in debt must end."[59]

Not everyone agreed, of course. The bill's advocates criticized the objectors as heartless, and the funding, unnecessary parts and all, went through. New Jersey Republican Chris Christie led the pack, saying, "There is only one group to blame for the continued suffering of these innocent victims: The House majority and their speaker, John Boehner."[60] This type of political back and forth does not help our deficit problem, and it does not help disaster victims either. The political process adds additional time, which means that victims get less needed relief and get it later than they should.

An annual accounting would have an added advantage of clarity and transparency. Perhaps the American people are comfortable with the amount of federal money we as a nation spend on helping local areas deal with disasters and other acts of nature. As detailed above, the American people have certainly developed higher and perhaps even outsized expectations regarding disaster-mitigation efforts. But without that clear accounting, it is impossible to have the argument in the light of day regarding the appropriate spending levels for disasters. If the only conversation about spending comes in the aftermath of a tragedy, then it is clear that Congress will open its checkbook to provide financial assistance to suffering families, as well as whatever other priorities wily legislators can add to fast-moving aid packages. But such an approach fails to bring about an informed discussion on the proper role of government in coping with acts of nature.

One idea that could emerge from this discussion is the need for more resilience when spending at the local level. Such spending would typically be specified to the needs of the particular community. A coastal area prone to hurricanes needs to build in different resiliencies than another area vulnerable to mudslides, or earthquakes, or droughts. In addition, this discussion about local need would also help highlight the fact of differentiated risks. Different communities face different risks, and government funding decisions should take these risks into account. This does not mean that we should be ungenerous or indifferent to human tragedy in the wake of a disaster. But it does mean that communities more vulnerable to certain risks should be expected to do more to prepare themselves for the risks that they do face.

Clearly, our disaster planning needs rethinking—especially for the disasters that we are most likely to face. But in the course of that rethinking, presidents must not lose sight of the political ramifications of weather-based calamities. Presidents must recognize that weather events will happen, that the president will be judged on how he or she handles them, and that weather events will affect large numbers of Americans. According to one analysis by the Environment America Research and Policy Center, weather-based disasters affected 243 million Americans between the years 2007 and 2012. Eighty percent of Americans lived in counties subject to a weather-based federal disaster declaration during that span.[61] In a country as geographically vast as ours, weather disruptions are a given. In a nation as compassionate as ours, pictures of suffering Americans are galvanizing events. The message to presidents in response to weather disasters must be: long-term, rethink; short-term, ignore or be callous at your political peril.

Chapter Four

Economic Collapse

ONE THING THAT CONNECTS EVERY AMERICAN TO ONE ANOTHER IS the US economy. You can be a banker in New York or a farmer in Nebraska, and the state of the US economy will have a tangible impact on you and your well-being. While economic events are not technically acts of nature, they are sufficiently removed from the actions of any one individual that they are not quite acts of man, either. Presidents must prepare for economic disruptions regardless of their classification, if for no other reason than their own political well-being. Throughout our history, Americans have judged presidents on the basis of how they handled the economy. Economic fluctuations, many of them completely out of presidential control, have both made and destroyed presidential reputations.

For the most part, economic ups and downs are part of the normal order of business and do not fit into the disaster paradigm. Future presidents should make it a primary order of business to avoid having an economic downturn or, worse, an economic collapse occur on their watch. This cannot always be avoided, and navigating through economic difficulties requires both policy savvy and communications skills. On occasion, though, an economic collapse can be so overwhelming and so devastating that it completely changes the order of things, damages the well-being of nearly every American, and ruins the reputation of the sitting president in the process. In 1929 Herbert Hoover learned this lesson the hard way.

When Hoover was elected president in 1928, he was a national hero. In the 1910s and 1920s, Hoover had distinguished himself by taking on some of the most difficult policy and logistical challenges of his time. By the time he left the Oval Office in 1933, he was seen as a national scapegoat, a symbol of ineffectuality who helped bring about, and then failed to fix, the Great Depression.

Hoover's rise to prominence took him from Stanford University to international acclaim and success as a mining engineer by the age of forty. He was a logistical genius and lacked no confidence in his own abilities—and for good reason. During World War I he started and headed the Commission for Relief in Belgium, which helped feed Europeans, particularly Belgians, behind the German blockade. By 1917 he had become, in the words of historian George Nash, "the embodiment of a new force in global politics: American benevolence."[1]

His skill was recognized by President Woodrow Wilson, who put Hoover in charge of the United States Food Administration (USFA). After the war the USFA not only helped stave off starvation for many, but in doing so also helped stabilize nations threatened by the spread of the Bolshevik revolution in Russia. Later he helped direct food to victims of a famine caused by that very Bolshevik revolution, under the auspices of his American Relief Administration. He then became secretary of commerce under Presidents Warren G. Harding and Calvin Coolidge, and even had a popular nickname: "the Master of Emergencies."

This background is important because it highlights just how far Hoover's reputation collapsed as a result of the Great Depression. It is also a reminder of how unyielding the judgment of history can be when it comes to those unprepared for large-scale crises or disasters. Hoover provides an object lesson that even an internationally beloved hero, even one who specifically had a reputation as someone skilled in responding to crises, could suffer permanent reputation damage based on one event.

Very few nonlethal events in history have cast such a dark shadow and affected so many lives as the Great Depression. It became a worldwide economic collapse unlike any other in modern history. It destroyed businesses across the American economy. Tens of thousands of banks and businesses collapsed between 1929 and 1932. Net farm income dropped from over $6 billion to $2 billion. In terms of the housing sector, residential construction dropped 82 percent. The stock market fell to 41 in July 1932, down from 294 in the spring of 1930. Overall, national income fell from $87.4 billion in 1929 to $41.7 billion in 1932. These aggregate figures, as horrifying as they are, do not take into account the human toll of the Depression and its devastating impact on millions of American lives.[2]

History portrays Hoover as a man crippled by inaction. In reality, though, many of his responses to the incipient depression mirrored the future policies of his successor. In fact, Hoover has incorrectly gone down in history as some kind of free market absolutist. As the political humorist Jonah Goldberg joked, "The Herbert Hoover of popular imagination was a laissez-faire lickspittle of Adam Smith."[3] This perception, however, was not the reality. Hoover, an inveterate engineer, thought he could fix things by tinkering. His tinkering with the economy included decidedly non-laissez-faire positions such as increasing farm subsidies, hiking taxes, creating the Reconstruction Finance Corporation, and signing the Smoot-Hawley tariff. Whatever one may think of these policies, they are in no way the policies of a free market purist. As historian of the Depression Amity Shlaes has written, "Hoover spent decades underscoring his aversion to stark austerity and pure laissez-faire policy."[4]

Hoover also tried and failed to boost American morale in order to turn things around. His attempts to talk up the economy failed in the face of overwhelming evidence that things were getting worse, not better. In May 1930, just to take one example, the *New York Times* headline read, "Worst of Depression Over, Says Hoover . . . Recovery Near, He States."[5] This prediction, understandable as his effort may have been, proved remarkably off base.

In addition to poor prognosticating, Hoover also had some wider deficiencies on the communications front. For example, he claimed to welcome questions from the press, but only if they were first submitted to his press aide, George Akerson.[6] This approach to questions contributed to his notoriously poor relations with the press.[7] He tried, unsuccessfully, to use the new medium of radio to instill confidence, giving between eighty and ninety speeches over the radio as president. He did less well in the newsreel medium, where he would stiffen before the cameras. The newsreels also made him look older than his fifty-five years in 1929.[8] But

Hoover's poor communications skills were exacerbated by the fact that his 1932 opponent, Franklin Roosevelt, was so skilled in his use of the press, and especially in the use of radio. FDR not only had one of the best radio voices of his era, but he also understood the importance of the medium sooner than his contemporaries. He had to do this because most of his home state papers in New York were Republican leaning at the time. Mastering the new medium of radio gave FDR a path to go around the newspapers and straight to the people.[9]

Given this skill born of necessity, Roosevelt made the most of it. He spoke to the Democratic National Conventions in both 1924 and 1928, and had the key insight that in the radio era his speeches would reach a larger audience over the airwaves than in the convention halls themselves. Consequently, both his 1924 and 1928 speeches were groundbreaking: His 1924 speech introduced William Wordsworth's concept of "the Happy Warrior" into politics, and in 1928 he specifically tailored the speech to the radio audience, something that was innovative at the time.[10]

Faced with Roosevelt's media skill, Hoover could not keep up. One story that highlights the contrast between the two men as communicators is in their interactions with the biggest star of the day: Babe Ruth. In the fall of 1929, after things had turned sour but before the long-term effects of the Depression had fully set in, Ruth was asked about the difference between his $80,000 salary and Hoover's $75,000 figure. Ruth's immortal reply—"Why not? I had a better year than he did"—stuck with Hoover and would become symbolic of his ineffectuality.[11]

FDR, in contrast, got on just fine with Ruth. This was in part because Ruth, despite his high salary, was no Republican. In fact, when Warren Harding's team asked Ruth for an endorsement, Ruth replied, "Hell no, I'm a Democrat." But FDR showed significant aplomb in dealing with the prickly Ruth, corresponding with him, getting him to endorse Al Smith in 1924, and even throwing out the first pitch at the 1932 World Series game in which Ruth hit his most famous home run, the "called shot" against the Chicago Cubs.[12]

In addition to their divergent PR skills, there was also the perceived policy contrast between Hoover and FDR. Economic historians largely agree that FDR's policies were not that different from Hoover's. Simply put, FDR advocated government intervention on a broader scale. His policy prescriptions included Social Security, the Securities and Exchange Commission, and massive public works projects. But neither was a supporter of laissez-faire, and both were believers in the need for government intervention in the economy. As Davis Houck has written, both Hoover and Roosevelt "believed that public confidence was vital to economic recovery." In this, he wrote, both "could rightly be described as Keynesians, perhaps even Post Keynesians."[13]

This is not to say the men were the same in their aims beyond the historic moment of the Great Depression. Hoover certainly did not think so. "Hoover," Nash observed, "perceived in the New Deal of Franklin Roosevelt not a moderate and pragmatic response to economic distress but something more sinister: a revolutionary transformation in America's political economy and constitutional order."[14] No doubt some of Hoover's suspicions were elicited by political rivalry and partisan jealousy—and FDR did his part to exacerbate the bitterness. Roosevelt saw a tremendous advantage of setting up a contrast between himself and Hoover, and missed few opportunities to sharpen that contrast. This is, of course, a standard political strategy in running against an unpopular incumbent. Roosevelt, however, took this strategy past the campaign, continued it long beyond his electoral victory, and even inspired this line of attack in his loyalists in the administration and in academia.

In the transition between the Hoover and Roosevelt administrations, Roosevelt let Hoover feel every last bit of his lame duck status. When Hoover asked for bipartisan cooperation on an issue, Roosevelt would ignore the outgoing president's requests. When Hoover put forward ideas that Roosevelt would agree with, such as a national bank holiday, Roosevelt would not engage, even when he was only a few days from taking the reins of power. And then, when Roosevelt did assume the office, he put forward the very same idea, although this time under his own name. As financial historian Liaquat Ahamed has written, "Roosevelt maintained his hard line against cooperating with the out-going administration to the very end."[15]

Even once Roosevelt took office, he continued to press his upper hand against Hoover. In his inaugural address, with Hoover sitting nearby and 400,000 spectators in the crowd, Roosevelt said, somewhat rudely, "The money changers have fled from their high seats in the temple of our civilization. We may now restore that temple to the ancient truths." Roosevelt biographer Conrad Black described the scene: "The vast audience before him and the tens of millions listening on radio loved it, though Herbert Hoover, sitting six feet away, must have found it disconcerting."[16]

All of this maneuvering had a purpose. FDR was determined to make sure that he was seen by the American people, and remembered by the historians, as the president who ended the Great Depression. For the most part he succeeded, although he had to be the first president to go beyond two terms, and America had to get involved in a world war, for this to happen.

Eventually, the United States and the rest of the world emerged from the Great Depression. What is increasingly debated is whether FDR's policies succeeded economically, and not just psychologically. Many now believe that his varying (sometimes contradictory) courses of action were not as effective as once thought. What is beyond argument is that the Great Depression did not end until the 1940s—almost ten years after Roosevelt was elected—and that America's resurgence was driven in no small part by a war that mobilized the entire US economy.

Looking back with the perspective and equanimity that historical reflection provides, there are certainly reasons to believe that Hoover and Roosevelt both played a part in lengthening the downturn. As Amity Shlaes has written, "From 1929 to 1940, from Hoover to Roosevelt, government intervention helped to make the Depression Great."[17] In trying anything and everything, both presidents, to varying degrees, created a climate of uncertainty for the businesses, entrepreneurs, and investors who had the means to lead the private sector's efforts to reverse the course of the economy. Despite this uncertainty, Roosevelt was long remembered as the forceful leader who ended the Depression, and Hoover is still lambasted as the dupe who caused it. During the financial crisis of 2007 and 2008, President George W. Bush dreaded being tagged by history as Hoover and backed a dramatic and unprecedented plan that appeared to contradict his free market approach. In explaining his perspective, he told aides, "If we're really looking at another Great Depression, you can be damn sure I'm going to be Roosevelt, not Hoover."[18] Roosevelt, it must be said, deserves credit for understanding one of the key aspects of presidential leadership: If there is going to be a crisis on your watch, make sure you don't get tagged with the blame.

OUR ECONOMIC SYSTEM

The US economic system is, and has long been, the envy of the world. For generations it has contributed to bringing millions of people out of poverty, not just in America but around the world. This success has made many people around the world dependent on the vitality of the US economic engine. As the saying goes, America sneezes and the world catches a cold.

For the most part the primacy of the US economy has been a good thing for Americans and for the world. For the past two centuries, the spread of working market economies has generated untold wealth and raised living standards for hundreds of millions of people. In the period following World War II, US leadership and innovation has improved the destiny of billions of people all the way into the twenty-first century.

It is important to recognize just how significant and far-reaching this increase in economic opportunity and rise in living standards has been. The development of free markets and the rule of law, especially in Western countries and the freer parts of Asia, have reshaped international relations and the prospects of peace. The Hobbesian notion of life as "solitary, poor, nasty, brutish, and short" is no longer an accurate description of the life experiences of most citizens in developed nations. An earlier chapter discussed how the millennia-long quest for food and water is no longer a daily challenge in the modern world. One of the primary reasons for the lifting of that burden is the development of modern economic systems that allow for civilization-changing improvements in the production and distribution of food. Food is apparently so little of a concern in the United States these days that the country throws away about 141 trillion calories annually, about 1,249 calories per person per day. This is the equivalent of $161.6 billion worth of food, about 31 percent of our overall food supply.[19] This abundance (and waste), combined with the fact that Americans spend only about a tenth of their incomes on food, is mind-boggling. Even more extraordinary is that the vast majority of Americans do almost nothing in the production of that food, freeing people to pursue other opportunities and develop new ideas and innovations.

The apparent end of the quest for food, however, is only one component of the free market revolution. The development of comfortable living quarters, sanitation systems, hospitals, safe transportation, and extensive trade means that the lifestyles of the average American are far more comfortable than even members of the royalty from previous eras. In twenty-first-century America, for example, 99.7 percent of poor households have a refrigerator, 97.9 percent have a TV, 95.2 percent have a stove and oven, and 74.7 percent have air-conditioning. And these figures are for Americans at the lowest end of the economic scale. For average Americans the numbers are even higher, although it is difficult to get higher than figures like 99.7 percent.[20]

Free markets and the rule of law enable the human innovation and investment that create these material blessings and put them in the hands of more and more citizens. It is no exaggeration to say that the story of the postwar era in America has for the most part been consistent periods of growth, punctuated by brief recessions that bring increasing waves of opportunity and comfort. The most significant break in this cycle (since the Great Depression) was the housing collapse and recession of 2008. Before that, there appears to have been a far-reaching trust that policymakers either knew how to create fairly regular economic growth, or knew enough to get out of the way to let economic growth take place. Either way, growth was the key. Growth rates of 3 to 5 percent kept the US population largely well-off—recognizing, of course, certain large and inexcusable pockets of poverty—kept the US military well equipped, and allowed policymakers to push off difficult questions regarding competing spending priorities.[21]

US economic growth did more than just raise living standards in both the United States and the world. Steady US growth also contributed to global stability. Other countries, many of which had less developed political systems and were rife with more intense ethnic rivalries, could be made placid in circumstances of economic growth. In periods when US economic growth ground to a halt, the odds of bad things happening internationally significantly increased.

The linkage of material well-being and stability goes back centuries. Think back to the French Revolution. When the masses have food, political systems can manage strife. When basic necessities are lacking, it becomes much harder for governments to contain disagreements and class or ethnic hatred. As the *Wall Street Journal*'s Dan Henninger put it, "If the American economic engine slows permanently to about 2 percent, you're going to see more fires around the world like Ukraine and Venezuela. At the margin, the world's weakest, most misgoverned countries will pop, and violently."[22]

For all these reasons and more, the most important job of US presidents is to keep the US economy humming. If they manage to do so, the population will be happy, foreign conflicts will be less likely, the deficits will remain manageable, and both the electorate and the history books will look more favorably upon them.

Given this very stark reality, every president knows that he or she will be judged in both the short and the long term on how the economy is handled. If they are elected during an economic downturn, they are expected to improve things, and if they come to power during economic growth, they are expected to "prevent" a recession. While every president deals with economic variations, the normal booms and busts of the business cycle do not fit within the definition of a disaster. It is only a sudden and total economic collapse that truly counts as a disaster.

One problem with facing this challenge is that policymakers typically do not know when an economic collapse will occur, or how to prevent it. The 2008 catastrophe, for example, was caused at least in part by a housing bubble, yet government policymakers, on the left and on the right, in Congress and in the executive branch, had been steadily focused on increasing homeownership, even among those who could not afford it. Furthermore, once a crisis happens, the president's options for stopping or ending a collapse are limited. As Hoover and Roosevelt learned, it can take a long time to right the economic ship after things go horribly wrong.

Even in the case of 2008, in which some people did warn that there was a housing bubble, or that Wall Street was overleveraged with debt instruments, those people were not in the right places at the right times to do something about it. The president, as powerful as he may be, does not have control over all the levers of economic policymaking. The Federal Reserve arguably holds more cards than the president. And even in the case of Fannie Mae and Freddie Mac, which the Bush administration worried about and tried to reform, congressional resistance prevented any of the reforms from being enacted. For good or for ill, our system is designed in such a way that it would be extremely difficult for policymakers to effect rapid changes that could prevent a collapse, even if the policymakers knew that a collapse was coming and knew what steps were necessary to prevent that collapse.

For these reasons economic catastrophes, while rare, will almost always come by surprise. That said, there is at least one looming economic disaster that cannot be considered a surprise, namely the massive and unsustainable deficit that the United States is carrying. This figure, in excess of $19 trillion and expected to hit $27 trillion by 2024, is exacerbated by the long-term liabilities that the US entitlement programs face.[23] The Medicare program, which provides health coverage for America's growing sixty-five and older population, faces a short-term deficit larger than that of Greece, and long-term unfunded liabilities in excess of $35 trillion. All told, long-term US debt obligations are in the range of $80 to $100 trillion. By 2039 interest payments alone will cost 4.5 percent of GDP, potentially crippling the government's ability to spend money on anything else.

Our long-term unfunded obligations are a big number, but not a cause for immediate panic. After all, these obligations are long-term promises, not already incurred debts. The words *long-term* mean exactly that, taking place over a seventy-five-year period. And slight changes in growth rates, demographic trends, or policies can make big changes in what those long-term obligations will mean at the end of the seventy-five-year window.[24]

Even though we should not have to worry about paying this debt tomorrow, these long-term obligations remain a concern. Just as these numbers can change for the better, they can also change for the worse. And even if they don't change at all, they would constitute an unmanageable obligation. Furthermore, recent behavior by the US government does not inspire confidence regarding the ability of the United States to reduce its long-term obligations. Despite some recent improvement in terms of the size of our annual deficits, the overall debt has continued to grow, meaning that the problem is likely to worsen.

The debt problem is not only a problem for the United States, but also for the world, and the world is noticing. In 2011 Standard & Poor's downgraded the US government's AAA credit rating. Large holders of US debt, including Russia and China, are both increasingly nervous about being stuck with these obligations. They can hardly be expected to risk their own interests. This could carry severe consequences for America. Furthermore, the irresponsibility of accruing these trillions of dollars in obligations constitutes behavior that would not be tolerated elsewhere. As financial analyst Peter Schiff has written, "We owe trillions. Look at our budget deficit; look at the debt to GDP ratio, the unfunded liabilities. If we were in the Eurozone, they would kick us out."[25]

The accumulation of debt has thus far not caused an economic collapse, but that does not mean it won't happen. It only means that it has not happened yet. When it does happen, if it does happen, it will take place very fast. Our new globalized world, with instantaneous financial transactions and information alike, will mean that a financial crisis is far less likely to be localized and much more likely to be global. As former Treasury secretary Larry Summers has observed, "The problem of global financial markets is that they are like modern jet planes. They get you where you need to go faster, but the crashes are far, far worse."[26] This is even truer if the crisis begins in the United States, where the ripple effects will be felt more keenly.

There is no guarantee that the US debt will be the cause of the next economic collapse, but it clearly is a likely culprit. For this reason the only rational response would be to take serious steps to get our debt situation under control. This would include taking some unpopular steps, which would focus on reducing the size of our long-term obligations by adjusting inflation rates, means-testing benefits, and increasing the retirement age. Thus far, the US government has been unwilling to take such steps, but if they fail to do so before a debt-fueled crisis hits, the government's inaction will be revealed to have been extremely short-sighted.

Although the steps to alleviate the debt crisis would be painful, not preventing a debt-fueled economic collapse would be far more painful. In fact, one of the reasons given for the reluctance to trim back unrealistic entitlement promises is that such steps could harm the poor. If our looming debt crisis does indeed create an economic collapse, it will be a disaster to our nation and to our way of life. In such an economic catastrophe, those living at the low end of the economic ladder will be the first to suffer because they have so little to fall back on.

First, the loss of economic dynamism will mean the loss of economic opportunity for those who aspire to rise from poverty. Loss of jobs also means that low-skill, low-wage jobs will be the first to go. Even now, France's anemic, state-heavy economy hires only the most productive and well educated, while the poorly educated or those without social connections are left behind. In such cases of Eurosclerosis, the highly educated often seek government positions and pensions to protect them from economic displacement caused by excessive government.

In addition, if we don't trim our entitlement programs, they will collapse. In an economic crisis, programs for the poor will be eviscerated; they will not be sustained, as liberals want, and they will not be reformed, like conservatives want. They will be cut indiscriminately, because we will have no choice.

Finally, the poor will be disproportionately affected because they have no savings to fall back on. According to the Federal Reserve Board, families in the bottom income quintile had a median net worth of $8,500 in 2007; in 2010 the median net worth of the bottom quintile was $6,200, a decline of 27 percent. The recession reduced the holdings of the poor by a quarter of its value. If a complete economic collapse takes place, it will not only be a human tragedy, but it will also be a civic disaster, as the disproportionately affected poor could be a source of major civil and possibly global unrest. As disaster chronicler Joshua Cooper Ramo has noted, "Every once in a while the physics come along and munch away decades of civilized life, the way the 1929 stock market crash tightened Europe's downward economic spiral, helping to elevate Hitler and the whole horrible historical train wreck that came afterward."[27]

＊＊＊

Fortunately, disaster is not destiny, and it is far from too late to take steps to prevent one from happening. There is even historical precedent for getting our debt under control by taking a series of measured, non-radical steps to control spending and maintain revenue levels. According to former head of the Council of Economic Advisers Martin Feldstein, "It is worth remembering that after World War II we brought our national debt down from 109 percent of GDP to 46 percent of GDP in 1960." According to Feldstein, the United States accomplished this without major tax hikes or spending cuts, but by keeping spending steady while the economy grew.[28] Such an event is not just doable, though; today it is also necessary. Our economic future is dependent on the ability of our elected officials to manage our spending priorities responsibly and make the hard choices. Thus far they have not been up to the task.

Another possible solution to our debt and deficit troubles could come from renewed economic growth. Naysayers of previous eras suggested that the American moment might be over, only to be surprised by the manufacturing boom of the 1950s, corporate restructuring in the 1980s, or the Internet revolution in the 1990s. American innovation has defeated the nattering nabobs of negativism in the past, and could do so again. Former White House speechwriter David Frum has even identified three likely sources of an American economic resurgence: the discovery of new energy sources, renewed innovation in pharmaceuticals and biologics, and the revitalization of America's inner cities.[29]

Frum may be right, but there are a host of other possibilities as yet unthought of, as well. Economic changes often come from unantici-pated places. Policymakers must therefore understand that we do not and cannot know which innovations will prove to be transformative. Along with recognizing the importance of innovation, we need policies that prepare for disasters by enabling the investment and innovation that allow for human beings to create new products and processes without the government putting its thumb on the scale in favor of one kind of innovation or another.

CONCLUSION

Of all the scenarios laid out in this book, the most likely disaster that all Americans will face in their adult lifetimes is some kind of economic crisis. These have struck our economy with some degree of regularity throughout American history, and there is little to nothing to suggest that we as a nation have figured out some kind of formula that will prevent future downturns. The good news is that we have survived these downturns previously, and surely can do so again.

The fact that these types of incidents are likely and recurrent, however, does not mean we should blithely accept their arrival. US policymakers, and especially the president, should do everything to prevent them from happening. This should entail looking at the most predictable source of a future downturn—our excessive debt and future obligations. If some new economic crisis develops from an unexpected or unanticipated source, it is regrettable but understandable. If, however, the completely predictable and heavily discussed debt crisis is the source of the next economic collapse, American politicians will have no one but themselves to blame. And if this very predictable problem is the source of a disaster that brings down the American economy for good, it will be nothing short of a tragedy.

Chapter Five

How to Prepare for Acts of God

THE GOVERNMENT HAS MANIFOLD RESPONSIBILITIES WHEN IT COMES to protecting its citizens from all kinds of natural disasters or acts of God. But the government, and particularly the president, is focused on the health of the nation at large, and not necessarily the well-being of each individual citizen. Furthermore, as we have seen, there will be times when the government either cannot or will not step in. For all these reasons you cannot rely solely on the government in cases of disaster; you need to take steps to protect yourself. This chapter will examine the kinds of natural disasters presidents have faced and make recommendations for what you as an individual should do to protect yourself.

DISEASE OUTBREAKS

The first, and most basic, step in preventing disease comes in the area of hygiene. Previous generations may not have understood how germs spread. In the colonial period, for example, Philadelphia legislators once deliberated about firing cannons into the air to clear the "bad air" that caused yellow fever.[1] We do not have this excuse. Consequently, there is no reason for individuals to thoughtlessly spread potentially deadly germs. This should be true at all times, but especially in cases of an outbreak.

The steps to basic hygiene should not be a surprise to anyone. However, since they are so often flagrantly ignored, even today, they bear repeating here:

- Try to avoid close contact with sick people.

- Wash your hands often with soap and water. If soap and water are not available, use an alcohol-based hand rub.

- Avoid touching your eyes, nose, and mouth. Germs spread this way.

- Cover your nose and mouth with a tissue when you cough or sneeze. Throw the tissue in the trash after you use it.

- While sick, limit contact with others as much as possible to keep from infecting them.

- Clean and disinfect surfaces and objects that may be contaminated with germs like the flu.

- If you are sick with a flu-like illness, Centers for Disease Control (CDC) recommends that you stay home for at least twenty-four hours after your fever is gone except to get medical care or for other necessities. (Your fever should be gone without the use of a fever-reducing medicine.)[2]

None of these recommendations should come as a surprise. Everyone who has attended kindergarten has heard them. And yet they are so frequently violated that individuals who want to protect themselves and their families should make sure to keep these at the forefront of their minds in cases of viral outbreaks. While the recommendations are long-standing, these commonsense notions are more important than ever in this age of technology and smartphones. The smartphone is a classic fomite—medical speak for an item that attracts germs. The importance of smartphones in our daily lives means that we need to develop a social etiquette to deal with these hygienic issues, as well as government mandates and suggestions.

Beyond these basics, individuals should make sure that they don't do these steps half-heartedly. For example, people may say they wash their hands, when all they do is splash water on them. Effective handwashing requires hot water, soap, and a significant enough amount of time to kill the offending germs. The standard recommendation is that one scrubs long enough to sing the song "Happy Birthday" twice.

Another problem stems from lack of awareness regarding where germs reside. The microbiologist Jerry Bowman looked at germ distribution in a school cafeteria and found that the places people most worry about are not the dirtiest. For example, Bowman found that cafeteria trays were particularly problematic. Furthermore, and rather disturbingly, Bowman found that the water fountain spigots "had more germs than, say, a toilet."[3] These kinds of findings should make individuals think more carefully about the surfaces they encounter, and when they should wash their hands after encountering those surfaces.

In addition to personal hygiene, there is also the issue of taking smart precautions. The flu vaccine is a safe and effective way to prevent getting infected. While getting the vaccine is a smart move in general, some populations should be more vigilant than others in taking the shot. Seasonal flu, for example, tends to be more dangerous to senior citizens, and they should make a special effort to get the vaccine. Furthermore, as "the biggest spreaders of the flu," children should be at the front of the line to get vaccinated. According to Harvard Medical School's Dr. Kenneth Mandl, "three- and four-year-olds lead off the flu epidemic every year." Furthermore, when youth vaccinations went down in Japan, the incidence of flu went up. For these reasons high-risk individuals and children should be high priorities for vaccinations.[4]

Of course, the definition of high-risk individuals can change depending upon the flu strain. The 1918 flu disproportionately affected young adults. This leads to another key action. In times of crisis, individuals should carefully monitor the situation, not only for determining who needs to get priority in terms of vaccinations, but also to keep abreast of developments. There are many places to get flu information, including online at CDC.gov and flu.gov. If you are disinclined to go to government sites, there is always flufacts.com, which is sponsored by Genentech, or a site like WebMD. In addition, local public health offices can be helpful as well. In contrast to 1918, we are fortunate to have a host of sources of information that can update you and your family should a dangerous pandemic emerge.

Finally, there is the question of what, if any, materials to stockpile. It is always a good idea to have a well-stocked medicine cabinet, with aspirin, acetaminophen, decongestants, and the like. Also, as with any emergency, you should maintain a stockpile of canned food and bottled water that can tide you over in case the supply chain breaks down. In terms of flu, though, there is also the question of whether to stockpile anti-viral drugs. Many employers and local governments have chosen to take this step. For individuals it is a personal decision, made more complicated by the fact that these drugs generally require a prescription, and doctors are not supposed to prescribe medicines to asymptomatic individuals. The federal government has looked in the past at the question of creating home medkits, which would be tailored to include countermeasures that could respond to a variety of ailments. The government still has a number of steps to go in this regard (see chapter 7, "The Bioterror Threat"), but should these medkits go on the market, purchasing one designed to combat flu would be a smart idea.

FOOD AND WATER SHORTAGES

Presidents are unlikely to devote serious resources or attention to the problem of food insecurity before a crisis hits. There are too many other competing priorities, and too many other more likely scenarios to expect the government to spend scarce time or resources on worrying about the possibility of large-scale food shortages. In addition, the United States does not maintain a strategic food supply. Petroleum and biological countermeasures, yes. Food, no.

This is not to argue that the United States should have some kind of strategic food supply. The logistical challenges are great, the risk of spoilage constant, and the likelihood of a famine low. In addition, figuring out how to distribute stored food, as well as to whom to distribute it, are difficult questions. Even if we could manage the distributional aspects, the ethical challenges of deciding who should get food in a crisis are enormous. In case of a bioterror attack, the US government prioritizes countermeasure distribution to high-priority officials, first responders, and high-risk populations. In case of a food shortage, everyone is equally at high risk of starvation from food deprivation.

Logistical and ethical challenges aside, the fact is the US government does not maintain an emergency food supply to support the entire population. What this means is that in the case of a famine, you and your family are largely on your own in terms of finding sufficient food. The government is more likely to intervene in the case of tainted or diminished water supplies, as we have seen in West Virginia and California. In case of wide-scale food shortages, you should not and cannot rely on government assistance.

The absence of a government plan to feed the population means that individuals need to come up with their own plans. The plans differ somewhat based on whether we are talking about a short-term tainting or a price spike versus a long-term shortage. They are similar, however, in that both approaches require individual ingenuity and resourcefulness to get by.

If there is a short-term disruption in the food or water supply, the best way to deal with it is to have planned ahead. Your house should be stocked with enough food and water to get you and your family through a week, or at the bare minimum a long weekend, without access to new provisions. Others, like disaster preparer Sam Sheridan, believe you should be stocked with enough food and water to last you and your family for a month.[5] Regardless of the amount, you should have these provisions right now. When I say *right now*, I mean it. If you feel that you are unprepared to handle a snowstorm or other disaster that traps you in your house for a multiday period, you should put down this book and stock up on the necessary provisions. This book will still be here waiting for you when you return.

Now that you have replenished your larder, you need to consider some of the following suggestions as part of your short-term food shortage strategy. First is storage. Unless you live in an area prone to frequent blackouts, you should purchase and freeze enough meat to get you and your family through a short-term shortage or price spike. Similarly, you should also maintain a store of in-season produce, 100 percent fruit juices, and agricultural products you rely on that come from drought-stricken California. In addition to maintaining a store of staples for emergencies, these storage techniques can help you and your family ride out a short-term food or water crisis with minimal disruption.[6]

For longer-term food problems, most modern, nonagricultural members of our society are largely not equipped to grow, find, or forage for food on their own. But that does not mean they cannot learn to do so. Start by growing a garden. It is the simplest and easiest step. Regardless of where you live, everyone can grow some foods, which they can also store and freeze. In addition, growing your own food is a renewable form of food, something that can help deal with food shortages, even if it can't fully replace all of your sustenance needs.

Beyond a garden, there are other ways to bolster your food supply. One possibility is learning to fish. Not everyone is close enough to an appropriate body of water to do so, but many are. Fifty percent of the world's population lives within three kilometers of a freshwater supply, and almost 40 percent of Americans live near the Atlantic or Pacific coasts. Fishing would not work for everyone in an emergency, but it would for many people.

Beyond fishing or gardening, there is also hunting. I recognize that many people have ethical problems with hunting, and many—often but not always the same people—are uncomfortable with owning firearms. The point is not to mandate any one method of food procurement. You should consider the method that works best for you and your family, based on your own skills, preferences, and geographic location. If everyone tries the same method, it will exacerbate whatever food crisis we are already facing. If everyone seeks outside food sources based on their diversity of interests and talents, it could alleviate the challenges the government faces in trying to feed a hungry population in the face of a crisis. As Sheridan put it, "If everyone in the country could become just a little more self-reliant, we could defuse this thing before it happens. If everyone lived with a few months' worth of food and water in their house or apartment, we could delay that competition for resources, and probably avoid a lot of the problems following something like an EMP attack, a solar flare, or even an economic crisis."[7]

WEATHER CATASTROPHES

More than any other potential disaster, weather disruptions are not in the realm of speculation. They will happen in this country during the course of your lifetime. They will happen multiple times, and the odds are they will happen to you.

Therefore, it is incumbent upon you to be ready to deal with a weather-based disaster. You owe it to yourself and to your family to prepare for this scenario. This should not be an "it won't happen to me" kind of analysis. The overwhelming likelihood is that it will happen to you, to people close to you, or both.

The first thing that everyone should do is have some kind of emergency kit. This kit should include basic necessities such as food, water, flashlights, spare batteries, a first-aid kit, and a radio. FEMA and the Red Cross have information regarding already-prepared kits. The problem here is that people have been told multiple times from multiple sources that they need to have these things on hand, but few people actually do it. According to one recent estimate, only about 10 percent of households are prepared to deal with disasters.[8]

Lack of personal preparation is a real problem, with real implications. The more prepared individual Americans are at times of crisis, the fewer the burdens will be on overtaxed local, state, and federal governments when disaster strikes. As Jonathon Links, director of Johns Hopkins' Center for Public Health Preparedness, has said, "It's really in the personal preparedness phase rather than the response phase that we need to be paying more attention."[9]

Personal preparedness, however, is largely beyond governmental control. The government can issue warnings, but people will not act unless they believe that the event will actually happen to them. But fear is only part of the equation. People also need to believe that their actions can mitigate the impact of the event that will happen to them. As Dr. Links put it, "The essence of the model is you have to convince people that there's a threat, and that there's something they can do about it."[10]

Preparedness officials clearly have work to do on that score, but readers of this book likely already believe that they need to take action. Just because 90 percent of Americans are not taking the necessary steps does not mean that you can't step up and do your part. In fact, stepping up and doing your part is doubly advantageous, as it not only relieves some of the burden on government, but also gives you a leg up on the vast majority of Americans who are unready for a disaster.

Beyond the emergency kit, which will serve you well in a variety of possible disasters, there are a number of steps you can take to prepare for weather-based contingencies. Since extreme weather often disrupts power service, considering a home generator is an important step. Generators are not without their disadvantages. They are costly, must be kept fueled up, can be noisy, and are dangerous if not handled properly. People have been asphyxiated when running certain types of generators in insufficiently ventilated areas. That said, they bring a great number of advantages as well. They can keep your house warm or cool—depending on the need—keep your food from perishing, and allow you to maintain contact with the outside world. For peace of mind in a crisis, generators cannot be beat.

Weather events like hurricanes also require specific types of preparation. If you live in a house surrounded by trees, for example, you should keep the tree branches trimmed and safe. Take extra cash out and have it handy. Tie down loose lawn furniture. Garage doors should be fortified so they do not blow away in high winds. Maintain an inventory of possessions so you can file an insurance claim for damaged property afterwards. This inventory should include photos of key items, value estimations, and make and model numbers. Keep both paper and electronic copies of the lists, and keep the paper copies inside a waterproof plastic sleeve.[11]

These things cannot be done at the last minute. First of all, they take time, and time may be in short supply when a storm is coming. In addition, the needed items will not always be available. Stores like Home Depot typically see a run on items like flashlights, batteries, and generators in advance of a storm. Getting ready for disasters takes careful preparation, and it must be done in advance.

All of the above-mentioned items can help you cope with a weather-based catastrophe should it take place. But beyond coping with disasters when they strike is the higher order of preparation in which you reduce your odds of being hit by a major storm. Certain parts of the country are more prone to certain types of weather patterns. You can and should engage in a risk-based analysis of where you and your family choose to live. Sandy notwithstanding, hurricane activity on the East Coast is typically south of North Carolina. Earthquakes happen in

California, but less so in the rest of the country. You will rarely see a blizzard in the South. All of these factors should go into your decision of where you might want to live. As disaster expert Amanda Ripley has written, "Your fate in a disaster in America depends to a large degree on where you live."[12]

Despite the fact that fate relies on location, Americans are particularly poor at assessing risk. According to Rutgers' Lee Clarke, Americans tend to "live in dangerous places (Malibu, New Orleans, West Palm Beach, central New Jersey)." Sometimes the most attractive places from some perspectives are also the most dangerous places. As Clarke put it, "We concentrate ourselves, and the mere fact of concentration makes for greater calamity when the hazard, whatever it is, strikes."[13]

The climatological risks of your region are only one aspect of this analysis. Some regions are just better than others at dealing with disasters. States like California or Florida are known for being more prepared for disasters than others. This is not an unmitigated good, though. As Ripley noted, "One reason California and Florida are so good at responding to most disasters is that they do it all the damn time." Other places have both problems: dangerous climates combined with suboptimal disaster planning. According to Ripley, "If the skies open up in, say, New Orleans, Dallas or Oklahoma City, all places with less-than-impressive emergency plans, then you could be in serious trouble."[14]

Of course, there is only so much one can do as an individual. Sometimes the best disaster planning for individuals can be to band together in a community. You must count on yourself for some kinds of preparation, but you can't count on just yourself for everything. And you certainly cannot count on overtaxed government officials who have competing priorities in times of crisis. As a FEMA training document states, in a disaster, "Local residents will be the first responders."[15] (Not a very comforting thought coming from FEMA.) Local residents can keep each other safe from external threats, have a better sense of the situation on the ground than government officials or outside organizations, and can take care of each other after the nation's attention span moves on to other issues. Individual preparation is essential for dealing with disasters, but building ties with neighbors and your community is necessary for getting through a longer-term event. In the case of a truly community-devastating catastrophe, the words of the great poet John Donne come to mind: "No man is an island."

ECONOMIC COLLAPSE

There are two levels of economic disaster. One is a severe downturn, such as the Great Depression or the 2008 recession. These could be characterized as "normal" economic collapses. They are certainly not "normal" for those trying to live through them, and they are not normal in the sense that they do not happen regularly. That said, they can be classified as normal in that they have happened before and will almost certainly happen again, but our society and our system will survive them and continue on after they are done, albeit with significant and tragic dislocations. In a normal economic collapse, the basic institutions of society continue to function, and families need to find a way to cope with job or income loss.

The second level of economic disaster, which we as a society have not faced, and hopefully never will face, is an utter and complete economic collapse. In this type of disaster, society would lose basic functionalities. The government would not issue checks, bank deposits and equity investments would no longer be recoverable, and most people would be reduced to subsistence levels. What the president does or does not do in this scenario would probably matter very little in your daily life. The impact of this would be far more devastating than a normal economic disaster. Fortunately, the risk of such an event taking place is lower as well.

Most of the strategies laid out here will address the lower-risk possibility of the normal economic downturn, although some will be applicable to both. A complete economic collapse is so much more severe, and difficult to plan for, that it is similar to the military maxim that battle plans go out the window once the shooting starts. You can plan for a complete economic collapse, but the rules of the game under that scenario will be so vastly different that one cannot be sure how effective any strategy will be beyond the short term. In that short term, however, preparation can make a huge difference. Once your stored food, water, and ammunition run out, it is unclear where you will be able to obtain more of life's necessities. Maintaining good relations with one's neighbors is also important and can help with warding off common threats and pooling resources.

When it comes to a normal downturn, the first step of preparation is to get your financial house in order. This is a wise step to take even in the unlikely event that there is no economic disaster during your adult life, which itself is unlikely. Getting your financial house in order means doing the standard things you should be doing, which can be found in any investment book. I am not an investment strategist and will not pretend to give complex financial advice, but there are certain steps that everyone should and must take. First among these is getting your debt under control or, better yet, eradicating it. As we learned in the 2008 recession, being burdened by debt makes it that much harder to make it through a financial crisis. It also leaves you vulnerable to collection agencies, which, feeling similarly squeezed, can resort to rather unsavory tactics in tough economic times.

The second key preparatory step is having a sound investment strategy. This includes having a balanced, diversified portfolio. Assume any one investment can disappear, so it is best to have a variety of different investments or different levels of liquidity. The portfolio should have a mix of stocks and commodities, and both international and domestic investments. You should also have an appropriate stock/bond mix, traditionally determined by subtracting your age from one hundred; the resulting number is the percent of your portfolio you should have in stocks.[16] When it comes to stocks, unless you are Warren Buffett, you should assume that you cannot outsmart the market. Therefore, low-cost index funds are typically the best bet. Finally, you should not take investment advice from me, your underemployed brother-in-law, or some guy you met at the racetrack. Take the time to find a qualified financial adviser.

Many people like gold as a hedge. Gold can be a good investment for difficult economic times, but it is also quite volatile if you are seeking high returns. Whatever you do, you should have gold only as one option in a diversified portfolio. Furthermore, you may be better off hedging with a variety of precious metals, and not limiting yourself to gold alone.

If there is a severe downturn, it is also essential to have the resources to carry you through it. For this reason you should have some kind of emergency fund that can carry you through a difficult period. This fund should be in an extremely safe and liquid form—no debt instruments or stock certificates. While you should have some cash reserve on hand, the fund should not be exclusively in cash. Cash, while extremely useful, is extremely problematic. A number of bad things can happen to it. First, and most likely, is that it could get stolen. Cash is an attractive target for thieves, and it is hard to hide large quantities of it in a safe location. In addition to these problems is the fact that cash's value does not remain steady over time. In fact, according to investment adviser Kevin Freeman, one of the worst things you can do with cash is to hold onto it for long periods of time. According to Freeman, "No fiat currency has ever held value" over time. Cash can also be destroyed, in a fire or by bugs, and it can also be lost. Many of us have heard the story of the woman who stored her cash in an old mattress, only to have her husband surprise her with a new mattress.[17]

An even better story illustrating the dangers of wealth hoarding comes from the Battle of Lepanto. In *Carnage and Culture*, the military historian Victor Davis Hanson explains how a modern banking system enabled the Venetians to defeat a powerful Turkish fleet at Lepanto in 1571. To illustrate the point, Hanson explains that Ali Pasha, the head of the Turkish fleet, brought all of his worldly wealth with him to the battle, as the Ottomans did not have a secure banking system at the time. When the battle was lost, the fortune was lost as well. Hoarding cash opens you up to the very same risk.[18]

The story of Ali Pasha raises another point that is important in a crisis: the need to have alternatives. Having alternative sources of income is extremely important in times of crisis. This could be having a side business so that you are not solely reliant on your job, some kind of investment income that could carry you over for a time, or a pension or annuity that carries you through retirement. Many people will not have this option; however, if you can develop it through one of these methods, you will be that much better off come crunch time. This also raises the issue of having usable or translatable skills, such as the ability to fish, hunt, sew, repair mechanical objects, or cook, among others. Furthermore, people who have a "tentmaker skill"—welders, plumbers, car mechanics—can get by in a severe recession more easily than symbolic analysts, that is, paper shufflers. In addition, to the extent that one has these capabilities, it is a good idea to pass them on to your children.

Finally, one crucial piece of advice in an economic crisis is not to despair. As discussed above, previous economic panics, as painful as they have been, all ended. The odds are that the next recession or depression will be bad, but it will not be permanent. It is important not to panic or give up hope. In fact, many recessions have also been investment opportunities. In 2008 investment guru Warren Buffett famously took to the pages of the *New York Times* to declare, "I've been buying American stocks."[19] People who took that advice and bought stocks at the height of the 2008 recession ended up doing very well for themselves; in 2015 the Dow Jones Industrial Average hit highs unseen even before the crisis, something unimaginable at the time.

SECTION TWO:
ACTS OF MAN

"Master of Emergencies" Herbert Hoover visiting Mississippi in 1927. President Calvin Coolidge put Hoover in charge of relief efforts, making him the first disaster czar in this nation's history.

President George W. Bush, joined by retired firefighter Bill Beckwith, on top of a destroyed fire truck at Ground Zero in New York City, September 14, 2001. Bush spoke from the heart when he said: "I can hear you. The rest of the world hears you. And the people who knocked these buildings down will hear all of us soon."

President George H. W. Bush and his wife, Barbara, visiting Florida in the aftermath of Hurricane Andrew in 1992. The coverage of Andrew had a heavy overlay of politics and of the political motivations behind Bush's actions. In detailing the administration's response efforts, *New York Times* reporter Edmund Andrews felt the need to indicate that "Florida, the nation's fourth most populous state, is considered crucial to Mr. Bush's re-election."

President Franklin Delano and Eleanor Roosevelt in Philadelphia, September 20, 1940. FDR was determined to make sure that he was seen by the American people, and remembered by the historians, as the one who ended the Depression. For the most part he succeeded, although he had to be the first president to go beyond two terms, and America had to get involved in a world war, in order for this to happen.

President Franklin Delano Roosevelt laying a cornerstone in Washington, DC, on April 16, 1936. FDR was a master communicator. He not only had one of the best radio voices of his era, but he also understood the importance of the medium sooner than his contemporaries. He had to do this because most of his home state newspapers in New York were Republican-leaning at the time. Mastering the new medium of radio gave FDR a path to go around the papers and straight to the people.

Robert F. Kennedy's gravesite in Arlington National Cemetery. Kennedy was in Indianapolis on April 4, 1968, and was advised by Mayor Richard Lugar not to speak. Kennedy not only spoke, but had the difficult task of announcing King's death to the crowd. Kennedy's words soothed the crowd, and Indianapolis, like New York, remained largely calm, in stark contrast to the dozens of cities that erupted in violence that night. Part of his speech is inscribed by his grave in Arlington National Cemetery.

President Lyndon Johnson in Marine One overlooking the damage on the ground in Washington, DC, on April 7, 1968, three days after Martin Luther King's death. The photo is remarkably similar to the famous photo of George W. Bush looking out over New Orleans after Katrina. The photo did not become as iconic as the Bush photo, but it does show a similar impotence of a president looking down from the air at devastation on the ground.

COURTESY OF THE LYNDON B. JOHNSON LIBRARY

Iconic photo by Dorothea Lange of a destitute mother and her children in the Great Depression. The Depression was an economic collapse unlike any other seen in American history. It destroyed businesses across the economy. Tens of thousands of banks and businesses collapsed between 1929 and 1932. Net farm income dropped from over $6 billion to $2 billion. The stock market was down to 41 in July of 1932, down from 294 in the spring of 1930. Overall, national income fell from $87.4 billion in 1929 to $41.7 billion in 1932. These aggregate figures, horrifying as they are, do not take into account the human toll of the Depression and its devastating impact on millions of American lives.

COURTESY OF THE FDR PRESIDENTIAL LIBRARY

General press briefing at the White House. The United States encountered two bioterror incidents under President Ronald Reagan: the Tylenol poisonings in Chicago and the salmonella infestation in Oregon. Reagan wisely let Johnson & Johnson run the response to the Tylenol case, although he did later sign a law that made tampering with medical products a federal crime.

COURTESY OF THE RONALD REAGAN PRESIDENTIAL LIBRARY

Walter Reed General Hospital in the midst of the Spanish Influenza outbreak of 1918, which had a devastating impact on the United States and around the world. The virus infected more than a quarter of the US population and was so severe that it reduced the national average for life expectancy by an entire decade. Nearly 675,000 Americans died from the disease, almost six times as many who died fighting World War I.

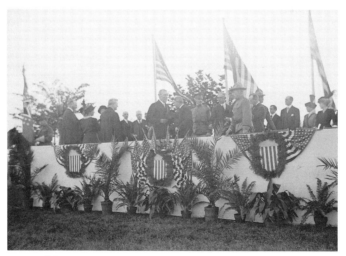

President Woodrow Wilson conducting a cavalry review. When the Spanish Flu epidemic broke out during World War I, Wilson allowed the war effort to trump public health. Besides one feeble attempt to question the wisdom of continuing troop transports that were spreading the disease, he does not appear to have said anything else about the disease, publicly or privately.

President George W. Bush visiting victims of Hurricane Katrina. The storm, which struck in August of 2005, killed over 1,800 people and caused over $100 billion in damages. It also had a crushing impact on the Bush presidency itself. In his own memoir, Bush wrote regarding Katrina that "the legacy of fall 2005 lingered for the rest of my time in office."

West Virginia National Guardsman taking water samples. The tainted water in West Virginia, which caused nausea, vomiting, dizziness, diarrhea, and rashes, closed schools and restaurants, sent dozens of people to area hospitals, and led to official warnings not to use the water for anything besides flushing toilets. Unsurprisingly, these announcements led to a run on bottled water, as stores quickly ran out of supplies.

Mississippi River flood damage in 1927. On April 16 the collapse of a levee in Illinois brought enormous flooding along areas near the river. Five days later another levee, in Mississippi, burst, exacerbating matters further. The effects of the flooding were devastating: 16.5 million acres flooded; 637,000 persons dislocated; 41,000 destroyed buildings; and an unknown number of deaths, usually estimated to be in the range of 250–1,000.

COURTESY OF THE LIBRARY OF CONGRESS

Johnstown Flood damage. In May of 1889, the area around Johnstown, Pennsylvania, was hit with extremely heavy rains. When the nearby South Fork dam broke, much of the town of Johnstown was washed away. Over 2,200 people died, and bodies were discovered as far away as Cincinnati—some 350 miles away.

COURTESY OF THE LIBRARY OF CONGRESS

President Lyndon Johnson and staff watching television news coverage of Martin Luther King's death. On April 4, 1968, at 7:30 p.m., Martin Luther King was murdered by an assassin's bullet. Race riots broke out in 125 cities across the country, killing 39, injuring over 2,600, and causing damages in excess of $65 million. Johnson understood that the riots would be politically damaging to him, but he also was unable to do much to stop them.

COURTESY OF THE LBJ PRESIDENTIAL LIBRARY

Debt Clock by Union Square in New York City. Huge and unsustainable US deficits bring with them the potential for a massive economic disaster. The total US debt, in excess of $19 trillion and growing all the time, is exacerbated by the long-term liabilities that the US entitlement programs face. A debt catastrophe could bring down the US economy, and potentially the world economy with it.

COURTESY OF MATTHEW G. BISANZ VIA WIKIMEDIA COMMONS

President Calvin Coolidge giving an award to the winners of a spelling bee. The standoffish Coolidge, famous for his taciturnity, believed in limited government. He was concerned about the precedent of federal involvement after the great Mississippi flood in 1927. He sent his secretary of Commerce, Herbert Hoover, to help with relief efforts. Coolidge's concerns about increased federal involvement in disasters have been borne out over time.

COURTESY OF THE LIBRARY OF CONGRESS

SOME RELEVANT STATISTICS OF THE 1965 AND 1977 BLACKOUTS

	1965 (November 9/10)	1977 (July 13/14)	Normal 24-Hour Period (1977)
Duration of Blackout	12 hours	26 hours	NA
Location	9 Northeastern States 2 Provinces of Canada	5 Boroughs of NYC Westchester County	NA
Arson and Looting	Negligible	1,809 Incidents	*
Arrests	*	2,931	647
Deaths (blackout related)			
– Civilian	None Reported	2	NA
Injuries			
– Civilian	*	204	*
– Police Force	*	436	*
– Fire Fighters	*	80	5
Fires (reported)	241	1,037	350
Alarms			
– Single Alarms	662	2,724	1,262
– Multiple Alarms City Wide	6	54	12
Personnel			
– Civilian Volunteers	*	*	NA
– Red Cross Volunteers	*	120	NA
– Police Force/Officers	*	17,411	4,715
– Firemen/Officers	4,773	7,427	5,034
"911" Emergency Calls	*	70,680	18,500

* – Data not readily available
NA – Not Applicable

Sources: New York City Fire Department, New York City Police Department (Reports, Informal Interviews)

Comparison of the damage from the blackouts of 1965 and 1977 in New York City. The blackouts of 1965 and 1977 had dramatically different effects on New York City. The 1977 blackout occurred much later in the evening, once it was already dark. This, plus the economic downturn and civil unrest at the time, spurred a night of looting, arson, and other violence. The contrast to the near crimeless blackout in 1965 stunned New Yorkers and Americans across the country.

"IMPACT ASSESSMENT OF THE 1977 NEW YORK CITY BLACKOUT," SCI ENERGY SYSTEMS DIVISION 1977, WWW.FERC.GOV/INDUSTRIES/ELECTRIC/INDUS-CT/RELIABILITY/BLACKOUT/IMPACT-77.PDF, ACCESSED SEPTEMBER 2, 2014

Chapter Six

Terror Attacks

Before the morning of September 11, 2001, Americans were understandably somewhat blasé about the possibility of a terrorist threat. On that morning that period of domestic focus ended violently and graphically. At the time President George W. Bush was famously reading to a group of schoolchildren at the Emma E. Booker Elementary School in Sarasota, Florida. The book he was reading, as most people now know, was *The Pet Goat*.[1] As he was reading, White House chief of staff Andrew Card came over to the president and whispered to him, "A second plane hit the second tower. America is under attack."[2] Card's statement was the first (and a remarkably prescient) articulation of the fact that the assault on the Twin Towers had surprised the nation's top leadership. At that moment it was clear that America had failed the first test: the ability to prevent a terrorist attack and protect its people.

The second test came right after: How should a president react to a crisis? On this test Bush's initial reaction has been heavily debated. Should he have immediately gotten up, potentially panicking the children and those watching on TV, and stepped into the role of executive leader and commander in chief? Or was he right to remain where he was, finish the eleven-page story, and then calmly excuse himself before assuming command? The truth is that any leader, and certainly the president of the United States, has countervailing and sometimes conflicting responsibilities in the wake of a crisis. It is vital for a president to assume command. At the same time, he must do so in such a way that reassures his fellow citizens, reinforces the markets, and strengthens institutions. Bush was right not to instill panic in a class-room full of students, especially knowing that the cameras were focused on him the entire time, and that the images they would convey would be projected to the entire nation.

A bigger concern was with what Bush did afterwards. Bush and his team were unsure of where to go and of what message to put out to the nation. In fact, Ari Fleischer, Bush's savvy press secretary, held up a makeshift sign for Bush to see with the words "DON'T SAY ANY-THING YET" printed in block letters.[3] Bush pushed for going back to Washington, but the Secret Service, still unaware of the nature and the magnitude of the attack, understandably vetoed an immediate return to the capital. Hindsight reveals that the Service acted wisely, as United Flight 93 was headed for either the White House or the Capitol Dome before the Todd Beamer–led insurrection brought the plane down in Shanksville, Pennsylvania.

While the Secret Service was right to be concerned, Bush had the right instincts for a leader. Unfortunately, his zigzag path across the country that day—initially to no destination other than in the air, then to Barksdale Air Force Base in Louisiana, and then Offutt Air Force Base in Nebraska—did not instill confidence. Bush himself recognized this problem, telling Secret Service director Brian Stafford in no uncertain terms that he had "decided to speak to the nation, and there was no way I was going to do it from an underground bunker in Nebraska."[4]

All of this was worsened by the fact that Bush did not seem to be in control of where he was and where he was going. In his own memoir he notes that he told his wife, Laura, who was in Washington, that "everyone was urging me not to return, but that I would be there soon. I had no idea whether that was true, but I sure hoped so."[5] Furthermore, his first two public statements were also less than fully inspiring. The nation had suffered its worst attack since Pearl Harbor, with three thousand Americans dead, with the iconic Towers One and Two of the World Trade Center lying in rubble, and the Pentagon burning. As the nation sought to separate truth from rumor and hold off panic, Americans keenly felt the absence of the president's voice and presence.

It was in the aftermath of this unsteady response, on September 13, that the nation began to see what White House speechwriter David Frum called "a new Bush." The first inklings of this different presidential response came with a short but powerful speech at the Washington National Cathedral. Then the president flew to New York, where he visited the Ground Zero site for the first time. At the site Bush was pressed by the rescue workers assembled there to give impromptu remarks. He joined Bill Beckwith, a retired firefighter, on top of the ruins of a fire truck. Bush borrowed a megaphone to address the first responders and workers sifting through the remains. Bush had not been prepped and had no remarks. He seemed unsure of what to say, when a voice in the crowd spoke for almost the entire country: "We can't hear you!" The comment inspired Bush to speak from the heart, and he replied, "Well, I can hear you. I can hear you. The rest of the world hears you. And the people who knocked these buildings down will hear all of us soon."

The crowd loved it, and the chants of "USA! USA!" showed that the president had given the nation the reassurance it needed that justice would be done.[6]

Bush found his voice and created an iconic image, standing on that destroyed truck that day. But one of the reasons it took so long for this moment to arrive was that the attack had come as such a surprise, both to Bush and to our national security establishment. The entire country was unprepared, and the assault caused Americans everywhere to rethink their fundamental assumptions about the nation and the world they were living in. This applied not only to America's now-pierced sense of invulnerability, but also to its ability to respond to such crises. In George Packer's *The Unwinding*, one of the Americans he profiles, a man named Kevin Moore, reacted to the 9/11 attacks by saying, "In a crisis you realized that society operated without anyone knowing deep down what the hell was really going on."[7]

After the attacks Bush changed the focus of his presidency. What was initially supposed to be a domestic issues presidency became one dedicated to protecting the homeland. The change in focus was almost immediate. FBI director Robert Mueller, who had just been sworn in on

September 4, recalled getting a call from Bush only minutes after the attacks. "This is what we pay you for," the president told him. As author Garrett Graff put it, "Mueller's term, President Bush's term, the FBI, and the nation were transformed."[8]

Bush's focus on fighting terror after 9/11 often crowded out other considerations. Both the domestic and foreign agendas changed in the aftermath of the attack. Bush even changed the configuration of government, creating a Department of Homeland Security (DHS) and a Homeland Security Council at the White House (since folded into the National Security Council). As Mueller described Bush's post-9/11 focus to a confidante, "You have to understand Bush. He's not a lawyer. He doesn't know what you shouldn't do. All he cares about is doing whatever he thinks is needed to keep people safe."[9]

9/11: WERE WE READY?

As the Bush story indicates, Americans were not ready for the major terrorist attacks on September 11, 2001. This lack of readiness was a fact at both the governmental and the individual level. And yet, a terrorist attack is the type of attack that is most prevalent in people's minds. I recall sitting in a conference room at Hudson Institute in the late 1990s, listening to a presentation on global trends in the decade ahead. The analyst, Gary Geipel, made an offhand comment about a terrorist attack on the US homeland. I asked him what he thought were the odds of a catastrophic terror attack sometime in the next decade. Without missing a beat, he responded, "100 percent." So it cannot be said that no one was thinking we were facing the prospect of an attack.

Similarly, much has been made of the supposed intelligence failure that preceded 9/11. As the journalists Matt Apuzzo and Adam Goldman have noted, what happened before 9/11 was not an intelligence failure. According to Appuzo and Goldman, "All the signs of an impending attack had been there" and "the system was blinking red." Our various intelligence agencies had picked up the scent of something. Unfortunately, they did not understand what it all meant. As Apuzzo and Goldman put it, "Al-Qaeda's plan succeeded because the United States did not understand what it was seeing. It was a failure of analysis."[10]

Since that day the people and government of the United States have spent hundreds of billions of dollars on addressing the possibility of terror attacks on the US homeland. We have changed laws, restructured our government, and altered our views about civil liberties in the process. We now know that a failure of analysis can bring devastating consequences. Fortunately, we have made improvements in this regard. While strategic analysis was an underpopulated backwater in earlier times, the Federal Bureau of Investigation changed its approach after 9/11, doubling its analysis section and getting the pick of eager graduates from elite universities.[11]

In the intervening decade we have learned that imminent terror attacks are not as frequent as initially feared. At the same time, we have also learned the troubling lesson that all our efforts have still not made us safe. There have been a significant number of terrorist near misses in the United States, including the "Underwear bomber," the Times Square car bomb, and Richard Reid's failed midair shoe bomb. The fact that bad luck (for the terrorists—good luck for us) or individual action rather than government efforts led to the failure of these attempts should not be reassuring, and suggests that the time has come to rethink our approach to dealing with terror threats to the US homeland. As the 2010 Abbot-Keating Commission on Department of Defense capabilities found, "There is currently no comprehensive national integrated planning system to respond to either natural or man-made disasters."[12] In addition, governmental agencies are not doing all they should to share hazard plans.

At the same time, it is vitally important that we remember the lessons of the past to "stay calm and carry on." We cannot assume our enemies are more powerful than they really are. As Apuzzo and Goldman have noted, "Though America has a perception of al-Qaeda as a limitless army of holy warriors, the truth is that finding people willing to kill themselves for God was hard, particularly in the United States."[13] In addition, the US government's many efforts to fight terror do produce results, even if they may be insufficient. As Yale professor Edward H. Kaplan has estimated, "at least 80 percent of all jihadi plots have been detected or deterred before anyone got hurt."[14]

As with all leadership and risk management, how you view this figure depends on your general outlook on life. An optimistic sort would take comfort in knowing that the vast majority of jihadist terror plots are stopped before anyone gets hurt. A more pessimistic sort might note that one-fifth of terror plots appear to cause at least some harm. This dichotomy is somewhat reminiscent of Ronald Reagan's tale of the optimistic and pessimistic brothers. The pessimistic brother refuses to play with his new toys because he is afraid they might break, while the optimistic brother gleefully jumps into a pile of excrement, convinced that there has to be a pony in there somewhere.

Regardless of your disposition, the United States needs to find a workable comprehensive approach for dealing with terror. At the same time, individuals need to prepare themselves and their families for the very real possibility that their government may not be able to fully protect them.

STEP 1: PREVENTION

The most important thing a president must do when it comes to fighting terror is to prevent it. It is impossible to prevent every attack, but this remains and will remain the standard by which people judge their government. While there are certainly serious and intense disagreements about how to prevent attacks, there are also broad areas of agreement. In fact, the very fact that President Barack Obama continued with or even expanded so many of President George W. Bush's policies in the War on Terror—from Guantanamo Bay to the Patriot Act to drone strikes—suggests how much overlap there is among the broad swath of not only Americans but also experts on how to deal with this problem.

In 2010 John Brennan, while serving as anti-terror adviser for the Democratic president Obama, suggested three main policy planks for fighting terror:

1. Take the war to al-Qaeda, decimating al-Qaeda's leadership;

2. Work with other countries, such as Pakistan and Yemen, and build up their capacity to go after terrorists and their infrastructure; and

3. Improve America's image in the world, thus weakening the ability of terrorists to recruit potential attackers.[15]

One would be hard pressed to find an expert, on either side of the aisle, who disagrees with these basic ideas. Among these three, the most controversial is probably the third, regarding improving America's image in the world. As we saw in the 9/11 attacks, a small number of terrorists can cause tremendous damage. Effective prevention of attacks must include some degree of successful efforts to improve America's image abroad. Even if such efforts manage to turn only a handful of people away from radicalism, every attack prevented is a victory that saves lives.

Image improvement does have its limits. As Garrett Graff has pointed out, the Obama administration did make a concerted effort on this front. He appointed a US special representative to Muslim communities and gave a high-profile speech in Cairo in which he never uttered the words *terror*, *terrorist*, or *War on Terror*. And yet, according to Graff, those who hate us were unappeased. Al-Qaeda's Ayman al-Zawahiri acknowledged the attempt, but dismissed it, saying that "America has put on a new face but its heart is full of hate."[16] Furthermore, Obama's softer words did little to stop the rise of ISIS and its anti-American ideology.

Still, the three Brennan points would probably generate wide agreement among the American people. This does not mean that everyone would agree on the tactics needed to carry out these goals, or that the Brennan goals are comprehensive. But it does suggest there are basic areas of agreement that every American president, of whatever ideology, could pursue in fighting terror.

In addition to the Brennan list, there are other anti-terror goals that would easily achieve broad consensus. In recent years the nature of terrorist attacks has been changing, shifting from group-sponsored to "lone wolf" or homegrown attackers. This would necessitate a fourth crucial plank: to improve our immigration and visa screening procedures so as to keep potential terrorists out. One need not take Donald Trump–style blanket bans on whole categories of people to tighten screening so as to include social media profiles or to ask more pointed questions from potential immigrants or visitors from countries with problematic records on the terror-producing front.

Another important step is the need for better information sharing among intelligence and law enforcement entities. Most people are aware of the problems that took place between the FBI and the CIA in the period leading up to 9/11. The Clinton administration created a wall between the agencies that prevented the sharing of information that could potentially have averted the terror attack.

This wall became known as the "Gorelick wall," after Clinton deputy attorney general Jamie Gorelick. Gorelick wrote an infamous 1995 memo in which she told FBI director Louis Freeh and US attorney Mary Jo White that "we believe it is prudent to establish a set of instructions that will more clearly separate the counterintelligence investigations from the more limited, but continued, criminal investigations." After the attacks the 9/11 Commission specifically identified this memo as creating the kind of "confusion" that prevented the CIA from telling the FBI that 9/11 hijackers Khalid al-Mihdhar and Nawaf al-Hazmi were already in the country in the summer of 2001. The commission, of which the ubiquitous Gorelick was a member, at the same time denied that the wall had the deleterious effect that former attorney general John Ashcroft claimed it did. According to *Wall Street Journal* columnist Gordon Crovitz, the Gorelick memo exemplified "the sort of pre-9/11 thinking that made the attacks possible."[17] Interestingly, according to former Bush national security aide Michael Allen, Gorelick herself "commented that there were no incentives for agencies to work together; there was no one in charge."[18]

The wall, however, is only part of the story. Even without policy barriers, many security and law enforcement entities refuse to share information. In Christopher Dickey's *Securing the City*, about New York City's anti-terror unit, he describes how New York officials felt the need to create such a unit specifically because they did not trust federal law enforcement and intelligence entities to give the NYPD actionable intelligence on a timely basis. After the 2004 Madrid bombings, the NYPD sent its own liaison to Spain because they knew that the FBI would not give them a full briefing on the terror attacks there.[19]

The problem of information withholding is a serious one, and deserves more than lip service. Post-9/11 reforms led to the creation of the Director of National Intelligence as an attempt to address this problem. Still, the government now puts out so many intelligence reports that, as Appuzzo and Goldman put it, it is "impossible to digest them all."[20] The next president needs to assign his top law enforcement, intelligence, and security officials to find a way to improve cooperation among the thousands of government employees tasked with preventing the next terror attack. In addition, finding information is not enough. We need to understand what to do with the information when we find it.

At the same time, adding lots of people into the national security state presents challenges of its own. There are now four million people with clearances, and as the massive Edward Snowden leaks indicate, that number is far too many.[21] The president needs to figure out how to have enough people to do the job without having so many people that we are tipping off our enemies, either via espionage efforts or eager journalism.

This leads to the question of the optimal size of government. According to the polls, almost three-quarters of Americans fear big government as the top threat to America's future. This 72 percent number is up considerably from the 65 percent figure Gallup found in 1999 and 2000, before the 9/11 attacks.[22] While many people believe that big government is worrisome, this sentiment is less prevalent when it comes to discussing the national security state. While it is clear that before 9/11, the United States devoted too little time and attention to the problem of terrorism, this does not mean that post-9/11 we should no longer have discussions about the optimal size of the security state.

Even within these discussions, the truth is that in the post-9/11 environment, presidents tend to err on the side of security over privacy. We saw this in the administrations of both the conservative George W. Bush and the liberal Barack Obama. In fact, Obama was regularly challenged for his apparent acceptance of the national security state. In June 2013, for example, Obama argued that "you can complain about Big Brother and how this is a potential program run amok, but when you actually look at the details, then I think we've struck the right balance." He also added, "Nobody is listening to your telephone calls."[23] The fact that Obama had to deny that he was Big Brother itself made news—think of the "Senator Denies Beating Wife"-type headlines—but as things played out, he needed to deny his Big Brotherhood on multiple occasions.

In a December 2013 press conference, *Fox News* White House correspondent Ed Henry said to the president, "You claimed to the American people that you had already reformed many of these surveillance programs, that you came to office, quote, 'my team evaluated them; we scrubbed them thoroughly; we actually expanded some of the oversight.'" Obama responded, "When it comes to the right balance on surveillance, these are a series of judgment calls that we're making every single day 'cause we've got a whole bunch of folks whose job it is to make sure that the American people are protected." Obama also added that he was aware that "people right now are concerned that maybe their phone calls are being listened to, even if they're not, and we've got to factor that in." In sum, however, and despite these concerns, Obama recognized that the bottom line is presidents are judged on whether they protect the nation from terror attacks. As Henry put it, "God forbid there's another terror attack. Every one of us is going to be second-guessing you, and that is extremely difficult, to be in the Oval Office." To this Obama replied, "That's OK. I volunteered."[24]

As these different stories show, there is some significant overlap between what Democrats and Republicans think needs to be done to prevent terror attacks. At the same time, and despite this appearance of agreement, we need to get rid of soft-headed thinking that limits our ability to confront the very real threats that we face.

We saw some evidence of this at the beginning of the Obama administration. Then Department of Homeland Security secretary Janet Napolitano briefly—and embarrassingly—flirted with calling acts of terror "man-caused disasters." Her justification for the use of this euphemism was that the term "demonstrates that we want to move away from the politics of fear toward a policy of being prepared for all risks that can occur." A report by DHS that same spring of 2009 warning of the threat posed by "right-wing extremism" only added to the perception that the federal government could not or would not maintain its focus on addressing terror threats by Islamist extremists.

The "man-caused" usage received a fair bit of (deserved) criticism. Heritage Foundation security expert James Carafano took the sober approach, arguing that "by deliberately trying not to use the T word they run a serious political risk. If something does happen, they'll be accused of taking their eye off the ball and no amount of explanation after the fact will suffice."[25]

Carafano's criticism accurately highlighted the risk that the euphemism created for its users, but other critics used ridicule to make the point. Combining both the "man-caused" usage and the classification of Nidal Hasan's murder of twelve service members at Fort Hood as "workplace violence," Victor Davis Hanson claimed that "since 2009, various members of the administration collective have sought, each according to his station, to bring us into the network of not associating Islamism with terror." While it is important that the US government not target a specific religion and that it avoids religious bigotry, the president of the United States does have an obligation to recognize the origins and the causes of Islamist attacks. Denying that terror attacks come from radical Islamist ideologies does no good to anyone. Hanson does, however, make the point that whatever the rhetorical contortions of the Obama administration, it actively prosecuted the War on Terror against its purveyors. As Hanson put it, "Obama may have killed ten times as many suspected Muslim terrorists by drone as did Bush, but we were to assume that the fact that there were no Christian, Jewish, or Buddhist victims of Hellfire missiles was irrelevant."[26]

The euphemisms did not escape ridicule. One editorial cartoon by Michael Ramirez highlighted a series of terrorist attacks and suggested euphemisms for them. Next to a picture of the Twin Towers burning, he wrote, "This is not called 'terrorism,' it's called a 'man-caused disaster.'" Next to a Fort Hood victim, he wrote, "This is not called 'terrorism,' it is called 'work place violence.'" And next to a burned-out embassy building in Benghazi, he wrote, "This is not called 'terrorism,' it is called a 'spontaneous protest.'"[27]

Euphemisms, it should be noted, are a standard feature of government. Everyone has seen them, in administrations on both sides of the aisle. But if euphemisms cause us to lose sight of the threats we are facing, then they stop being useful and can actually be detrimental to our security efforts. In addition, euphemisms not only become a problem themselves, but they also do not satisfy critics who have been "euphemized," to coin a term.

The euphemism strategy is destined to failure. Well into the second Obama term, the world was continually beset by problems caused by radical Islam; from Hamas's terror rockets in Israel, to ISIS slaughtering non-Muslims and beheading Americans on tape, to Boko Haram kidnapping young girls in Nigeria, to increasingly bold ISIS attacks in places like Paris and San Bernardino, the murderous excesses of radical Islam have not abated. Regarding ISIS—the Islamic State in Syria—President Obama said, in his address to the nation, "ISIL is not Islamic," despite the fact that the word Islamic is precisely how they choose to define themselves. As Peter Berger wrote in the *American Interest*, "Viable policy depends on a clear view of the empirical realities. One reality is that we are in effect at war with Islamist radicalism; it is very unhelpful if this reality is denied."[28]

Arguments about rhetoric aside, a review of the proposals of left and right reveals that there are many more areas of agreement than disagreement when it comes to combating and preventing terror. In fact, both sides even agree about the nature of the threat itself. In a 2013 report the liberal Center for American Progress's Peter Juul identified two "basic facts" about terror. First, despite gains in the struggle against al-Qaeda, "violent Islamist extremist groups will remain a security threat in many regions of the world." (Note his willingness, in contrast to the Obama administration, to use the phrase "violent Islamist extremist groups.") In addition, Juul noted that "the tactic of terrorism will unfortunately remain a tool for violent extremists of varying and diverse ideological persuasions for the foreseeable future." Once we can agree on the problems, it becomes somewhat easier to agree on solutions. In this regard Juul wrote that we need "a counterterrorism framework in which the logic of 'armed conflict' no longer applies because Al Qaeda has been effectively defeated." In this effort he wrote that the United States "should view specific groups espousing violent Islamist extremism as threats to its national interests, the security of its allies and partners, and human rights in the local and regional contexts in which they arise."[29]

Juul's search for a new framework presupposes an effective defeat of al-Qaeda, ISIS/ISIL, and any other radical Islamist group that seeks our destruction. Once that victory has been achieved, the next steps would include, for example, "adopt[ing] a high threshold when considering the use of drone strikes as a counterterrorism tool" and "promot[ing] counterterrorism cooperation and capacity building across US allies and partners." Even though Juul took some shots at conservatives in writing his piece, his analysis and the recommendations would be unlikely to raise hackles on the right.[30] In fact, many would see his voice as a valuable critique of the isolationist left.

As for conservative analysts, their recommendations focus on the need to maintain vigilance against attempted terror attacks, something that the vast majority of Americans—and even experts—would no doubt agree with. As for specifics, Heritage Foundation analyst Jessica Zuckerman wrote in 2012 that an effective anti-terror strategy would include continuing to insist on and reexamine interagency information-sharing efforts, the maintenance of tools like the Patriot Act (which Obama, to his liberal critics' chagrin, has done), and direct action to counter violent Islamic radicals both at home and abroad.[31] Additional Heritage proposals, put forth in other papers, include being more vigilant regarding stopping potential threats from flying on planes, remaining committed to preventing Afghanistan from becoming a terrorist haven, resolving the issue of holding and interrogating terrorists, and being more proactive regarding state-sponsored terrorism.[32] While some of these suggestions may be slightly more controversial, they are unlikely to be unpopular, and not out of the realm of possibility for either a Democratic or a Republican president to pursue.

This commonality, of purpose and policy alike, presents a real opportunity for our next president. Although much of the nation seems disgusted by partisan infighting and ineffectuality in Washington, DC, presidents—of whatever party—know that the American people for the most part will support aggressive anti-terror efforts. More importantly, presidents understand that they will be judged by their ability to prevent terror attacks from succeeding. The approach, summed up by President Bush, is that "we need to do everything in our power to stop the next attack."[33]

Unfortunately, it is far from clear that we are doing "everything in our power to stop the next attack." On the tenth anniversary of the 9/11 Commission report, cochairs Lee Hamilton and Tom Kean penned an op-ed in *USA Today* in which they admitted that we had made a great deal of progress in combating terror, but that more work remained to be done. According to Hamilton and Kean, the establishment of a Director of National Intelligence and National Counterterrorism Center belonged on the plus side of the ledger. At the same time, they argued, threats such as ISIS, homegrown terrorists, and cyberattacks had proliferated. Furthermore, they discussed the unwieldy nature of the ninety-two committees and subcommittees with jurisdiction over homeland security. This figure had increased from eighty-eight in 2004. In sum, Hamilton and Kean found that "the 'generational challenge' against terrorism we anticipated 10 years ago has entered a new and dangerous phase. America cannot afford to let down its guard." It is clear from their analysis that a stronger defense against terror is necessary.[34]

Just playing defense is not enough. While the American people may not give much credit to a president solely for not having a terror attack take place on his or her watch, presidents can be quite sure that the American people will blame them if they fail to prevent the next 9/11. And they can also be certain that the American people's judgment will be particularly harsh if they are seen as insufficiently vigilant in this regard. This knowledge gives presidents a fairly clear path regarding what kind of policies to pursue to prevent an attack from taking place.

STEP 2: REACTION

Presidents know that they must do everything in their power to prevent a terrorist attack from taking place. But what if they fail to do so? How should presidents react to a terror attack that takes place on US soil? If such an event does occur, the reactions of President Bush, both good and bad, give us some guidance regarding how presidents should react after an attack takes place.

First of all, the president's top priority is to reassure the nation. Assuming the attack is a conventional one, it is likely that the impact would take place in a limited area. A radiological, or dirty bomb, would both spread farther and induce more panic. In either case the president must convince the vast majority of Americans outside the affected area to remain calm, while at the same time getting every bit of available help and assistance to the affected region. In the 9/11 circumstance, as we have seen, President Bush was found wanting on the score of immediately reassuring the nation. There are a number of reasons for this failure, including the confusion immediately after the attack and the Secret Service's insistence that he not travel back to Washington immediately.

It is hard to blame Bush for those problems. At the same time, he did experience a rhetorical disconnect in the early going. He had trouble—understandably—finding the right words to soothe the nation. This challenge was exacerbated by his inability to return to the seat of government. Still, the early reviews of his first two statements to the nation were not good: His own speechwriters called his speech to the nation the night of 9/11 the "Awful Office Address."[35]

Fortunately, Bush was able to right the rhetorical ship with his speech at the Washington National Cathedral and then the "USA! USA!" moment at Ground Zero. But it is important to remember that while the Cathedral speech was a carefully crafted attempt to reassure Americans after a rough period, the "USA! USA!" moment was an improvised one. This underscores an important lesson. Presidents can have the best speechwriters and prepare all they want, but ultimately leadership depends on the unique abilities the president brings to the table, and what presidents do when they do not have their words and movements choreographed.

Beyond reassurance the president must also direct coordination of relief efforts. As we shall see, each kind of disaster brings its own kind of challenges, but we have learned a number of lessons over the past decade. First is that there needs to be better coordination among government agencies in managing the federal response. Having worked in the federal government during and after the 9/11 attacks, I saw that there was no cabinet department, no matter how removed its mission appeared to be from the crisis, that did not play a role in response. While Defense, Justice, and Health and Human Services (HHS)—and now Homeland Security—are logically the first agencies that come to mind in dealing with disasters, the Department of Labor, Department of Housing and Urban Development (HUD), and the Environmental Protection Agency were all assigned duties and responsibilities. The president needs to make sure that his White House is coordinating the efforts of all these agencies in addressing the crisis. This entails selecting one entity within the White House to take lead on the issue, and receiving regular briefings from the senior aide responsible for that entity.

Another recurrent issue is that disasters bring out all kinds of offers to help, from the bizarre to the jaw-droppingly generous. The American people, and indeed people around the world, want to help in a crisis, but it is very easy for the kind offers to come to naught if there is no one to sort through them and apportion them appropriately. There is even a foreign policy aspect to this. Many foreign governments call with requests to provide assistance in times of disaster. These requests, while appreciated, bring with them challenges of both the legal and political variety. From the legal perspective, there are limitations on what the US government can accept from foreign governments, limitations that tend to be so complex that State Department lawyers need to sort out what kind of help can be accepted and what must be politely turned down. From a political perspective, there are nations from whom it may occasionally be imprudent to accept assistance, either because they may be suspected in involvement with the attack, or because of other complications taking place with US relations with that nation at that time. This example is just one of the myriad complications the US government faces just in terms of accepting help from fellow nations. The president must handle the issues of government response efforts and external attempts to assist on separate tracks.

With terrorism and other so-called man-caused attacks, the president cannot just be focused on relief; he must also decide how to respond to a successful attack.

Immediately after an attack the president must make sure his law enforcement agencies are identifying the source of the attack, are making sure there are no additional attacks imminent, and are finding and arresting the perpetrators. In this age of cell phones, traffic cameras, and social media, he must lay out the protocols to gather and sift through information from the public. To do this, coordination among law enforcement officers is essential. As discussed above, this has been a recurrent challenge for the US government. We have made important strides in this area since 9/11, but clearly more work is needed. Assuming law enforcement officials are able to capture the attackers, our intelligence agencies need to determine what, if anything, we can glean from them to prevent other attacks or disrupt the terror networks that may have financed or planned the attacks.

If the attack is a suicide bombing in which the direct perpetrators die in the attack, the job of law enforcement and intelligence offices becomes more complicated, but no less important. Even in death terrorists leave behind clues that can help prevent future attacks, ascertain terrorist methods, and capture or kill other terrorists who mean to do us harm. All these actions, while incredibly important, are also complex and difficult. A president must stay on top of all these complicated activities, while at the same time projecting a calm and reassuring air to the nation.

Finally, a president must lead the effort to build resilience, the ability to bounce back after taking a blow. In this, Americans can learn important lessons from the embattled Israelis. Americans can tick off the major domestic terror attacks the country has faced on one hand: 9/11, Oklahoma City, the Boston Marathon bombing, San Bernardino. Israel has suffered through far too many terror attacks to count. Furthermore, these attacks have been from a multitude of types: suicide bombings, bus attacks, missile launches, hijackings, attacks on Olympic athletes, assassinations, and many more. But Israel has shown a remarkable resilience in the face of these attacks. After a terror attack the authorities respond, clean-up crews spring into action, and storeowners—sooner, rather than later—reopen shuttered establishments.

This kind of resiliency does not emerge accidentally. Israel puts both resources and effort into its resiliency project. According to Meir Elran, director of Israel's Homeland Security Program, resilience among the civilian population requires preparation, information dissemination, and leadership, especially at the local level. It also helps to have a relatively wealthy population with a high percentage of veterans from universal military service. After Israel's 2014 war with Hamas, Elran noted that the Israeli populace maintained the necessary emergency routines while also returning to normal behavior immediately after disruptive events. During Operation Protective Edge, as the Israelis called it, there were eleven ceasefires when people went back and forth. Eighty percent of the people in the affected areas left when hostilities began, but 95 percent of them returned to their homes within two days after the last ceasefire took force.[36]

Israel's civilian reaction to the Gaza War demonstrates at least three key lessons in resilience. First, resilience is not a given; it can and should be built and enhanced continuously in advance. In addition, civilian resilience is more complex and challenging than infrastructure resilience. It should be handled in accordance with the relevant threats and specific circumstances. Third, and perhaps most importantly, strong societal resilience is a primary leverage for countering terror and attenuating its intended impact.[37]

The preparation and thought Israel puts into resilience means that the kind of citywide shutdowns that took place in Boston after the marathon bombings would be unthinkable in Israel. Attacks take place, and far too often, but the citizens move on. Presidents need to lead by example and make sure that even if we are attacked, life goes on, and that terror cannot defeat our will to live, and to fight.

CONCLUSION

Despite the limitations on the scope of terrorism's reach, individuals should not understate the danger of terrorism. Our enemies are determined to do us harm, and at any one moment are actively engaged in efforts to bring about that harm. The danger is clearly higher in areas like New York and Washington, but terrorists know that any blow to the US homeland, wherever it takes place, serves their purposes. The October 2002 Washington sniper attacks, in which John Allen Muhammad killed ten people over a three-week period, terrified an entire region. The panic this incident caused raises the question of the effectiveness of terror attacks in general. According to a study by terror analysts Max Abrahms and Matthew Gottfried, terrorist incidents can have the effect of making the civilian population angrier and more resilient. As Abrahms and Gottfried put it, a successful attack "significantly lowers the likelihood of bargaining success."[38]

Of course, not every terrorist wants to bargain. This fundamental insight so penetrated American culture it was given voice in the blockbuster film *The Dark Knight* by Alfred Pennyworth (portrayed by Michael Caine), who said stoically, "Some men just want to watch the world burn." But substantial evidence exists to show that millions more want to see the world spin on in peace. One well-regarded study found that Western nations are more resilient in the face of terror than is typically thought, suggesting that citizens of free nations are on the winning side in the war against terror. As Johns Hopkins University's Steven David has said, "There have been very few tangible, long-term gains for terrorists." This is in large part due to Western societies'—and their citizens'—ability to cope with terror threats while remaining true to their core values.[39] Individual resilience in the face of future terror threats is essential to maintaining those values.

CHAPTER SEVEN

The Bioterror Threat

THE MOST FAMOUS INCIDENT OF BIOTERRORISM CAME IN THE AFTER-math of the 9/11 terror attacks. A series of letters filled with anthrax were mailed to prominent Americans in government and the media. The attacks killed five people and shut down parts of Capitol Hill. Coming in the wake of the destruction of the Twin Towers and the strike on the Pentagon, the anthrax letters contributed to the perception that the nation was under assault. Compounding the sense of vulnerability was the fact that the government had no idea who had mailed the letters. More than a decade later, there is still considerable doubt about the perpetrator. One suspect committed suicide in 2008, but uncertainty remains as to whether the departed was the actual culprit.

While the anthrax letters were both well-known and relatively recent, it was not the only bioterror incident in American history. In fact, they were not the only bioterror scare in that time period. According to author Garrett Graff, within days of the anthrax letters appearing, there was a botulinum scare at the White House. A "suspicious substance" triggered the White House biohazard detectors and was thought to be the deadly botulinum toxin. The FBI tested the substance on laboratory mice, and for a difficult twenty-four hours, it was unclear whether some top officials would live or die. Deputy National Security adviser Stephen Hadley described the test to National Security adviser Condoleezza Rice in stark binary terms, "If the mice are *feet up*, we're toast. If the mice are *feet down*, we're fine." Fortunately, the mice lived, and Rice told the president that all was well. "Feet down, not feet up," she memorably put it.[1]

Going back further in history, in 1763, British forces gave Delaware Indians smallpox-infected blankets, and they may have engaged in similar attempts against Continental troops during the Revolutionary War. (George Washington took his own precautions against this biological warfare by working diligently to inoculate his troops with weak strains of the virus.) In the Cold War, the United States built stocks of bioweapons, although President Richard Nixon agreed to destroy them in 1969. And in the 1980s, while Ronald Reagan was president, there were two actual bioterror attacks on US soil.

The first one is the better known. In September 1982, a number of people in the Chicago area mysteriously became ill after taking extra-strength Tylenol. No one knew that was the cause at the time, however. When twelve-year-old Mary Kellerman's parents gave her an extra-strength Tylenol to deal with a cold, they had no idea there was anything wrong with the medication. Nevertheless, Mary collapsed on the bathroom floor and later died at the hospital. Adam Janus, a twenty-seven-year-old, also died after taking a Tylenol capsule. Following Adam's death, his brother Stanley Janus and his sister-in-law, Theresa, took Tylenol to cope with headaches. They died as well.

Officials had little idea what caused the deaths. Initial speculation looked to the possibility of poison gas as the culprit. Northwest Community Hospital's Dr. Thomas Kim checked with Rocky Mountain Poison Center's John Sullivan, who dismissed the gas theory and instead pointed to cyanide. While blood tests checked on the cyanide theory, firefighters at two separate stations compared notes about the incidents and eventually discovered that all the victims had taken Tylenol. Cook County toxicologist Michael Schaffer tested the pills and found that the tainted Tylenol had more than ten thousand times the average lethal dose of cyanide. Unfortunately, a reporter at Chicago's City News Bureau found out about the Tylenol connection, which led to a panic in Chicago. Mayor Jane Byrne gave a press conference in which she asked that Tylenol products be taken off shelves. After some initial hesitation, McNeil Consumer Products, the Johnson & Johnson subsidiary that distributed Tylenol, issued a recall on the product. Despite this action, three more people died from capsules poisoned with cyanide.[2]

As this story makes clear, the bulk of the responsibility and effort for identifying some kind of biological attack begins at the local level. Local officials are critical to spotting the problem, determining the source, and then warning national companies and federal officials about the situation. Once that happens, the levers of the federal government may get engaged.

In the Tylenol case the two key federal offices were the Food and Drug Administration (FDA) and the Federal Bureau of Investigation (FBI). The FDA makes recommendations about product recalls and the FBI is supposed to catch the culprit. In neither of these cases does the president of the United States have much to say. Despite this, the Tylenol case did touch President Reagan in a number of ways. First, he was subjected to a threat in the case. Someone, who may or may not have been the poisoner, sent a number of extortion letters related to the incidents. The one that went to the White House threatened more tampering, as well as a bombing of the White House itself, if Reagan did not change his tax policies.

Reagan did not change his tax policies, but he did turn his attention to health policies. The next year, in January 1983, Congress passed legislation making Tylenol-style poisonings against the law. According to Congressional Quarterly, the anti-tampering provisions were "largely a response to the seven deaths that occurred in October when unsuspecting consumers ingested Extra-Strength Tylenol capsules that had been laced with cyanide." Reagan, however, vetoed the bill because of a provision in it that would create a new federal officer, a "Drug Czar," to coordinate intra-governmental anti-drug efforts. In a statement, the administration argued that such a position was unnecessary because it would create "another layer of bureaucracy within the Executive Branch." Furthermore, the statement called attention to the "overwhelming opposition to this provision by the Federal law enforcement community" and the fact that the idea was not properly vetted in congressional hearings. Despite these objections, Reagan's vice president and successor, George H. W. Bush, would later create such an office, and former education secretary William Bennett would serve as the first drug czar.[3]

Reagan opposed the drug czar concept. He was not, however, opposed to anti-tampering legislation. When he vetoed the larger bill in

January, his veto message noted that "I share the widespread public desire for new legislation on tampering and will work with the new Congress to produce an acceptable bill on that subject."[4] In October 1983 he signed similar legislation, but without the drug czar position, that made it a felony to tamper with food, drugs, or cosmetics, subject to a $100,000 fine and life imprisonment. Reagan's signing statement explicitly discussed the Tylenol case as the rationale for the bill, noting, "Last year about this time, the Nation was shaken by the Tylenol tragedy in Chicago." The statement added, "The repercussions of that tragedy were felt far beyond the boundaries of Chicago." In terms of federal engagement, Reagan said that "the FBI was heavily involved in the investigation of the Chicago tragedy" and that "the Department of Justice quickly realized that Federal jurisdiction in such cases was questionable." For these reasons the Senate unanimously passed the bill, and Reagan signed this revised version.[5]

Reagan discussed the poisonings in 1986, when he invited Johnson & Johnson chairman James Burke to a meeting in the White House. Burke had taken a strong stance in response to the tampering, pulling thirty-two million bottles of Tylenol from the shelves, at the considerable cost of more than $100 million. The effort worked, and Tylenol remains a respected brand today, something that was far from certain at the time. Burke, for his part, earned the moniker the "Tylenol hero."

Burke's handling of the entire incident was so successful that it is used as a textbook business school case study of how to handle a crisis. At the meeting in the East Room of the White House, Reagan specifically called out Burke, saying "Jim Burke of Johnson & Johnson, you have our deepest appreciation." The president added that Burke had "lived up to the highest ideals of corporate responsibility and grace under pressure." Burke, who died in 2012, said he was "flattered that he was complimentary in Johnson & Johnson's handling of the case, and I was a little tongue-tied."[6] After the White House meeting, Burke expressed optimism that the culprit would eventually be caught, but the AP noted that he also acknowledged that "he had no inside information to support such hopes."[7]

Reagan's praise of Burke for handling the case is instructive. The Tylenol attacks were targeted at a specific company, and not only that, but at a specific product. Some federal agencies, like the FDA and the FBI, had investigative roles to play. The legislative responses to the Tylenol scare were squarely within Reagan's bailiwick. Presidents regularly decide whether and how to work with Congress on developing legislation, and the ability to sign or veto legislation is enshrined in the US Constitution. The other main responsibility of the government once the attack took place was to track down the perpetrator. In this, they failed. The culprit has never been identified, let alone brought to justice.

In terms of immediate action in response, though, Reagan recognized that the primary response had to be undertaken by both local officials and Johnson & Johnson. The direct Tylenol connection meant that when dealing with the crisis, the eyes of the nation were on Johnson & Johnson; CEO James Burke was in charge of the response, not US president Ronald Reagan. Many leaders would have had the instinct to try to take charge of the situation, but Reagan was instead willing to take mediated action. He let the company itself withdraw the product from the shelves, and trusted them to manage the fallout safely and efficiently.

The second biological attack during the Reagan years is far less well known. But in this case the problem was worse than not catching the culprit—the government did not even detect that an attack took place. In 1984 members of the Buddhist Rajneeshee cult spread salmonella out of plastic bags at restaurants in The Dalles, Oregon, east of Portland. While we do not know what motivated the Tylenol killer, we do know the intent behind the Oregon poisoning. The cult wanted to influence local elections, and hoped that sickening non-cult members would improve their electoral prospects.[8]

The attacks, which *Time* magazine called "the first large-scale bioterrorism attack on American soil," caused no fatalities. The cult members spread their noxious cocktail, which they nicknamed "salsa," in ten different locations, as well as to select local officials. Their methods were decidedly low tech. A member of the cult would take the material in the plastic bag and put it on a salad bar at a Shakey's,[9] or on the salsa and salad bar at a Taco Time.[10] The poisonings sickened about 750 people and hospitalized 45 individuals. Fortunately, none died.

The initial reaction of public officials was that the illnesses derived from unsanitary food handling at the restaurants in question. Despite the fact that some locals suspected the Rajneeshees had something to do with the illnesses, the official FBI history has recorded that "initially, health officials thought the outbreak was the result of unsanitary conditions at the restaurants."[11]

One federal official did suspect the Rajneeshees. Local congressman Jim Weaver (D-OR) complained about the situation on the floor of the House of Representatives and expressed skepticism about the Centers for Disease Control's belief that the illnesses came from food handling at the restaurants.[12] But the fact is that law enforcement did not believe there was foul play at work until the Rajneeshees themselves owned up to what they were doing. The FBI's own official history notes that investigators only discovered salmonella samples at the Rajneeshee compound "in 1985[;] when the Bhagwan Rajneesh announced that some of his followers were responsible, a joint Oregon State Police and Portland Division [of the FBI] investigation turned up salmonella samples and other evidence at the commune." This joint task force did not enter the Rajneeshees' ranch until October 2, 1985, two weeks after the Bhagwan spoke up, and more than a year after the attacks first took place.

What this means is that the largest bioterror attack on US soil had taken place, yet federal officials designated to deal with this kind of attack did not even know it had happened. While the Tylenol murderer escaped justice, at least officials knew within a few days that the poisonings had taken place. In the case of the Oregon salmonella attacks, it is impossible to judge the reaction of the president or of the White House. Through no fault of his own, the president of the United States did not know that hundreds of citizens of the United States had been subjected to a bioterror attack on US soil.

Ignorance of this incident did not last long, however. As *Food Safety News*'s Dan Flynn has written about this attack, "Far more people know about it now than did at the time."[13] This clearly would not be the case today. Even though the Rajneeshee attack was not that long ago, so much has changed, in the form of Twitter, Facebook, and twenty-four-hour media coverage, that an incident of this magnitude would not escape attention. In addition, it would likely cost corporations billions of dollars in lost business. Far more concerning, however, is that when looking at the three most prominent bioterror incidents in our history, it is clear that in two of the cases the culprits were never caught, and in the third, federal officials did not know the incident even took place.

REACTING TO BIOTERRORISM

Bioterror is one of the most frightening public health scenarios we face. The biological and pharmaceutical agents themselves are relatively cheap and easy to produce. The attack itself is difficult to detect. And the consequences could be devastating. According to pollster and statistician Nate Silver, "A singular nuclear or biological attack, meanwhile, might dwarf the fatality total of September 11."[14]

The threat of a bioterror attack does not exist in the realm of idle speculation. In fact, we know with certainty that ISIS—the Islamic State in Syria—is looking into the use of bioweapons. A captured laptop from ISIS terrorists revealed that ISIS was examining how to weaponize bubonic plague, which killed tens of millions of people in the fourteenth century. One document found on the laptop noted that "the advantage of biological weapons is that they do not cost a lot of money, while the human casualties can be huge." Bubonic plague itself is treatable by antibiotics, so it is not a top concern. Still, ISIS has demonstrated a capacity—and a willingness—to murder not only Americans, but anyone who does not worship as they do. The prospect of ISIS terrorists with a biological weapon is truly a frightening prospect.[15]

Furthermore, biological agents are silent killers. As our previous experiences with bioterror have shown, one of the biggest challenges with bioterror is detecting it. Detecting has three levels: discovering that an attack has taken place, determining what the agent is, and identifying the perpetrator. Government officials have yet to succeed on all three fronts in any of the previous biological attacks. Fortunately, all of those attacks, although tragic, were relatively small in scale. Unfortunately, a future attack could very well be of greater magnitude.

On top of these challenges, there is also the problem that we are not ready for such an attack should it take place. According to former senator Joe Lieberman and former Homeland Security secretary Tom Ridge, co-chairs of a recent Blue Ribbon Study Panel on Biodefense, "The United States is underprepared for biological threats. Nation states and unaffiliated terrorists (via biological terrorism) and nature itself (via emerging and reemerging infectious diseases) threaten us. While biological events may be inevitable, their level of impact on our country is not." As the introduction makes clear, this Blue Ribbon examination, in which the author participated, examined the state of US bio-preparedness and found it wanting.[16]

Fortunately, there are steps a president can take to make our nations better prepared to deal with potential bio-attacks. The first step is to make sure the government is actively engaged in prevention efforts. This entails aggressive intelligence and swift action against potential attackers, along the lines discussed in the chapter on terrorism. It also requires detection programs to identify that an attack took place as soon as possible. This is indeed a challenge. Mexican officials, for example, were slow to detect the outbreak of swine flu in 2009. At the same time, there are a number of new private-sector capabilities, from detection systems like air-quality monitors to search engines like Google, that can help us detect problems earlier than in previous eras.

In addition to these private-sector tools, there is also BioWatch, a dedicated government program to detect possible airborne attacks. Under BioWatch, signed into law by President George W. Bush in 2003, the Department of Homeland Security coordinates interagency efforts to maintain vigilance against biological attacks. Agencies like the Environmental Protection Agency (EPA), the Centers for Disease Control (CDC), and the FBI contribute their respective expertise. So, for instance, the EPA examines air quality, while the FBI stands poised to react to any attack and search for the responsible parties. The program was formed in reaction to the still-unsolved anthrax attacks of 2001, and President Bush referred to it in his 2003 State of the Union address, stating that the United States was now "deploying the nation's first early warning network of sensors to detect biological attack."[17]

Despite all these positive developments, the system is far from foolproof. For example, BioWatch airborne detectors would not have detected a food- or product-borne attack, such as the Tylenol or Rajneeshee attacks of the 1980s. And it probably would not detect a mail attack, such as the 2001 anthrax letters attacks. In addition, an attack on a large building's ventilation system, which could potentially kill thousands, might not be picked up either. For all the progress we have made with both technology and government programs like BioWatch, there is a significant chance that a biological attack would not be detected before people became symptomatic. Furthermore, recent mishandlings of pathogens by federal scientists—such as the discovery of smallpox vials in an insecure lab or the accidental exposure of eighty-four federal workers to live anthrax—only highlight the degree to which federal officials are far from infallible.

Once a biological attack is detected—however that detection may take place—a new set of problems emerge. First, the government must determine the nature of the attack. At this point responsibility goes from the EPA, which detects anomalies in the air, to the CDC, which has to identify the pathogen—and the counteragent required to combat it. Though technological improvements have made this far easier than it once was, it is not always an easy task. The difficulty of the task is compounded by the fact that there is a time sensitivity at work. The longer it takes to discover the agent, the harder it is to save lives with the appropriate countermeasure. In fact, scenarios involving US responses to various bioterror attacks show steep inclines in mortality rates the longer a pathogen-based infection remains untreated. This is especially true with anthrax, which needs to be treated within forty-eight hours.

Compounding this is the possibility that the terrorists could send a false flag to stymie government scientists. Combining two different pathogens or, worse, two strains of the same pathogen would complicate response efforts. Since time is so essential in responding to a bioterror incident, anything bioterrorists do to slow our reaction time has the potential to increase the death rate of any attack.

Assuming CDC identifies the pathogen, the FBI will use that information in the hunt for the responsible party. As we have seen, the odds of catching a bioterrorist are relatively low, largely because the actor spreading the agent can choose to be far removed from its victims, and the act of spreading a pathogen recruits a more calculating and designing perpetrator. In addition, the distributor has the advantages of not just distance, but time—the perpetrator will likely be far away when the symptoms finally manifest themselves in the targeted area. Despite these challenges, the FBI is best equipped to continue to handle the law enforcement aspect of a bioterror incident. But no matter how the FBI proceeds, it will have little to do with the immediate need for the full apparatus of government to deal with the attack itself.

The three stages of detection of a bioterror attack—understanding that we are under attack, identifying the pathogen, and catching the responsible party—take place at the non-political, career level among officials assigned and (hopefully) trained to work on these activities. These individuals might have other day-to-day responsibilities, but should a bioterror attack happen, they would spring into action. The president would be unlikely to get involved in any of these early activities. But if there is indeed a large-scale bioterror attack, things get more complicated, and the president would have to get involved, at least on the communication and coordination level initially. As the University of Colorado's Richard Hoffman has written, "Elected political leaders [would] be in charge of response to the attack, rather than the health commissioner or the state epidemiologist." Hoffman further added that in the instance of a bioterror attack, "the president, governor, or mayor will assume leadership roles, and public health agencies will need to carry out their duties within an incident command structure."[18]

With much of the bioterror response taking place on autopilot, the president may be at a loss for what to do. The number one thing that must happen in response to a bioterror incident is to determine the level of governmental response. If the pathogen threatens to spread, the president may need to consider imposing quarantine on the affected area. Step two would entail communicating with all relevant elected executives at each level and coordinating an internal governmental response. Step three would be communicating to the larger populace the rationale for swift and decisive action.

Another key decision regards the need for the government to get the appropriate countermeasures to the affected areas. The entire basis of our bioterror-combating strategy is based on the accumulation of counter-measures that would be distributed when needed. For this purpose the US government has created a Strategic National Stockpile (SNS) of countermeasures—antibiotics, vaccines, and a variety of other life-supporting drugs and devices—to be deployed in time of need.

Established in 1999, the SNS evolved from the National Pharmaceutical Stockpile (NPS), headed by the Centers for Disease Control and Prevention within the Department of Health and Human Services (HHS). Its purpose, as directed by Congress, was to "provide a re-supply of large quantities of essential medical materiel to states and communities during an emergency within twelve hours of the federal decision to deploy."[19] Following 9/11 and the 2001 anthrax attacks, President George W. Bush signed the Homeland Security Act of 2002, which transferred responsibility of the NPS to the Department of Homeland Security, and changed the name to the Strategic National Stockpile in March 2003.[20]

President Bush took another step to bolster preparedness against bioterrorism with the enactment of Project Bioshield in 2004. This project restored jurisdiction of the strategic stockpile to the CDC—which is part of HHS, not the Department of Homeland Security. Project Bioshield called for the strengthening of the national capacity to store and distribute countermeasures such as vaccines and drugs in the event of a bioterror attack. It also put the country on the path to develop a Bioshield Special Reserve Fund to encourage private business involvement by offering a guaranteed federal market for medical supplies.[21] Establishing such a market was, and is, essential for national stockpiling efforts. In the absence of such incentives, individual citizens are unlikely to purchase many of the key countermeasures needed in case of a biological, radiological, or chemical incident. Since developing these countermeasures is both costly and time intensive, manufacturers are similarly unlikely to develop them unless they know that they have a reliable customer in the US government. In many ways this Strategic National Stockpile is a cardinal example of the role of the federal government in protecting the citizenry.

Developing a stockpile is incredibly costly. The expense of a stockpile is a challenge in these days of high budget deficits and even higher government debt. Recent appropriations for the SNS are lower than they were in 2011: $591 million in 2011, but $571 million in 2016, and as low as $486 million in 2013.[22]

The SNS's arsenal of drugs and vaccines has been deployed only a few times since its creation. SNS was deployed as a response to the attacks on September 11, 2001, the anthrax threat in October 2001, and Hurricanes Katrina and Rita in August and September 2005.[23] Even when unused, however, the SNS serves a valuable purpose. Its very existence enables government officials to focus on other priorities, knowing that there is a stockpile of key countermeasures available in case of a crisis. Similarly, it provides private citizens some peace of mind, knowing that they do not have to purchase every conceivable countermeasure for every possible contingency. Furthermore, the SNS creates a marketplace for many relatively rare or expensive medical products that would not be manufactured otherwise. The SNS marketplace also enables manufacturers to innovate, creating lifesaving, life-extending, and life-improving products that could be useful even in the absence of a crisis.

When a crisis does strike, however, the Strategic National Stockpile is even more valuable, allowing government officials to send needed countermeasures anywhere in the United States on very short notice, thereby reducing the danger of a bio-event's spreading out of control. Once the secretary of Homeland Security or the secretary of HHS recognizes that there is an emergency, the appropriate medical supplies can be dispensed by the SNS and delivered to citizens within a prompt time frame. Unlabeled, secret stockpile warehouses are strategically placed at twelve locations throughout the country to ensure the efficient delivery of the supplies, with a goal of being able to get a crucial countermeasure to any location in the country within twenty-four hours. The first provisions to be deployed are twelve-hour "Push Packages" that provide an extensive array of drugs and rations within the early hours of an immediate threat. In the event of a bioterror attack, antibiotics hypothetically would be distributed to a designated metropolitan area within forty-eight hours of the determination to deploy countermeasures after an attack.[24]

One of the best examples of the stockpile's potential benefit is in the area of anthrax. And, of course, this example is not hypothetical as the attacks via the US Postal Service showed us in the autumn of 2001. Anthrax, an infectious disease that affects the skin, gastrointestinal tract, and lungs, can spread rapidly, over great distances, in relatively minute amounts. In 2009 the National Security Council reported that a biological attack with an agent such as anthrax could cause casualties in the "hundreds of thousands of people and [could] cost more than $1 trillion."[25] Anthrax, while indeed a deadly disease, is relatively treatable with ciprofloxacin in the first forty-eight hours after exposure to the bacteria. After the first forty-eight hours, however, inhalational anthrax (the type that would likely be used in a biological attack) develops a 95 percent mortality rate.[26] Should there be an anthrax outbreak, having ciprofloxacin already stockpiled and ready to deploy could help ensure that a deadly attack does not become a mass-casualty disaster.

Given the protocols already in place directing the use of the Strategic National Stockpile, once a bioterror attack happens, the president has very little to do with the distribution of the needed countermeasures. The president's role is paramount in the period before an attack, should it take place. Each president needs to make the funding and management of an efficient and up-to-date stockpile a priority. As part of this effort, he must also explain to Congress and to the American people why the stockpile is a priority. If the president does his job correctly in advance, should an attack take place, the system should be able to respond quickly and decisively.

With this in mind, the president's most important activities will occur before an attack takes place. He will still need to handle the messaging aspects of dealing with the crisis, but he must also step back and let the emergency response mechanism kick into gear. There are a number of steps that presidents can take now to improve the operations of the stockpile should its services be needed. The SNS faces a number of challenges, including a limited ability to determine the disposition of products. For example, we did not know for more than five years what happened to a large percentage of the Tamiflu that was sent out to states during the 2009 H1N1 (swine flu) outbreak. At the start of the outbreak, eleven million courses, amounting to 25 percent of the entire supply in the stockpile, were sent out to the states, and thanks to a poor tracking system and subpar communication with the states, it took four years to learn the ultimate disposition of those courses.[27] Stockpiling antivirals such as Tamiflu did help deal with the crisis at that time. On the other hand, knowing quickly exactly what happened to the distributed courses would help us plan better for future events and might incidentally help the SNS better defend its budget in the face of legislators who demand accountability.

Beyond the big-picture goal of the distribution of large quantities of lifesaving medicines over a large area, there is the question of how best to distribute product to the specific people in need. The president should engage in a high-priority, top-down effort to make sure we have the best possible distribution system. Currently, the primary method for dispensing SNS supplies is by the Points of Dispensing (POD) system. The drugs are delivered to a central location (schools, public spaces, etc.), and people are given the responsibility of accessing them on their own. While this method on the surface seems fair and low-maintenance, it raises some significant concerns. First, such a method discriminates against people who lack the means to drive or transport themselves to acquire the drugs.[28] Furthermore, rural Americans are at a disadvantage, as they are located the farthest from cities, where medical provisions are primarily centralized.

The POD method is also a "blind" distribution. In aiming for fairness, it does not necessarily target those who require the countermeasures the most. If there were an especially high-risk population, the POD method might not reach that particular population. The government does in fact draw up lists of priority recipients of crucial countermeasures, including first responders, vulnerable populations, the military, and a select few key government officials. POD-based distribution, however, does not coordinate with that kind of prioritization.

The president should look at two main categories of proposed solutions to the distribution problem: improved versions of the POD method, and completely changing the current approach. One of the most talked about methods of distribution involves the US Postal Service and its fleet of approximately 300,000 mail carriers nationwide. Utilizing the Postal Service to dispense medical supplies makes a certain amount of logistical sense: It is perhaps the only service that literally goes door-to-door and reaches each household within entire communities. This process also covers those who lack the means to drive to pick up supplies, especially high-risk elderly people. This method of distribution would allow the government to efficiently target affected areas of the nation.

At the same time, there are some problems with this approach. The American Postal Workers Union has expressed understandable concern over the safety of their employees when handling highly sought after supplies during periods of tension, high risk, or contagion. To ensure the safety of the workers, the union has demanded that a public safety officer accompany each worker. This would create an unrealistically high demand for police officers at a time when they are most needed elsewhere. Furthermore, there remains the very real possibility that a portion of public safety workers could potentially be unavailable in the event of a national emergency. During the Hurricane Katrina disaster, for example, an estimated one-third of the members of the New Orleans Police Department, approximately five hundred officers, abandoned their posts.[29] It is unclear if the desertion rate would be this high during a national emergency, but public safety officials do have to account for at least some drop-off in their modeling.

Another possible approach to the distribution problem is using polling or other community sites as PODs. Polling sites in particular are typically more numerous within communities than the standard public PODs (high schools, pharmacies, etc.); their locations are specifically designed to efficiently handle large crowds of people during a short, discrete time period (e.g., Election Day) and to provide service to a significant, but unknown, number of citizens in a timely manner. Typically, the locations are convenient and familiar to people, and are designed to prevent congestion and limit long lines. Election personnel, moreover, are experienced in handling crowds and equipment at sites, and would presumably work well in conjunction with public health officials. They are also predisposed to volunteer and are engaged in their communities. Overall, employing workers or volunteers already used to staffing community centers for civic purposes could address the potential shortage of public health workers who could quickly and efficiently distribute drugs in case of emergency.

While the polling place POD method has many advantages, it presents some challenges as well. Increasing the number of locations may reduce congestion, but it also requires more complex logistics for organizers.[30] In addition, the heavy reliance on volunteer, civic-minded, non-health experts might cause some consternation with the recipient population since the volunteers would be inexperienced in the administration of the materials. It probably would not require too much time and effort to train them, but any additional tension during an already high-stress scenario requires careful consideration.[31]

Another promising distributional approach would be to employ the private sector through retail stores and drug manufacturers. Most retail pharmacies have experience with administering flu vaccines, so they already possess basic skills with medical supplies and civilians. Furthermore, they are ideal for handling large crowds looking to procure specific items—that is what they do. Their resources for doing so include large parking lots, storage units to receive large shipments, extensive indoor space laid out for the purpose of dealing with customers, and an available and expandable supply of staff. Perhaps most importantly, retailers also have experience dealing with sales crunches, which a countermeasure supply effort would resemble. On the other side of the equation, retail stores are also familiar and convenient for people. If there is one thing the American people like to do, it is shop. Consequently, there is a retail store within five miles of 95 percent of US residences. Furthermore, web-based retailers such as Amazon could provide invaluable expertise on how to distribute products to millions of Americans in very short time periods.

This idea, while promising, has challenges as well. Primary among them is the question of liability. If someone were to be injured during the distribution process, or even by the administration of the countermeasure, who would be held liable? As nongovernmental employees, the private-sector retail workers would face significant liability exposure. Furthermore, the retail stores themselves, as well as their parent companies, could also have some exposure, which would likely make them extremely wary of participating. In fact, it is likely that the only way that the retail store option could be utilized would be if Congress were to pass, and the president were to sign, blanket and explicit liability protection for the workers, the individual locations, and their parent companies.[32] Fortunately, Congress has already passed similar legislation that exempts volunteers from liability in the event of a national crisis. In 1997 Congress passed the Federal Volunteer Protection Act (FVPA), granting immunity to public health volunteers from nonprofits. The FVPA is limited, though, for it fails to include punitive or noneconomic damages.[33] So while some legislation has been passed with the intention of providing volunteer health workers with liability protection, presidents should support more comprehensive liability protection to entice corporate entities to lend a hand.

Another, somewhat similar, private-sector option is to utilize drug manufacturers' preexisting commercial routes to distribute drugs to recipients. This approach is particularly attractive because it employs routine, pre-established methods of distribution: The manufacturers' commercial channels have already been put to use multiple times. This option also allows for a single, central dispensing method to avoid the confusion and complexity of various separate allocation modes.

The way this option could work is as follows: A manufacturer of a particular countermeasure gets a contract with the Biomedical Advanced Research and Development Authority (BARDA) to provide a specific product to the SNS. Depending on the arrangement, the manufacturer might not even have to provide the physical product itself to the twelve distribution hubs but would instead sell the government a guarantee that they would provide the product to the requested location in case of emergency. In doing so, the manufacturer could use its existing logistics, storage, and security operations to hold on to the product until needed, at which point it could serve as the single distributing force when directed by the SNS, or even after a signal from the marketplace that commercial supplies had been depleted to a prearranged degree. The necessary supplies would be dispersed to communities via manufacturers' existing commercial modes of transportation.

None of these methods is perfect, but they all provide some type of improvements to our current approach. Thinking about them also reminds us of the purpose and appropriate focus for federal efforts. The competing forces in preparing for bioterror challenges mean that there needs to be more strategic thinking. It is here that presidential leadership can be important in figuring out how we will handle the question of countermeasure distribution in case of a bioterror event.

Another area where the president can play a role is in the area of SNS funding. The difficult budget environment we face (see chapter 4, "Economic Collapse") means that SNS, as with nearly all government programs, will likely experience budget cuts. But there is a strong case to be made that while some of the potential crises we face should be handled at the local level, the bioterror threat is one that demands federal involvement. Preparing for and preventing possible bioterror incidents and maintaining a national stockpile are the kinds of responsibilities that appropriately fall within the presidential purview. Given this, the outstanding question is whether the SNS budget cuts will threaten the efficiency of the program. As Ali Khan, director of CDC's Office of Public Health Preparedness and Response, has said, "The [stockpile] will be buying less. There's no doubt about it."[34] The president must make the case for maintaining a robust SNS even while coping with limited resources and competing interests.

Of course, the entire discussion about improving the SNS presupposes that we should continue to keep such a stockpile. While most analysts on both sides of the political aisle agree on the value of the SNS, it is not a unanimous view. FDA economist Marta Wosinska, for instance, has argued that the government can't accurately predict which countermeasures will be needed in a crisis, and that stockpiling only serves to drive up prices for the specific countermeasures the SNS does select. This argument may make some sense at a theoretical level, but fails to take into account the state of the American mind-set after a decade that revealed both internal and external threats capable (and desirous) of inflicting mass casualties. Furthermore, she argued, stockpiling cannot realistically cover the entire population of the United States, resulting in prioritizing populations that will receive SNS supplies versus those who will receive nothing.[35]

The SNS, while not perfect, goes a long way toward alleviating public concern by ensuring that the federal government won't be helpless in the case of a crisis. The existence of the SNS itself even arguably deters terrorist bio-threats, since the impact of an attack will be mitigated by the medical countermeasures. Theorists can debate whether there should be a stockpile, or whether government should provide public goods at all, but the most responsible way to arm ourselves against unknown future threats is to make sure that we have the best, most robust, and most efficient SNS possible, and that it is coordinated with the larger intelligence effort to anticipate the most likely line of attack in criminal enterprises and asymmetric terrorist ventures.

CHAPTER EIGHT

Loss of the Power Grid

AT 8:28 P.M. ON JULY 13, 1977, THREE SEPARATE LIGHTNING BOLTS struck and destroyed three power lines in Westchester County, New York. These three strikes, together comprising a statistical improbability though obviously not an impossibility, conspired to throw America's largest city into darkness.[1]

The 1977 New York blackout was not New York City's first blackout. In 1965 there had been another blackout, affecting thirty million people across the Northeast. This blackout was recalled nostalgically by city residents: People got along splendidly—arrest totals that day were below average—the power was restored in about thirteen hours, and some tittered that the hospitals had experienced a slight baby boom nine months after that November day.[2]

The 1977 blackout did not induce nostalgia. In contrast, it led to lootings, destruction, arson, and fear. New York in 1977 was a very different place than in 1965, poorer, more crime ridden, more volatile, and struggling to overcome bankruptcy. When the lights went out for more than twenty-four hours that July, over 1,600 stores were looted or damaged, arsonists set over one thousand fires, and over 3,700 people were arrested, overflowing the city's jails. All told, the mayhem caused over $300 million in damages.[3]

New York's embattled mayor, Abe Beame, struggled to deal with the situation. As Beame said that night, "We've seen our citizens subjected to violence, vandalism, theft and discomfort. The Blackout has threatened our safety and has seriously impacted our economy. We've been needlessly subjected to a night of terror in many communities that have been wantonly looted and burned."[4] Beame did not call out the National Guard, although the Guard had been notified. This left the New York Police Department in charge of public safety during the blackout, a daunting and overwhelming task.

Part of the problem was a loss of social order. The *Daily News* quoted eighteen-year-old looter Cheryl Ross, who said, "You take everything you can get. Look, dungarees are $17.99 and sneakers are $24. Who wants to buy sneakers for $24? Carter is not giving us what we want. He ain't giving us nothing. So we have to take it."[5]

This breakdown in the social order highlighted the thinness of civilization's veneer. George Will, at the time a *Newsweek* columnist, observed that the episode provided "vivid evidence that today nothing, not even petroleum, is more essential than electricity, or has done more to transform the world." A blackout one hundred years ago would have meant little, as society had not yet become dependent on electricity. "Before electricity was harnessed a century ago," Will wrote, "conditions of life were more like those of Julius Caesar's day than of Jimmy Carter's day." Will's analysis spoke not only to the way electricity had transformed modern life, but also to the erosion of order that had taken place in the process.[6]

As New York was erupting in chaos, the new president, Jimmy Carter, did surprisingly little. Mayor Beame declined to call in the National Guard, and the power was restored within twenty-five hours, so there was little to do in that initial period. After the blackout ended, however, Carter mismanaged his relations with New York City in a number of crucial ways. First, despite the damage, he refused to designate New York as a federal disaster area, which would have made it eligible for badly needed disaster relief funds.[7] Mayor Beame noted, correctly, that "the costs when finally tallied will be enormous."[8] Beame was right about the costs, and Carter's decision was detrimental to New York's ability to recover, especially given New York's near bankrupt status at the time.

A few days after the blackout, President Carter gave an interview on the subject with Joe Brown of the National Black Network. In it he argued that it is "important that public officials like myself try to understand the reasons for it." In Carter's opinion one of the causes was "high unemployment among young people, particularly those who are black or Spanish-speaking or in a minority age or group."[9] These statements made Carter sound both condescending toward youth, and exculpatory of their actions.

Carter also blamed the power companies for the problem, saying, "I think had the power companies notified homeowners immediately to turn off air conditioners, TV sets, and cut down on power consumption, the crisis could have been avoided."[10] From the perspective of the power companies, the blackouts were a perfect storm of compounding problems leading to the meltdown. As author James Goodman put it, "A dozen things went wrong on the evening of July 13, 1977, from multiple lightning strikes to circuit breaker failure to backup generator failure."[11] Still, while Carter was not wrong to call attention to the power companies' deficiencies, these comments were a bit of a preview of the sweater-wearing scold Carter would become later in his presidency during the 1979 energy crisis.

Beyond his messaging challenges, Carter also left the city feeling unsupported in the aftermath of the blackouts. Carter's refusal to grant disaster-based aid raised the uncomfortable specter of Gerald Ford's refusal to help bail out New York from bankruptcy, an action immortalized—somewhat unfairly—by the infamous *Daily News* headline: "Ford to City: Drop Dead." Carter had promised "never to tell New York to drop dead" (words that, for the record, Ford never uttered), but his actions made it seem as if he was reneging on his promise.[12]

In addition to not granting federal funds, Carter also failed to visit the city in the immediate aftermath of the blackouts. In fact, he would not visit the city until the fall, when he came to town for meetings at the United Nations. While there, under pressure, he made a high-profile trip to the South Bronx, a symbol of urban blight. The visit made the front page of the *New York Times*, but failed to alleviate the bad feelings stemming from his inattentiveness to the blackout. The trip would also backfire on him in a political sense. In 1980, GOP presidential nominee Ronald Reagan pointedly made his own visit to the Bronx, where he recalled that he had not "seen anything that looked like this since London after the

Blitz." The lack of progress three years after the Carter visit was manifest. Reagan ended up winning New York State in that election, something unlikely for Republican presidential candidates today.[13]

The New York City blackouts highlighted just how dependent society had become on electrical power to maintain order and calm. As Will put it, the episode showed that "extinguishing street lights is enough to crack the thin crust of civilization in whole neighborhoods."[14] Over the next two decades, however, the United States would become even more dependent on our electronic infrastructure. The development of the personal computer, the Internet, and early cell phones meant that America was significantly more wired than it had been in 1977, and therefore had more to lose from some kind of a power grid meltdown.

The increased dependence on electricity put added pressure on the power companies and the government alike to make sure America's power stayed on. As the year 2000 approached, though, the US government had a problem. Twentieth-century computer systems tracked years in a two-digit format, so that "67" would refer to 1967. With the onset of a new millennium, computer experts were afraid that systems would not be able to handle the confusion between 1967 and 2067, and that there was the potential for an epic crash.

This fear may sound trifling today, but we should not underestimate the levels of concern prevalent at the time. A November 1999 *Law Tech Journal* piece observed that "Y2K problems will occur, and they could affect anyone, in limitless ways." The piece even speculated that "Perhaps they could create the next Great Depression."[15] Areas of particular concern included power, utilities, communications, transportation, and banking. And it was not just technical journals looking at the problem. *Newsweek* ran a story on the problem called "The Day the World Shuts Down." *Newsweek*'s Steven Levy asked, "Could the most anticipated New Year's Eve party in our lifetimes really usher in a digital nightmare when our wired-up-the-wazoo civilization grinds to a halt?" His answer, after consulting with experts, was not only yes, but "yes, yes, 2,000 times yes!"[16]

All the mainstream papers covered it, providing breathless updates on the efforts to head off the problem. And the government focused vast amounts of resources on the problem, spearheaded by President Bill Clinton. Most of this effort went into programming fixes to adjust the Y2K glitch. At the end of the day, Y2K was about the relatively dull and obscure work of software coding, and spending the money to both hire and, in the private sector, encourage the coders to do that necessary work.

While Clinton did spend a lot of effort on the Y2K effort, there is a real question as to whether he got on the case early enough. The initial warning bell on the Y2K problem was sounded by Peter De Jager, in *Computer World*, in 1993. Companies started looking at the problem shortly after. In 1998, before Clinton even mentioned the problem, 86 percent of companies reported having ongoing Y2K strategies.[17] And in 1999, *CIO Magazine*'s Scott Kirsner wrote, "For months, if not years, Y2K experts have been calling for President Clinton or Vice President Gore to draw attention to the millennium bug, wake up the American public and elevate the problem to a national priority."[18]

Congress appeared to take on the Y2K problem before the White House engaged on the subject. In 1996 Democratic senator Daniel Patrick Moynihan sent a letter to Clinton requesting that the military be in charge of dealing with the problem, and that the president establish a special Y2K commission.[19] Other legislators pressed the issue as well. In 1998 Republican congressman Steve Horn said that "we urge [President Clinton] again to use the bully pulpit. Not to create public panic, but to explain the nature of the issue."[20]

Clinton's Y2K response began in earnest in July 1998. He gave a major speech on the subject, where he laid out the initial governmental response to the issue. To his credit he began with a joke, calling the moment "one of those days that I never thought would ever arrive, where Al Gore has to listen to me give a speech about computers." To top off his one-upsmanship of the self-proclaimed tech geek Gore, he added: "Being President has its moments."[21]

More seriously, he announced a series of steps that the government would be taking to address the Y2K issue, most importantly the appointment of John Koskinen as the Y2K czar. Koskinen is perhaps better known today as the replacement IRS commissioner appointed to deal with the 2013 scandal of the politicization of IRS reviews of organizations with Tea Party affiliations. Before becoming theY2K czar, he had a distinguished career in both the government and the private sector. A graduate of Duke University and Yale Law School, he worked on Capitol Hill and for New York mayor John Lindsay, before working on corporate turnarounds for the Palmieri Group. Interestingly, Koskinen did not have technical expertise. As recently as five years before his appointment, he was unable to use something as simple as a computer word processing program.[22]

In addition to appointing a czar, Clinton also set a government-wide goal of complete Y2K compliance by March 1999. He made a similar request of our allies abroad, in the IMF (International Monetary Fund) and Russia, and he called for spending $12 million to help developing countries address the issue. Other steps included calling for legislation to encourage businesses to share readiness information, as well as a call to businesses to make sure their systems would be Y2K compliant as well.[23]

Presidential speech making is important, to be sure, but is not a substitute for action. Clinton's initial speech was only one component of a larger effort to address the Y2K problem. The Y2K response continued in what appeared to be a step-by-step manner over the next two years leading up to December 31, 1999. In December 1998 the White House announced that it had successfully addressed the Y2K problem with respect to Social Security, which provided regular checks to forty-eight million Americans. As President Clinton said in making this announcement, "The system works, it is secure, and therefore older Americans can feel more secure."[24] A few months later, in March 1999, the administration announced contingency plans to keep social programs working in case of a computer system failure. Under the plan, even if the state computers stopped working, the government would continue to be able to distribute checks.[25] While these issues might not be the first thing disaster planners consider in coping with a crisis, the distribution of benefits—regardless of your position on the size and the nature of the social safety net—is a good indicator of government functionality, and a stabilizing influence in difficult circumstances.

In April 1999 the White House issued a status report on where nuclear plants stood on the Y2K issue. This was important because some of the oft-stated Y2K concerns related to the possibility of an accidental nuclear launch, or a meltdown at a nuclear power plant. These kinds of disasters had the potential to take a nuisance like a power failure and make it into a catastrophic event. Furthermore, one of the areas of concern stemmed from Russian-made nuclear plants, which were operational at the time in nine countries, not to mention in Russia itself.[26] One of the Russian plants was in far eastern Russia, perhaps close enough to Alaska so that Sarah Palin could see it from her house. As for the accidental nuclear launch, that was apparently less of a concern: A White House report on the subject declared that "Y2K problems will not cause nuclear weapons to launch themselves," as a "nuclear weapons launch requires human intervention." Good thing, that.[27]

Dealing with Y2K also required legislative efforts. In October 1998 Clinton signed into law a bill, the Year 2000 Information and Readiness Disclosure Act, which granted antitrust exemptions and additional liability protections to companies trying to cope with the Y2K issue.[28] Then a few months later, in July 1999, Clinton signed the Y2K Act, which provided legal protection against frivolous lawsuits associated with Y2K.[29] It is important to note that Clinton signed into law these kinds of liability limitations in the face of real political risk. The trial bar is one of the largest donors to the Democratic Party, and signing this bill irked both the members of the bar as well as some Democratic legislators. Furthermore, the fact that this is an issue points to a real problem in our society, as well as in our disaster preparedness efforts. The threat of lawsuits, frequently frivolous ones, informs so much of government and business thinking that it is hard to get these sectors to move on a problem for fear of litigation. It is only in the aftermath of specific protections or legislative carve-outs that businesses are able to cooperate in disaster preparedness efforts. More problematically, the severe increase in partisanship in recent years means that it would likely be much more difficult today to get a Democratic president or legislators to accede to liability protection efforts against the wishes of the trial bar, something that could harm disaster preparation and response efforts in the future.

As the Y2K deadline neared, Clinton stepped up the preparation and communication efforts. In November Clinton expressed optimism that the United States would avert the most feared consequences of Y2K. As Clinton put it, "When it comes to financial services, power, telecommunications, air and rail travel, leading organizations report they have completed nearly all of their Y2K work."[30] When asked about the issue in an online forum, Clinton said, "I wouldn't hoard food and I wouldn't hide. I would be trusting because I think we're going to make it fine." His administration also issued a booklet to citizens, called *Y2K and You*. Despite the president's suggestion that people not hoard food, the brochure recommended having "at least a three-day supply of food and water on hand." Other suggestions included having "half a tank of gas in the car, and jot[ting] down the direct phone numbers for police, fire and ambulance services in case 911 systems do not work."[31] Despite these warnings, Clinton's overall attitude was that Y2K would be recalled as the "last headache of the twentieth century, not the first crisis of the twenty-first."[32]

In December the government issued its last Y2K report. The report said that of the government's 6,167 top systems, all but eight were ready for the date changeover on January 1. And those eight, the report assured, would be ready in time. This included Department of Defense (DOD) systems: The Pentagon reported that the military had checked four million weapons systems with embedded microprocessors to make sure everything was prepared. This overall considerable effort no doubt was expensive. According to the report, the government spent $8.38 billion in preparing for Y2K.[33] By December 1999 Koskinen's staff had grown to about two hundred people. Beyond that, the private sector spent about $100 billion on the effort. Koskinen called the Y2K preparations "the most significant management challenge confronting the world since the Second World War."[34] Responding to this challenge was costly, and we will never know if it was necessary, but the government was able to report that the nation was ready.

After the millennium came, and the disaster didn't, the administration continued its communications efforts. In February the administration took credit for fixing the Y2K problem. Clinton invited Koskinen and the Y2K team to the White House for a group photo and to congratulate them. At the event White House press secretary Joe Lockhart boasted, "We averted what could have been a big problem in many of our economic sectors and government institutions."[35]

There was a political component to this, of course. The Clinton administration had expended a great deal of capital in addressing the Y2K issue and wanted its political due. Furthermore, Clinton wanted Vice President Gore to succeed him, and the political fortunes of the administration were crucial to that effort. That Gore was unsuccessful in his effort does not change the fact that Gore's election was a consideration in the thinking of the Clinton White House in the year 2000.

In contrast to the New York City blackouts, the after-action report on the Y2K effort is mostly positive. Once Clinton did direct White House and governmental resources toward the effort, he by most accounts did a good job on the issue. In fact, his method for dealing with the issue can serve as a template for crisis management efforts to address a looming challenge. He identified the problem, selected a respected point person to lead the issue effort, worked together with Congress, states, the international community, and the private sector on the problem, devoted resources to addressing the problem, and communicated regularly with the nation about the problem. In addition, by going sector by sector and giving frequent progress updates, the president gave the American people a sense that there was a strategy at work, and that they were developing momentum in their efforts to fix the problem. As a result of these efforts, the country was made ready for Y2K, regardless of the level of threat it truly represented.

While the Clinton/Y2K episode is instructive, there are at least two limitations to its applicability to other disasters. First, we don't know, and can't know, if the Y2K problem, had it remained unaddressed, would have had the disastrous results some predicted. It is certainly a good thing that the dire consequences did not take place, but since the consequences were not certain, it remains unclear whether the situation constituted a true potential disaster. Second, more than any other disaster that we will ever face, Y2K presented us with a date certain for when we would face the potential consequences. New York City, in contrast, had no warning before the lights went out in 1977. Going forward, if America faces a cyberattack or an electromagnetic pulse (EMP) attack, we would similarly not get advance warning that it was coming. In addition, even though Y2K was not that long ago, we as a civilization have become far more dependent on computer-based systems in just the short time between then and now, and far more so than New York was in 1977. If a system failure were to take place now, the consequences would be far worse than they would have been at the dawn of this millennium.

Still, there is much we can learn from both Carter and Clinton. Carter, on the one hand, had a harder job in that he had to face a surprise disaster. Unfortunately, he handled it poorly, with negative consequences for both New Yorkers and his political career. Clinton, in contrast, faced a theoretical threat yet handled it well. Clinton's approach shows the importance of preparation in dealing with potential problems before they occur. Carter's situation informs us about the kind of meltdown we might face after a cyber or an EMP attack. To deal with this possibility, we need the kind of advance planning, cooperation, and focus seen in the Y2K situation in order to prevent it from happening. And if it were to happen, we would need to step up national resilience efforts to deal with the consequences.

COPING WITH AN ATTACK ON THE GRID

The New York City blackouts happened. The Y2K crisis did not. But both incidents highlight concerns about the loss of our electric grid and our electronic systems in general. These concerns continually remain high in the public consciousness. As Peggy Noonan wrote about these fears in the *Wall Street Journal*, "All our essentials and most of our diversions are dependent in some way on this: You plug the device into the wall and it gets electrical power and this makes your life, and the nation's life, work. Without it, darkness descends."[36] The Brookings Institution's Joseph Kramek expressed this sentiment in more sober, academic language, concluding in a 2013 report that "Utilities provide services which, if disrupted for long periods of time, may result in economic chaos and may even lead to social unrest."[37]

The author John Steele Gordon encapsulated our level of dependence on computers in the following "thought experiment": "Imagine it's 1970 and someone pushes a button causing every computer in the world to stop working. The average man on the street won't have noticed anything amiss until his bank statement failed to come in at the end of the month. Push that button today and civilization collapses in seconds." The starkness of our dependence happened, Gordon explained, "because the microprocessor is now found in everything more complex than a pencil."[38]

These fears have lately been manifesting in the realm of popular culture. Some kind of attack that takes out power, utilities, and our entire computer-based system remains a constant concern in movies, TV, and popular books. In *Die Hard 4: Live Free or Die Hard*, cyberterrorists attack every aspect of the web-based grid in order to pull off a massive heist. In the remake of *Red Dawn*, our nation becomes vulnerable to outside attack when an EMP disrupts all our advanced weaponry, taking out the electricity in the process. In a host of recent TV shows, including the *Walking Dead*, *Revolution*, *Dark Angel*, *Falling Skies*, and *The Last Ship*, humanity must cope with a world in which most if not all of our pre-existing systems are no longer available. And the 2009 book *One Second After*, specifically designed to scare Americans about the prospects of a successful EMP attack, became a best-seller. Wikipedia even has a page dedicated to "Electromagnetic pulse in fiction and popular culture."[39] Outside of the realm of fiction, former *Nightline* anchor Ted Koppel's best-selling *Lights Out* warns of the likelihood of the loss of our electric grid, and urges both government and individuals to do more to prepare for this eventuality. Clearly there is a growing fear in the collective consciousness of the nation regarding the devastating impact such an attack could have on our way of life.

Beyond the fictional and hypothetical concerns, though, there is some evidence that we do face a very real threat. In the winter of 2014, it emerged that there had been a systematic effort to disrupt the power in the area of Silicon Valley. Some unknown assailant or assailants cut fiber optic cables and fired bullets from an AK-47 into seventeen of twenty-three transformers at the Metcalf power substation in San Jose, California. Other than the damage it caused—which took a month to repair—the general public heard little about this attack. If the upper echelons of government know more, it remains a mystery.

There were a number of worrisome elements to this attack. First, it appears to have been well planned and strategically placed. Attacking Silicon Valley, our cyber-intellectual capital, would have a disproportionately large impact on the nation as a whole. The effects of a coordinated power attack could have national implications. According to the *Wall Street Journal*'s Rebecca Smith, disabling as few as nine of the fifty-five thousand electric-transmission substations in the United States on a high-usage day could lead to "a coast-to-coast blackout."[40]

While this attack appeared focused on a single area, the attackers seem to have known what they were doing and planned the attack to inflict the maximum possible damage. As former Federal Energy Regulatory Commission head Jon Welinghoff said, it was a "purposeful attack, extremely well planned and executed by professionals who had expert training." Compounding all this was the fact that the attack happened in April 2013, and the general public did not find out about it until February 2014. And yet, despite that enormous time lag, the FBI still did not have any idea who had carried out the attack, and were unwilling to characterize it as terrorism.[41]

Beyond this mysterious assault on one of our physical power stations, we also face the constant threat of cyberattacks against our power supply, against weapons systems, and against our information systems. Cybercrime alone costs the United States $100 billion annually, and $575 billion worldwide. Another estimate, by the Center for Strategic and International Studies, found that cybercrime and economic espionage combined cost the world economy some $445 billion annually.[42] Whichever number you pick, the sheer scale of cyberassaults is staggering. According to *Politico*'s Tal Kopan, "If cybercrime were a country, it would have the 27th largest economy in the world."[43] While cybercrime itself does not rise to the level of disaster, its existence speaks to the prevalence of hacking, which is the method by which an attack on the grid could happen.

Government officials are seriously concerned about this problem. The 2008 Obama presidential campaign was hit by a significant cyberattack, so top campaign officials knew about the danger even before they knew they'd be serving in government. Furthermore, according to the *New*

York Times's Peter Baker, the outgoing George W. Bush administration provided contingency plans to the incoming Obama administration on about a dozen possible scenarios that the new administration might face in its early days, among them "a cyberattack on American computer systems." (Although that did not happen at the start of the administration, one of the other possible scenarios, renewed instability in the Middle East, did take place in Obama's first term).[44]

In addition to the problems of espionage and theft, there is also the certainty that the United States would come under cyberassault in any future military action. This is especially so if the dispute were to be against Russia or China, or against their interests or allies. In the case of any attack by us, or against us, we could count on the fact that our opponents would use cyberattacks to harass and frustrate our economic and military capabilities. This is no longer in the realm of theory; it is a reality of modern warfare. Israel, for example, regularly experiences attempted cyber disruptions during flare-ups in conflicts with terror groups like Hamas. During 2014's Operation Protective Edge, Palestinian hackers, with an assist from Iran, attempted what Israel characterized as "a major attack" on Israeli operations. That attack, which aimed to disable Israeli websites, failed, as did a 2016 attack on Israel's power grid, but Israeli security forces now recognize that cyberdefense is a standard part of modern warfare. The Israeli Defense Forces even have a division specifically dedicated to cyberdefense. According to the unnamed head of that division, in this latest war, "for the first time, there was an organized cyberdefense effort alongside combat operations in the field. This was a new reality." The Israeli official expected the cyber struggle to intensify over time. "I won't be surprised if, next time, we meet [terrorists] in the cyber dimension," he warned.[45]

Because of the intensity of these threats, Israel is a global leader in cybersecurity efforts. This leadership is in both the private and the military sector, as there is a great deal of migration between elite military units and cutting-edge technology firms. As a result, according to Dudu Mimran, CTO of the Cyber Security Research Center at Ben-Gurion University, "Israel is one of the few countries positioned to become a worldwide cyber leader. In the world of cyber (where there is a) high threat level, such leadership is much needed."[46] Going forward, the United States must be prepared to provide this kind of leadership as well.

In addition to the certainty that we are already facing—and will continue to face—a variety of cyber threats, there is also the problem that branches of the US government do not seem prepared to work together to address these perils. Former US secretary of defense Bob Gates recalled in his memoir that the nation has been "dangerously vulnerable" to the threat of a cyberattack. He even mentioned that there were warnings of "a major cyber attack" planned against the United States in the fall of 2010. Despite this obvious weakness, Gates saw "a deep division within the government—in both the executive branch and Congress—over who should be in charge of our domestic cyber defense." Compounding the problem was the fact that multiple players thought it was in their bailiwick: "government or business, the Defense Department national security agency, the department of homeland security, or some other entity." In addition, Gates found that the government could not agree on what the strategic priority should be, national security or civil liberties. According to Gates, "the result was paralysis."[47]

These intra-governmental divisions were not just an abstract concern. They had real-world ramifications. Gates said that he specifically requested an opinion from the DOD General Counsel's office on the question of what level of cyberattack would prompt military retaliation. According to Gates, in a somewhat chilling passage, "I was still waiting for a good answer to that question three years later." What this means is that separate and apart from our capacity to respond to an attack, the security establishment was unable or unwilling to grapple with the question of whether we should respond if hit with a crippling cyberattack. And although Gates included some obligatory language about having seen "considerable progress" on his watch, the overall picture he paints of our cyber preparedness was not remotely comforting.[48]

As Gates understood, proper US response to state-based incursions is essential to deterring future attacks. These things are hard to measure, but there is some indication that the indictment by the US of Chinese People's Liberation Army officials suspected in cyberattacks against the US did lead to some short-term reduction in the number of incidents.

The indictments are a public act, but there is a variety of covert activities that US cyber forces can also engage in to discourage state-to-state cyber activity.

State-based cyberattacks are only one part of the problem, though. The dangers to our power systems are multifaceted. The primary threats to America's electrical grid come from three very different sources— cyberwarfare, a physical assault, or an EMP from above. This diversity of threats indicates how difficult it is for the president, or anyone, to prepare for this challenge. But the difficulty of the challenge is no excuse for failing to address it. In fact, the ability of the threat to come from so many different directions increases the likelihood that it could happen.

It is this very question of likelihood of attack that the president should assess first. While there is lots of discussion on the severity of the threat, there is less so on how realistic the various threats are, or on the solutions. For this reason the president needs to be wary of what analysts Jerry Brito and Tate Watkins call "threat inflation."[49] In an era of limited budgets, government officials use threats like cyberwar to secure funding for their agencies. We should fund efforts to protect the nation and our infrastructure, but we need to make sure they are not duplicative or wasteful, and are based on the severity of the threat itself.

The first step in this process is to do a cost-benefit analysis of the various threats and the steps needed to counteract them. Cyber threats are a sexy topic in Hollywood, but presidents need to deal with the real-world likelihood of such threats. With respect to a full-on EMP attack, for example, there would be no ambiguity about level of response. Such an attack would be considered an assault on the sovereignty of the United States, and would be dealt with accordingly. It would almost certainly be treated as severely as a nuclear assault, which would turn this attack into a Mutual Assured Destruction scenario.

The attackers might assume that the EMP would take out our response capabilities, including about ten thousand nuclear warheads, but they could not be sure this would be the case. In fact, because no one has ever tried a large-scale EMP attack, no one can know what the results would be. Perhaps our nuclear subs would sink to the bottom of the ocean after an EMP, as in the fictional *One Second After*, but perhaps, as is likely, they would not, and they would then respond with overwhelming and destructive force. Any nation-state contemplating a full-scale EMP attack would have to assume it would lead to its own destruction. This does not mean that it can't happen. But it does mean that nation-states—those most capable of carrying out such an attack—would be quite wary of doing so.

As for the physical attacks, it is true that a widespread attack on many power plants on a high-usage day could potentially take out the power grid. But such an attack would have to be extremely well coordinated and well timed. As for the 2013 California attack, that dry run—if indeed that is what it was—may have helped those planning to do us ill, but it also alerted the potential victims. It is a safe bet that even without government coordination, power plants across the country beefed up security in response and are now more prepared for some kind of physical attack than they were beforehand. Again, this does not mean that it cannot or will not happen, but that the likelihood of success for a physical attack may paradoxically be lower, not greater, after the previous attack.

This leaves the question of a massive cyberassault on the power grid. According to the US Cyber Consequences Unit's Scott Borg, "An all-out cyber assault can potentially do damage that can be exceeded only by nuclear warfare."[50] As Borg suggests, there is little doubt that we face considerable cyber weakness. Every individual, every private institution, and every government agency is vulnerable to a computer network–based attack, and seemingly all have faced them, including tens of millions of government workers whose data was on the Office of Personnel Management system. Furthermore, there is no doubt that the government should do more to protect both its own resources as well as help the private sector in its cyber-protection efforts. Before getting into the specifics of those efforts, however, it is important to get a sense of how realistic a threat is some kind of coordinated assault that shuts down all our major systems, including the power grid. A number of analysts have looked at this question and determined that the overwhelming, science fiction movie–type of attack is a low-probability event. According to Brandon Valeriano and Ryan Maness, writing in *Foreign Affairs*, "fear of a lone cyberterrorist—like the recent Bond villain in *Skyfall* who is capable of bringing a government to its knees—is unfounded." As Valeriano and Maness put it, "To be effective, cyberwarfare requires substantial infrastructure, money, and ground operatives."[51] As with EMP attacks, an all-out cyberassault is far more likely to come from a state actor than from an individual assailant. This means that they would likely be more easily identified, and therefore similarly vulnerable to retaliation, be it of the cyber or the kinetic variety.

Other analysts agree about the unlikelihood and difficulty of the cyber blitzkrieg. IT security expert Bruce Schneier acknowledged to the *Economist* that future wars will include cyberattacks, but that an all-out attack that takes down our whole system is both technically complex and "movie-script stuff"—unlikely in the real world.[52] The Center for Strategic and International Studies' James Andrew Lewis, writing in the *Washington Post*, agrees that "truly destructive attacks are hard to pull off." *Politico*'s David Perera talked to a half-dozen security experts and concluded that "it's virtually impossible for an online-only attack to cause a widespread or prolonged outage of the North American power grid."[53] Notwithstanding the difficulty of such an action, though, Lewis thinks we do need to do more to prepare for such an eventuality, noting that "if somebody decides to attack us, we are in no way ready to protect ourselves in cyberspace."[54]

Dismissing the threat, however, is not a strategy. Presidents must deal with Black Swans, events that no one expects but happen anyway. Beyond getting a realistic sense of the nature of the threat, presidents can and must take a number of key steps to increase our security in the face of possible threats to our infrastructure and power system. It of course goes without saying that we should bolster our physical and computer security to prepare against attack. But the president is not involved in security protocols at power plants or writing code to combat viruses. Presidential involvement is crucial, though, in a number of key areas.

The second area of presidential involvement, beyond the assessment of the threat, is in the determination of a doctrine of war. As Secretary Gates noted, we do not know how we could or should respond to an attack on our infrastructure, and the bureaucracy has been resistant to determining that doctrine. This is not surprising. Determining how to respond to new and asymmetric attacks is not a job for the bureaucracy. But it is important for the president to do so, in coordination with appropriate cabinet level officials—State, Defense, Justice, Treasury, and Homeland Security—as well as with our diplomatic partners.

Article 51 of the United Nations charter does grant states the ability to respond to a nation's cyberspace, but it does not and cannot determine the level of the response.[55] This determination needs to include some kind of scale of intensity for figuring out which attacks warrant hitting back. This review should also create a risk-benefit scale for opposing entities that we would target in response. Cyberwarfare differs from conventional warfare in that counterattacks can have many more unexpected ripple effects. Taking out an electrical station that powers a military base could also affect hospitals or schools in the same grid. In addition, the United States' use of offensive cyber capabilities can bring about their own retaliatory efforts, and can also break down standards of restraint that currently do exist between nation-states. These kinds of decisions cannot be made by military personnel on the ground, but need to be considered by senior military and political officials.[56]

Another problem with these kinds of new and difficult questions is that traditional defense and political officials will almost certainly not have experience with them. For this reason the president needs to consider a designated office to cope with these questions and to lead our cyber-security efforts. Such an office could be modeled on the Department of Homeland Security in its effort to have a crosscutting overview of US government agencies, but would need to avoid the cumbersome and bureaucratic aspects of DHS as it has come to be.

However the president decides to go, he must be careful of useless deck chair rearranging. Changes in doctrine, tactics, and organization must be made with security, not politics, egos, or committee jurisdictions, in mind. Furthermore, the president must be wary of empty government declarations. As Secretary Gates recalled about the various and periodic national strategy directive documents that emerge from the bureaucracy, "I don't recall ever reading the president's National Security Strategy when preparing to become secretary of defense. Nor did I read any of the previous National Defense Strategy documents when I became secretary. I never felt disadvantaged by not having read the Scriptures." Obviously, some new document that goes unread by senior officials will do little to prepare the US government for the real threats that we face to our infrastructure.[57]

In short, we should not overestimate the threats to our power grid. According to former DHS official Perry Pederson, "the grid is a little more robust than what we give it credit for. It's not quite so fragile."[58] But even if a grid takedown is low probability, at the same time it remains a high-impact event. It is unlikely to happen, but if it were to happen, the effects would be devastating. Presidents and their disaster planners need to prepare accordingly.

CHAPTER NINE

Civil Unrest

THERE HAVE BEEN HUNDREDS OF RIOTS IN THE HISTORY OF THE UNITED States. The causes have been manifold: race, poverty, unhappiness with the draft, and even sports victories (or defeats). The vast majority of these, while unfortunate, are brief and settled at the local level, by standard law enforcement intervention, or at times nonintervention. Riots become a national problem when they are so large that they cannot be contained by local officials, or when they become so widespread that they take place in multiple locations across the nation. In the 1960s President Lyndon Johnson often had to deal with both of these kinds of riots.

Urban riots put their indelible stamp on the Johnson administration in ways that are rarely discussed today. Daniel Patrick Moynihan, who served as urban affairs adviser to Richard Nixon, observed that "urban rioting had consumed the domestic energies of the Johnson administration in its last phase." According to Moynihan, upon entering the White House in 1969, the Nixon staff "was presented with pads of forms to be used in calling out the National Guard. Blank spaces were provided for date, time, and place."[1] Rioting was so pervasive that they even pre-printed forms for dealing with them.

Urban riots plagued the nation during every summer of Johnson's one elected term (New York City also saw a five-day riot in 1964, during the term Johnson inherited from Kennedy). The five years of summer riots in the 1960s brought about 225 deaths, four thousand injuries, and $427 billion in economic destruction.[2] Another estimate counts 329 racial disturbances in 257 cities, causing approximately three hundred deaths and eight thousand injuries in the three years from 1966 to 1968.[3]

The best known of the series of riots that became known as the "Long, Hot Summers" was the Watts riots. Unrest in Watts began on Wednesday, August 11, 1965, just five days after the passage of the Voting Rights Act. The spark that started the riot was an incident between the Los Angeles Police Department and a twenty-one-year-old African American named Marquette Frye. Frye was stopped for drunk driving; his mother got involved, and the police treated him roughly, angering neighborhood residents who had assembled to watch. The ensuing riots, which urban affairs expert Fred Siegel wrote were "sometimes better characterized as a 'rebellion,'" caused thirty-four deaths and led to more than 3,400 arrests, as well as $40 million in damages. As Sergeant Ben Dunn of the LAPD recalled, "The streets of Watts resembled an all-out war zone in some far-off foreign country; it bore no resemblance to the United States of America."[4]

Even though urban riots would come to define much of the Johnson administration, Johnson was slow to react to the situation in Watts. Joseph Califano, special assistant to the president for domestic policy, recalled that, initially "the event was unnoticed in the White House." After Califano had been alerted by California officials about the seriousness of the situation, he tried to get in touch with Johnson to discuss the situation. Califano further revealed that he was unable to reach Johnson, despite repeated attempts to call and get direction. According to Califano, this was the only period in his experience in the White House that Johnson did not respond to his phone calls.[5]

Compounding the problem in Watts was the fact that California governor Pat Brown was out of the country in Greece, leaving Lieutenant Governor Glenn Anderson in charge. Brown liked Anderson, but was not alone in considering him "a bit of a bumbler." Even though the incident happened on a Wednesday, Brown did not learn about the situation until Friday, August 13. His top aide, Hale Champion, interrupted him at a banquet and told the governor about the unrest, and that the LAPD was contemplating asking for help from the National Guard. Brown had seen a minor item about unrest in LA in the Athens paper that morning, but it had few details and he apparently thought little of it. After getting the call, he began planning a trip home, but did not get to Los Angeles until 10:45 p.m. on Saturday night, after twenty hours of travel. For the riot's first three days, Anderson was in charge.[6]

Bumbler or not, Anderson put the riots on the White House radar screen. Specifically, he placed the issue squarely in Califano's lap. Anderson wanted authorization for the use of Air Force planes to transport the National Guard to LA, and to bring needed army supplies on the planes as well. He put the issue starkly to Califano: "If you don't provide support, the violence will rest on the White House's head." Califano authorized the planes but, given his inability to contact Johnson, hedged in how he provided that support. According to his memoir, Califano told Anderson, "You've got White House approval." Anderson was not fooled by Califano's careful use of language and asked, "Do we have presidential approval?" Califano could not go that far, but he did repeat his initial OK, "You've got White House approval."[7]

Califano's dodge raises a key question: Why was Johnson so unavailable in this particular case? In Califano's telling, he mentioned at least six times that he was unable to reach his usually reachable boss.[8] The reasons for this apparent disappearance are unclear. At one point, Califano wrote that Johnson was "withdrawing into the bosom of his family and intimate friends and aides." When Califano finally did speak to Johnson, the aide noted that his boss's "voice was heavy with disappointment" and that he sounded depressed.[9]

Johnson went through a number of stages regarding the riots. First, according to Nick Kotz, both Johnson and civil rights leader Martin Luther King were initially "slow to comprehend" the impact of the riots. Once Johnson did realize what was happening, he seemed to feel that the riots were a rebuke to his civil rights accomplishments. This feeling led to his depression and his uncommunicative period, the period in which Califano took matters into his own hands, at considerable professional peril. Califano's White House colleague Jack Valenti had been with LBJ at the president's ranch, and he saw the depths of Johnson's despair. Johnson, it seemed, took the rioting personally, asking, "How is it possible? After all we've accomplished. How could it be?"[10]

In the midst of his frustration, Johnson expressed some extremely questionable thoughts about the developments in Watts. According to Califano, Johnson speculated that "Negroes will end up pissing in the aisles of the Senate." Califano explained that "Johnson feared that the reforms to which he had dedicated his presidency were in mortal danger, not only from those who opposed, but from those he was trying to help." Johnson also expressed his disgust with white liberals. When Johnson heard that presidential speechwriter Richard Goodwin was away at Martha's Vineyard, he mused, "We ought to blow up that God-damned island." Despite his sadness and frustration, Johnson did not lose his typical focus on the politics of the situation. He checked in to see if Governor Brown was following the situation closely enough to make sure that likely 1966 gubernatorial rival Ronald Reagan did not take political advantage of the situation.[11]

When Johnson did get involved, tentatively at first, he was fairly territorial with Califano. Johnson did not like having people act without his authorization. Once Johnson learned what Califano had done, Valenti had to intercede with Johnson to protect Califano's job. Johnson also issued a statement on the fourth day of the riots, saying, "We are deeply committed to the fulfillment of every American's constitutional rights. We have worked hard to protect those rights but rights will not be won with violence." Then, sounding somewhat like a cross between Voltaire and a Spiderman comic, he added, "Equal rights carry equal responsibilities."[12]

Johnson also spoke to Dr. Martin Luther King to get his advice. King's response to Johnson's request for a recommendation was to focus on economic deprivation as a cause of the violence. According to King: "Well, the problem is—I think the poverty—if they could get in the next few days this poverty program going in Los Angeles, I believe it would help a great deal."[13] King's feeling in the aftermath of the riots was that the civil rights movement needed a second act, one focused on economic improvements.[14] Johnson apparently agreed with King on the issue of poverty programs, saying, "We've got to have some of these housing programs, and we've got to get rid of these ghettos, and we've got to get these children out from where the rats eat on them at night, and we've got to get them some jobs."[15] Beyond verbal agreement with King, he also worked to move the federal government in that direction. In this effort he did what Lyndon Johnson did best: spend federal dollars. According to historian Robert Dallek, the White House instructed multiple federal agencies to direct funds toward Los Angeles. Within a month the federal government sent $29 million to Los Angeles.[16]

Despite Johnson's instinct to send money to address the problem, he also had significant concerns about the consequences of such an approach. Part of the reason for his initial reluctance to get involved was, as he told Califano, to avert having a "federal presence in Los Angeles." According to Dallek, the implication of this was that Johnson feared the "indication that his administration had contributed to the upheaval by indulging black anger."[17] As events would turn out, the additional federal funding did not help defuse urban anger, and may have even encouraged the subsequent riots, something LBJ himself feared.

Of course, the Watts riots were not the only riots LBJ would have to deal with. Summer riots took place in Cleveland in 1966 and in Newark and Detroit in 1967. The recurrence of urban violence led to a number of developments in the government's approach to the problem. At the local level, urban police departments began to militarize in order to deal with the threat of urban violence. This took place initially in reaction to Watts, but additional episodes added to the impetus. Police departments started to stockpile weapons and equipment designed for urban warfare. According to author Clay Risen, the defense industry encouraged these efforts, as these companies were happy to have a new market for their wares.[18]

At the same time, the Pentagon began incorporating urban warfare into its doctrine. Beginning in 1963 the Army Operations Center started developing plans to cope with domestic unrest. The operational plan, named Steep Hill, included twenty-one thousand soldiers encompassing seven brigades. Up until 1967 the group's activities were somewhat limited, including monitoring of dangerous situations and the provision of supplies for the National Guard in situations like the Watts riots. In 1967, however, things changed when the Michigan National Guard could not control the Detroit riots, where five days of unrest in that city caused forty deaths, one thousand arrests, and seven thousand wounded. Michigan governor George Romney requested federal assistance in the form of troops on the ground. With much reluctance, and perhaps after too long a wait, Johnson called in five thousand federal troops, including the 82nd Airborne Division, to restore order.[19]

Johnson's continued discomfort with the use of federal personnel to respond to local unrest was a recurring theme throughout the Long, Hot Summers. His recalcitrance in this regard was somewhat ironic, given his eager and some might say profligate use of federal dollars and laws to address the nation's social ills. Still, there was a philosophical as well as a political component to his stance. From a philosophical standpoint, he saw himself as a proponent of local government and, especially given his Southern origins, was wary of federal intercession in local policing.[20] On the political side, as noted above, he feared the implicit rebuke to his social policies that the riots represented.

Despite Johnson's concerns about encouraging future riots, he himself exacerbated the problem. On August 26, 1965, at a bill signing for the Public Works and Economic Development Act, Johnson used what the *Washington Post*'s Karen Tumulty later called "apocalyptic" terms to warn of the consequences of not pursuing more social legislation. At the ceremony Johnson said, "I want to warn you this morning that the clock is ticking, time is moving, that we should and we must ask ourselves every night when we go home: Are we doing all that we should do in our nation's capital, in all the other big cities of the country where 80 percent of the population of this country is going to be living in the year 2000?" Johnson referenced what had happened in Watts and added, "Let's act before it is too late." Future president Gerald R. Ford, then the House minority leader, warned that the president's words constituted "an invitation to trigger terrorism in the streets."[21] Johnson did not think much of Ford, and had once made a disparaging and damaging comment about Ford's intellect that became widely circulated.[22] As it turned out, though, Ford would be proven right. Advance justification of violence can serve as an invitation to engage in violence, something Johnson and the country would suffer through each of the succeeding summers of his presidency.

Beyond new laws, Johnson favored another ineffective government solution to try to prevent future outbreaks of unrest: studying the problem. A recurrent theme throughout the 1960s was the need for commissions to analyze urban violence and come up with recommendations for preventing it in the future. The first of these commissions was the McCone Commission, formed by Governor Brown in the wake of the Watts riots and headed by former CIA director John McCone and vice chair Warren Christopher. Their report, issued in December 1965, issued four primary recommendations: continued government efforts to advance African Americans, better integration of African Americans and Hispanics by both business and labor, more prudence on the part of the news media, and more restraint by African American leaders.[23]

Obviously, the McCone Commission failed to prevent the recurrence of urban violence. But that did not stop government officials from trying the same approach in the wake of the Detroit and Newark riots of 1967. On July 28, 1967, while the Detroit riots were still taking place, President Johnson appointed an eleven-person commission, headed by Illinois governor Otto Kerner, to investigate the cause of race riots and make recommendations for the future. The commission's report, written in large part by New York's John Lindsay and issued at the end of February 1968, became famous for its finding that "our nation is moving toward two societies, one black, one white—separate and unequal." The report quickly became, in Johnson aide Harry McPherson's words, "the Bible of the liberals" for its searing indictment of "white racism" and American policies toward the African American community.[24]

Others, unsurprisingly, had a different view. Writing in 1989, former LBJ aide Ben Wattenberg called Kerner "off-base factually" and argued that the report "sent out harmful messages to blacks and Americans generally." Wattenberg, who argued that Kerner was "politics not sociology," felt that the Kerner approach put too much emphasis on big government and not enough on individual responsibility.[25]

LBJ seemed to agree with the negative assessment of Kerner. A number of aides, including Califano, McPherson, and Attorney General Ramsay Clark, recommended that Johnson issue some kind of statement about the report, even if he did not necessarily embrace the Kerner recommendations. Johnson, however, refused, and initially ignored the report. As Wattenberg later put it, his response to the report was "to smolder in silence for a while." Under pressure to say something, Johnson tentatively referred to the report a week after its release, and offered faint praise on March 15 and 22, but he was clearly not a big fan. In fact, on the 22nd he allowed that the report was "very comprehensive," but made sure to add that "we did not agree with all of the recommendations, as certain statements have indicated." Johnson even refused to sign thank-you notes for the participants, telling McPherson that "I'd be a hypocrite" if he thanked them for the unwelcome report.[26]

Regardless of Johnson's reaction to the report, riots would remain a problem for the Johnson administration. At the end of March, beset by problems in Vietnam and one month after the release of the damaging Kerner report, Johnson made the surprising announcement that he would not be pursuing another term as president. His famous words—"I shall not seek, and I will not accept, the nomination of my party for another term as your President"—had a surprising impact. In the wake of his announcement, Johnson received positive press, including editorials praising his decision not to run again, and an unexpected bump in popularity—from 57 percent against to 57 percent in favor. At a visit to New York's St. Patrick's Cathedral for the installation of Archbishop Terence Cooke, Johnson received an ovation from the crowd, and was even greeted by cheering crowds in the streets of Manhattan. All of this was particularly surprising, as Johnson had been limiting his public appearances to apparently safe locations, such as military bases or American Legion posts.[27]

The respite, however, was too good to last. On April 4, 1968, at 7:30 p.m., Martin Luther King was murdered by an assassin's bullet. Race riots broke out in 125 cities across the country. Thirty-nine people died, over 2,600 were injured, and damages exceeded $65 million. Johnson, the political animal that he was, immediately understood their import. Back in Washington from his New York trip, he told staffers, "Everything we've gained in the past few days, we're going to lose tonight."[28]

Johnson was right. The 1968 riots destroyed what remained of his political standing. Once again the National Guard had to be called in to over half a dozen cities, including Chicago, Detroit, Boston, Jackson, Raleigh, and Tallahassee.[29] Three cities ended up getting federal troops, including Chicago, Baltimore, and Washington. In Baltimore, Maryland governor Spiro Agnew asked for assistance from federal troops, and

Johnson sent a contingent of three thousand, a number that quickly grew to five thousand. Baltimore imposed a curfew, but it failed to quell the looting. Snipers fired on public safety officials, including the troops trying to maintain order.[30]

Worst of all from Johnson's perspective were the riots taking place in Washington, DC, only blocks from the White House. On April 7, three days after King's death, a photographer took a picture of Johnson in *Marine One* overlooking the damage on the ground in Washington. The photo is remarkably similar to the famous photo of George W. Bush looking out over New Orleans after Hurricane Katrina. The photo did not become as iconic as the Bush photo, but it does show a similar impotence of a president looking down from the air at devastation on the ground.[31]

Johnson may have watched the situation from the air, but he also faced decisions on the ground. He was reluctant enough to send troops to other US cities, but sending troops into the nation's capital had additional implications for America's standing in the world, as it would be a propaganda defeat in both the Cold War against the Soviets and the hot war in Vietnam.

To help him make this decision, Johnson sent three senior officials—Deputy Attorney General Warren Christopher, DC Public Safety director Murphy, and General Ralph Haines—into the rioting areas to give him an assessment. Once they were out on the streets and saw the depths of the situation, they immediately understood that returning to the White House to report back to Johnson would be a challenge. This was in the era before cell phones, they did not want to indicate who they were to the angry crowds, and they quickly realized that placing a flashing light on their car wouldn't do any good. In order to notify the president of their findings, these three senior officials waited to use a pay phone on the street. When Johnson picked up on his end, he was irate, asking, "Where have you been! I've been trying to reach you for an hour." They explained their situation and recommended that Johnson call in federal troops. Johnson seemed none too happy to hear it, saying, "Fine. We'll send in troops," and then hung up.[32] Some thirteen thousand federal troops were sent to Washington, where twelve people died and over one thousand were injured before the riots subsided on Sunday, April 8.

Throughout all the chaos, Johnson still maintained a biting sense of humor. When he heard from Califano that the radical black activist Stokely Carmichael was going to be leading protesters into Georgetown, home to many members of the elite media, he joked, "Goddamn! I've waited thirty-five years for this day." And when Califano and Deputy Defense Secretary Cyrus Vance, who was suffering from a bad back, took a break from dealing with the riots to share a 3:00 a.m. scotch in the White House, they had the misfortune of being caught by the president. LBJ, clad in pajamas, looked at them and said, "No wonder the nation is going up in smoke and riots and looting. My two top advisers are sitting around drinking!"[33]

This humorous LBJ, however, was unknown to the nation. The American people saw their cities burning and a bedraggled president unable to deal with a difficult war abroad and civil unrest at home. When it came to making decisions—regarding the National Guard in Watts, or reacting to the Kerner report, or sending in troops to the nation's capital—he was dilatory, and he appeared out of touch. Furthermore, his social policies were seen as insufficiently generous by liberals and wrong-headed by conservatives. In both worldviews LBJ's policies contributed to continuing urban violence. In dealing with one of the worst periods of widespread civil unrest in our nation's history, Lyndon Johnson proved unequal to the task.

DEFUSING CIVIL UNREST

We as a nation have clearly made great strides in terms of racial progress since the 1960s. State-sanctioned racism is a vestige of the past, and most Americans seem to have progressed in their views enough that they elected and reelected an African American president without much difficulty, albeit much commentary. Furthermore, African Americans participate at all levels of society, and there is a large and thriving black middle class. This does not mean that racial disparities or tensions no longer exist. It does, however, mean that the regularity of the Long, Hot Summers is a thing of the past.

That said, urban, or even rural, unrest could emerge for a host of reasons. America's earliest civil upheavals, such as the Shay's Rebellion and the Whiskey Rebellion, had nothing to do with race. The Occupy movement in late 2011 did not descend into full-scale violence, but it did give us a vision of a class-based form of civil unrest that could reemerge in the future. Furthermore, we have had instances of racially based riots since the 1960s, most notably the post–Rodney King Los Angeles riots of 1992. Those riots caused over fifty deaths, over two thousand injuries, and more than $1 billion in damages. They necessitated the call-up of 9,800 National Guardsmen. Over 1,100 marines and six hundred soldiers would also help quell the disturbance.[34] The riots damaged President George H. W. Bush politically and contributed to him losing in his reelection bid to Arkansas governor Bill Clinton.

Even more recently, US cities such as Ferguson, Missouri, and Baltimore, Maryland, experienced weeks of racial unrest in response to police-involved killings of young black men. In Ferguson riots erupted after a police officer shot an unarmed black eighteen-year-old named Michael Brown on August 9, 2014. The violence flared up again after the grand jury, upon seeing the evidence that the officer in question had felt threatened, decided not to indict. The riots led to round-the-clock news coverage, cost St. Louis County over $4 million, and also opened a debate in the United States about the militarization of American police forces. Elements on both the left and right expressed discomfort with the militarization of American police forces. The images of police officers with heavy weaponry and body armor were disturbing to many, as were the revelations about the widespread proliferation of military-grade hardware to police forces around the country. President Obama called for a review of militarization, while the GOP's Senator Rand Paul said, "The images and scenes we continue to see in Ferguson resemble war more than traditional police action."[35] At the same time, many citizens, especially in Ferguson, were worried about the actions of a lawless mob, bolstered by agitators who came in from around the country, and wanted to make sure the police had the proper equipment to protect both the citizenry and themselves. What was most surprising about the post-Ferguson argument was the extent to which conservatives, who typically tend to side with the police, were divided over this question.

One other surprising aspect of Ferguson was its foreign policy implications. US rivals such as Russia and China used the unrest to point fingers at the United States and suggest that the country should take care of its own problems rather than focusing on human rights abuses elsewhere. Even so, the United States is far from the only Western country to experience civil unrest, including France in the *banlieues* (suburbs) outside Paris in 2005, and even Sweden in 2013. Looking beyond the West, the entire Arab Spring of 2010–11 was ultimately a series of civil uprisings that overturned, changed, or at the very least frightened governments throughout the Arab world. At least a dozen Arab countries saw some form of protest during this period. While pro-democracy Westerners likely have at least some sympathy for the sentiments driving the Arab Spring, we must also recognize from a governance standpoint that civil unrest can overturn democracies and dictatorships alike, and therefore it is the responsibility of the president to prepare for such an eventuality and be equipped to deal with it.

These incidents are in the past, of course, but we face an uncertain future. Billionaire investor Nick Hanauer wrote a 2014 piece in *Politico* in which he looked ahead and said, "I see pitchforks." Hanauer argued that economic inequality is going to drive unrest, and told his "fellow filthy rich," "Wake up, people. It won't last." According to Hanauer, continued economic inequality could lead to only two possible outcomes: "a police state. Or an uprising." Underscoring the point about unrest, he added, "It's not if, it's when." Hanauer may or may not be correct, but a responsible leader needs to be aware of these kinds of tensions and work to defuse them.[36]

The first thing a leader has to do when it comes to civil unrest is to prevent it from happening in the first place. As a constitutional democracy not subject to the whims of an arbitrary dictator, we don't have to worry about the same types of official abuses that ignited rebellions throughout the Arab world. Still, people in Western nations have plenty to get mad about, including inequality, high taxes, high prices, and intrusive government bureaucracies. In addition, crises often bring out the worst in people, and food shortages, power outages, and racial incidents all have the potential to bring about citizen protests, so presidents need to be aware of the potential for unrest and the tools they have for dealing with it.

One of these tools, monitoring the populace, has received a lot of attention following the Edward Snowden revelations. While the United States does not monitor citizens in the same way that a dictatorship does, the government does have those capabilities, and they are a double-edged sword. Maintaining awareness of the mood of the populace is a necessary skill for a politician. Politicians work hard to make sure they know the price of a gallon of milk to show that they are not out of touch. House majority leader Kevin McCarthy tells his fellow caucus members to read *People* magazine to be aware of the interests of their constituents.[37]

Keeping abreast of the people, however, has a dark side as well. Monitoring phone calls and private conversations are typically the hallmarks of a police state, and are generally unacceptable in our constitutional system. That said, presidents such as John F. Kennedy, Lyndon Johnson, and Richard Nixon are known to have authorized the taping of conversations. These and other actions in the 1960s violated constitutional protections but also failed to prevent or even mitigate the unrest of the 1960s. And Presidents George W. Bush and Barack Obama have allowed the national security state to collect data in an attempt to prevent terrorism in ways that make civil libertarians uncomfortable.

Even in the case of extraordinary and impermissible actions, there remains a limit to what preventative monitoring can achieve. In the Arab world, for example, the absence of personal freedoms did not prevent the civil unrest of 2010 and 2011. And the Soviet system collapsed despite—and perhaps because of—aggressive and intrusive government spying on its own citizens. In our own system, every president wants to avoid economic dislocation, racial problems, and unpopular wars such as Vietnam, which exacerbated the problems of the 1960s. But even assuming that presidents can't stop the sparks or underlying causes that lead to a conflagration, talented politicians can help shut down unrest before it starts. George Washington, for example, faced down a near mutiny of his troops in Newburgh, New York, in 1783 with a dramatic gesture. Before he began speaking, he made a point of reaching for his glasses, then said, "Gentlemen, you must pardon me. I have grown gray in your service and now find myself growing blind." That gesture of humility reminded the troops of his sacrifice and embarrassed the officers who had conspired against him. After his speech Washington's troops stood down, and the mutiny was no more.[38]

In 1968 two politicians faced down the crowds in two different cities and prevented post-King assassination riots from taking place. Mayor John Lindsay, who had worked on the Kerner Commission report and was said to be responsible for the commission's "white racism" finding, went out into the streets of Harlem after King's death. Lindsay left a Broadway play and overruled police objections in making the dangerous trip. According to Lindsay biographer Vincent Cannato, things were somewhat dicey for Lindsay while he was there, and there were a number of scuffles that appeared to threaten the mayor. Lindsay press aide David Garth even thought at one point that "my life is over." Still, Garth felt that Lindsay's visit to Harlem made him "the most courageous man I've ever seen," and his appearance tamped down, even if it did not eliminate, the violence. Cannato, who is highly critical of Lindsay, nevertheless concluded that "Lindsay's reaction to the King riots represented a high point of his administration."[39]

Another politician who showed that political skill and bravery, not to mention eloquence, can defuse an explosive situation was Robert F. Kennedy. Kennedy was in Indianapolis on April 4, 1968, and was advised by Mayor Richard Lugar not to speak. Kennedy, like Lindsay in New York, ignored the advice and not only spoke, but had the difficult task of announcing King's death to the crowd. After making the announcement, Kennedy then gave a speech on the importance of compassion and non-violence, and shared words from his favorite poem by Aeschylus. Kennedy's words soothed the crowd, and Indianapolis, like New York, remained largely calm, in stark contrast to the dozens of cities that erupted in violence that night.[40]

Even if a president is unable to stop violent outbursts, he must have a clear sense of what is taking place on the ground. Lyndon Johnson sending out three senior aides to report back on a riot taking place a few short blocks from the White House was unwise, unsafe, and largely ineffective. Today, with better communications tools, a president is far more capable of following the situation on the ground. Social media can allow a president and his aides to follow the absolute latest developments, and not just through the mainstream media filter, but from participants directly in view of the action. In addition, modern communications tools can allow a president to get messages out much more quickly.

Like communications, coordination is another area in which modern technology can help a president aiming to keep a situation under control. The president can give orders more quickly, more directly, and with more clarity than ever before. The fog of war is always difficult to deal with, but modern tools are extremely helpful for dissipating that fog.

Just because a president has new tools, however, does not mean that he will deploy them wisely. One problem that Johnson had, even with communications capabilities that his nineteenth-century predecessors would have marveled at, was his inability—or refusal—to make decisions during riots such as the one in Watts. Califano noted that he was always able to get in touch with Johnson except for the period during the Watts riot, which suggests a problem with the president's responsiveness rather than a technical issue.

Of course, a rapid answer is not always a good answer. The decision to send in federal troops is always a difficult one. Here it is important to remember that public safety issues are for the most part a local concern. The local police force is supposed to maintain order. If a situation is out of the control of the local police, the governor is supposed to provide additional assistance. Because of the Posse Comitatus Act, the federal government cannot send in troops without the permission and even the express request of the governor. In many cases governors are reluctant to have federal intervention for political reasons. While governors during the Long, Hot Summers appeared quite anxious to get this assistance, this is not always the case. At one point during Katrina, for example, President George W. Bush weighed sending in troops despite the fact that the governor failed to give permission for him to do so. Bush ultimately decided against it.

Either way a governor decides presents challenges for a president. If a governor refuses to give the OK, that places the president in the uncomfortable quandary of what to do if a situation escalates out of control. Sending troops without the approval of the governor could be politically unpopular and possibly illegal. And yet allowing a situation to get out of hand would be seen as shirking the president's responsibilities. Alternatively, sending in troops too quickly, even with gubernatorial approval, could be seen as bringing down the heavy hand of the federal government on the right of the people to assemble. In sum, a president is in much better shape acting if he has the governor on his side, but still needs to make plans for what to do in the absence of said approval.

Unfortunately, once riots begin, the president has only a few levers to address matters. Beyond the troops issue there is also the possibility of addressing whatever grievance has arisen. Sometimes the issue is too vague to address, such as the Occupy protest's generalized concerns. Sometimes the complaint is impossible to address easily, such as food or oil shortages. If such problems could have been eliminated in advance, they likely would have been. And sometimes addressing the concern would be contrary to administration policy. Lyndon Johnson, for example, was not going to end the Vietnam War just because protesters asked him to do so.

In addition, there is the issue of what to do in a riot's aftermath. It is close to a surefire certainty that any urban unrest will lead to some kind of high-level commission to examine the causes of the unrest and to recommend solutions for the future. This sort of commission cannot be avoided, but neither can it be counted upon to do much good. The McCone Commission after Watts did little to prevent the riots of Newark and Detroit. And the Kerner Commission not only failed to prevent the 1968 riots but, with its condemnation of American society, may have made the reactions to Dr. King's tragic death even worse than they might have been otherwise. Commissions will be convened, but they won't solve the problem.

Finally, it is important that the president pick good people to help sort through potential disasters. George W. Bush, for example, was famously ill served by Mike Brown after Hurricane Katrina. The Los Angeles riots in both 1965 and 1992 could have been prevented by more judicious behavior by the LA police. Warren Christopher, who worked on the McCone Commission that failed to prevent future riots after

Watts, later worked on hostage negotiations with Iran for the Carter administration and on the post-2000 election legal team for Al Gore, a spectacular record of continually failing upward. In picking staff to help deal with the worst crises a president has to face, presidents should be sure to look carefully at the track records of those who will be responsible for handling their most difficult situations.

CHAPTER TEN

How to Prepare for Acts of Man

TERROR ATTACKS

INDIVIDUAL AMERICANS CANNOT COUNT ON ANY OF THE VARIOUS LEV-
els of government to protect them in case of a terrorist attack, especially
in cases of a nonconventional attack. Local government officials recognize
this fact. The Government Accountability Office (GAO) interviewed
local officials in twenty-seven different large cities and found a disturbing
lack of faith in the federal government's likelihood of coming to their aid
in the aftermath of a terror attack. Furthermore, these officials did not
even know what kind of aid they should expect in such circumstances.
According to the report, "GAO found that federal guidance on the type
and timing of such assistance is not readily available or understood by all
emergency managers." More disturbingly, FEMA's reaction to the GAO
report was to bury its head in the sand, responding coolly that it "did
not concur" with the GAO's analysis. As anyone familiar with self-help
knows, the first step to recovery is recognizing that you have a problem.[1]

Regardless of who is right between GAO and FEMA, the safest
assumption you can make is that federal officials will be too busy in the
aftermath of an attack to worry about you and your family. This means
that you need to be ready to cope with any possible threat on your own.
For individuals, the first step in self-protection is to make a realistic
assessment of the danger you face. The president is under tremendous
pressure, as he has to protect every square inch of the United States, as
well as every American citizen or property around the world; on an individual level, the calculation is quite different.

In terms of preparing for an attack, individuals need to recognize that the danger to the nation is greater than the danger to themselves as individuals. Gallup has found that about 90 percent of Americans are concerned about additional acts of terror taking place in the United States, and about 40 percent of Americans are worried that they or a family member might die in such an attack.[2] The likelihood of any one person falling victim to a specific attack, however, is quite low. Furthermore, this likelihood varies according to where one lives and activities in which one engages. According to a Heritage Foundation breakdown of attempted terror attacks, there were seventy-five failed terrorist plots against the United States between 9/11 and 2015. A significant number of those—forty-eight—were aimed at military targets, New York, or mass gatherings (see chart).[3]

Terrorist Plots against the United States between 9/11 and 2015

Location	Number of Attempts
Military targets	19
New York	16
Mass gatherings	13
Mass transit	8
Critical infrastructure	6
Commercial aviation	6
Diplomats and politicians	6

In addition, terrorism is a global phenomenon, and only 7.8 percent of 38,345 terrorist incidents between 1969 and 2009 worldwide were directed at the United States. Before we get too complacent, though, the eleven terrorist attempts in 2015 were higher than in any year since 2001 and included more plots than the years 2012, 2013, and 2014 combined.[4] Still, Americans should be careful not to ascribe superhuman abilities to terrorist operatives. As Edward Kaplan has discussed, there are fewer than three terror plots in motion at any one time, and the plotters have a relatively low success rate. All in all, the odds of being killed in a terror attack were about one in twenty million in the years 2007 to 2011. Adding to this is the fact that since 9/11, our capabilities and our focus on stopping terror have vastly improved, making attempted attacks on the United States a far from certain prospect.[5]

In case of a conventional attack, the harm comes in a specific and circumscribed area. Dirty bombs, in contrast, are worse, as the physical harm can spread beyond the area in which the attack takes place. In either case, though, the vulnerability range is limited to at least some degree. There are also psychological and economic effects, but for the individual outside of the direct attack location, the physical dangers are relatively light. This does not, however, mean that individuals outside the danger zone have no responsibilities. Just as the government must remain vigilant to prevent attacks, so must individuals maintain high levels of vigilance both before and after a terror attack. "See something, say something" is not just a slogan, but an important way for citizens to contribute to the protection of the nation.

We saw this to some degree in the aftermath of the Boston Marathon terror bombings of 2013. The nation, and indeed the world, was watching, but it was Boston that was affected by the actions of the terrorists, and it was in Boston where individual citizens had the capacity to do the most good. One citizen in particular, David Henneberry, noticed that something was amiss with his boat. When Henneberry went out to investigate, he saw blood, and then discovered that the surviving bomber, Dzhokhar Tsarnaev, had hidden in his boat. Henneberry immediately returned to his home and called the police, which led to a gunfight with and the capture of Tsarnaev. Henneberry's action, which helped police capture the bomber, came at some cost to Henneberry. When police asked him how many gallons of gas he had in his boat, Henneberry was convinced that he was going to lose the boat. The explosion he feared did not happen, although the boat was damaged by bullet holes, and insurance ended up covering only $1,000 worth of damage. Henneberry had no regrets, though, and was even rewarded for his actions when generous and grateful fellow citizens donated $50,000 to help Henneberry buy a new boat. Henneberry, typically, wished that the money had gone instead to victims of the terror attack.

Henneberry's actions are instructive in explaining what individuals should do in case of a terror attack: stay calm, do not panic, listen to instructions from authorities, and help to the extent possible. Indeed, instructions for what to do in case of a terror attack from the Red Cross, the American Medical Association, and FEMA are all remarkably similar. In addition, many of the basic tasks carry over across multiple categories. Whatever the emergency, FEMA—and others—are likely to tell you to remain calm, to have an emergency plan for you and your family, to have an emergency kit containing food, water, toilet paper, batteries, a radio, lights, and first-aid equipment, and to listen to instructions from local and federal officials.

These are all good pieces of advice, and everyone reading this book should adhere to them. But it is also true that different dangers require different approaches beyond the basics. In case of a terror attack, citizens should be prepared, like Henneberry, to assist local law enforcement to bring the offenders to justice and the incident to a close. One never knows when the moment will strike, or how we will react when called upon. As John F. Kennedy, another Boston hero, said regarding his bravery while he commanded the destroyed PT 109 in World War II, "It was involuntary. They sank my boat."

THE BIOTERROR THREAT

While some disasters are best dealt with at the local level, the federal government should have primary responsibility for preventing and responding to bioterror. But the government, at whatever level, will have a lot of issues to deal with after a bioterror attack, which means that you need to think about how to protect your family and yourself.

There are a number of ways to protect yourself from a bioterror attack. One key way is through the use of home medkits. Medkits go beyond having the standard first-aid supplies—which you should have anyway—and contain countermeasures to address specific dangers: ciprofloxacin for anthrax, Tamiflu or Relenza antivirals for the flu, or even potassium iodide for a radiation attack. These kits would be stored at home, making them convenient and available for the entire population. Furthermore, the kits could be purchased by large companies and universities and distributed to large groups of employees and students. In addition to their utility for individuals, home medkits have a large social benefit as well. Citizens are more likely to remain calm during a pandemic knowing they have immediate access to health provisions within the safety and convenience of their own homes.

As with all potential solutions, home medkits have a few drawbacks. Most vaccines have specific requirements, such as administration by a health professional or storage in temperature-sensitive environments. Neither of these restrictions can be accommodated through the use of home medkits. Vaccines would therefore not be included in the kits. In 2008 Secretary of Health and Human Services Michael O. Leavitt met almost unanimous opposition regarding home medkits from public health authorities, who distrusted citizens' ability to handle the medkits properly. However, a 2006 study performed in St. Louis by the Centers for Disease Control and Prevention (CDC) revealed that when given the home medkits, 97 percent of citizens followed the directions of health officials.[6] These findings suggest that home medkits can be useful sources of basic provisions, although they obviously cannot cover the entire scope of emergency products.

Home medkits make sense, and are something you should consider, but it is an unrealistic expectation that every American citizen could or would purchase all of the potential countermeasures necessary in case of an emergency. Furthermore, home medkits would not have helped with the Tylenol or the Rajneeshee poisonings. And if bioterrorists disseminate a sufficiently obscure pathogen, the likelihood is that the government will not have the right countermeasure, and the near certainty is that your home medkit won't have it either.

For these reasons the unfortunate likelihood is that if you are exposed to a pathogen for which neither you nor the government have an appropriate countermeasure, there is little you can do about the exposure itself. As a result, the best things you can do to prepare for a bioterror attack are to work to minimize your potential exposure, and to figure out how best to cope in the aftermath of an attack to which you and your family were not directly exposed.

In terms of minimizing exposure, there are a number of preventative steps you can take to protect yourself, your family, and your place of business. To protect your home from taking in unwanted airborne agents, it is a good idea to weatherize your home to prevent air from getting in through cracks. As an added benefit, this could also help reduce your heating and cooling bills. You should also make sure that your air-conditioning filters are up to date and changed regularly. This will not prevent exposure outdoors, but at least your home will be safer.

Office buildings are much more target-rich environments for terrorists and require more serious protections. Office buildings should keep secure areas around the air-conditioning systems and air intakes. As with homes, places of business should be weatherized, and air filters should be kept up to date. In addition, large office buildings should have evacuation plans, as well as building procedures to fix or deactivate the air-conditioning systems in case of compromise.[7]

One can avoid exposure and still be affected by the ripple effects of a large-scale bioterror attack. Other chapters in this book address how to cope in case of some kind of larger societal disturbance, but there are a number of strategies that are particularly applicable in case of a bioterror attack.

Having a kit is crucial for any emergency, but particularly for an incident in which movement and travel may be significantly curtailed. For this reason, having a family disaster plan and being prepared to shelter in place are especially important. In case of a bioterror attack, particularly if the pathogen is contagious, understanding the concepts of quarantine and isolation are important, along with the ability to engage in those activities. Quarantine applies to people or things that may have been exposed to a pathogen, but are not definitively ill, or may not become so. Isolation applies to those who are certainly ill, and ill with a contagious disease. You may have to quarantine or isolate members of your own family, or even yourself. It is not easy, but be prepared to do what must be done.[8]

Bioterror is a particularly worrisome problem, one that could leave individuals and families feeling powerless before larger forces at work. It is true that we must put some measure of faith in our government intelligence agencies to prevent such an attack, and in emergency preparedness workers to distribute the appropriate countermeasures should an attack take place. But we are not helpless, and the steps laid out above can serve you and your family well if the worst happens.

LOSS OF THE POWER GRID

Of all the disasters discussed in this book, the destruction of the power grid and our computer networks is the most disruptive and carries with it life-altering potential. How such a collapse happened would matter to governments, but not to individuals. The complete loss of electrical power would send us back centuries, but put us in even worse stead because, unlike our ancestors in those times, we will have had no preparation for dealing with a world without power. Of course, there are numerous scenarios that could take place short of a complete loss of power, including short-term or localized power disturbances, but a complete loss of power across the whole of the United States is the most devastating possibility.

Obviously, the first thing to do is to pray that this does not happen. Furthermore, it is important not just to hope that it does not happen, but to support and elect leaders actively committed to making sure that it does not happen. If a grid failure does take place, it will require a level of preparation and response beyond what has been discussed previously.

First of all, you need to make sure you are safe and have food and water. Other chapters have discussed the need to store at least some food, water, and other necessities. A disaster of the magnitude of a grid shutdown would also require you to take some home security measures, including stiff locks on your doors, a safe room in your home if feasible, a security plan for you and your family, and whatever means of home protection you deem appropriate. I happen to believe that a firearm is good to have, but I recognize that both opinions and legal requirements differ on this point. If you do choose to purchase a firearm, be sure that you are proficient in its use and that you practice with it and keep it clean and oiled. A grid shutdown could lead to many unpredictable and dangerous consequences, and it is far from clear that all of your fellow citizens would behave appropriately in said circumstances.

A grid shutdown would have other consequences as well. Beyond the food and sustenance issues, individuals need to think about all the ways that they rely on electricity and other utilities in their daily lives. For basic lighting you should have candles, matches, flashlights, lanterns, and lots of batteries. If there is no water supply, a portable toilet or sanitation device is a good investment. Be sure to have lots of hand sanitizer as well.

A home generator is also an important tool. A home generator would survive a cyberattack or a physical attack on our power grid. It is not clear whether it would survive an EMP attack. There is a possible way, however, to protect home generators and other key electronic components from the effects of an EMP: by storing the electronic components when not in use in what is known as a Faraday Cage. If you are so inclined and have a working knowledge of physics, you can build your own Faraday Cage with the instructions available online. For the rest of us, purchasing a premade one is the way to go. An old microwave, designed to prevent the passage of radiation, could serve this purpose as well. There is, of course, no guarantee these measures would work, as a full-on EMP has not yet happened, and we hope it never will.

Securing a Faraday Cage is on a higher-level order of preparation magnitude, but it is an available option if you are interested. If you do go down this path, it would be a good idea to store some other basic electronic devices in the container, include backups of disk drives, an old laptop no longer in use, and a digital camera with pictures of your family and key possessions.

In a complete grid meltdown, just having food, water, and flashlights would not be enough. It's important to have a storehouse of key medicines, both in terms of prescription drugs for chronic conditions—as well as the details of prescriptions themselves in nonelectronic format—and other medications such as analgesics, anti-diarrheals, antibiotics and antibiotic ointment, bandages, antiseptics, hydrocortisone, antacids, and antihistamines. Maintaining a storage of cash and perhaps other tradable goods would help as well.

The Department of Homeland Security has little to say about preparing for an EMP, but it does have specific recommendations for what to do in case of a blackout. DHS recommends conserving energy and keeping your vehicles' gas tanks half full at all times, as gas stations won't be able to pump without electricity. DHS also has instructions about keeping the refrigerator and freezer as cold as possible for as long as possible, and making sure you can get in and out of your house without relying on an electronic garage door.[9]

One problem—unaddressed by DHS—that a grid collapse would present is the dilemma of lost assets. Since much of our wealth these days is recorded electronically and not in physical form, you need to have and store records in a nonelectronic format. You should have copies of key documents stored in a fireproof box, and make sure you have copies of those documents. Doing this is not a short-term solution, though. It is unlikely that you will be able to access your investments, CDs, bonds, securities, and so forth during the crisis itself. If we do sort things out and the system is put back on line, having these records will be essential to recovering assets in a post-crisis environment.

Overall, one of the frustrations of preparing for a grid meltdown–type of attack is the limited number of things individuals can do to prevent it. Protecting the grid from whatever attack may come is not in our hands as individuals, and reestablishing order after a collapse is not either. In fact, according to *Slate*'s David Shenk, the answer to the question of what can be done to prepare for this circumstance is a depressing "less than you think." As Shenk put it, when it comes to a cyber or EMP attack, "we have to rely on the professional paranoids—the software wizards in anonymous Virginia and California office buildings who are devising defenses against all the clever electronic assaults they can imagine."[10]

The problem with Shenk's analysis is twofold. First, no one wants to hear that there is little to do to protect themselves from dire circumstances. Americans prefer self-reliance, and a fatalism coupled with a blind reliance on the government to fix the problem is far from the American way. Second, and more problematically, if we do experience some kind of grid meltdown, then the very people who failed to prevent the problem from taking place will be the very same people we would be looking to for solutions. Not a very comforting thought.

CIVIL UNREST

Living through a period of urban unrest has a number of components. The key question individuals must face before deciding on a strategy is where they will be in relation to the unrest. Surviving on the front lines of riots requires one kind of approach, focused on mobility and survival skills. Hunkering down at home and trying to cope while walled up in your home or apartment is a very different kind of issue and requires a different approach, focused on protecting your home, driving away potential attackers, and having enough supplies to live through the crisis. There will be some overlap, but for the most part the two challenges are fundamentally different. For this reason each of the two scenarios will be discussed in turn.

If you are out and about when a riot breaks out, you need to be ready to fight for your very survival. But avoiding is better than fighting, and one thing to be aware of is that there are often warning signs that appear before a riot. Some of these signs will be hoary clichés, like housewives closing the shutters before a storm. Beyond such immediate signals, though, are more complex indicators, such as the local news. If you live in the area, you will probably be more attuned to what's going on, whereas a visitor may have to make more of an effort. In either case, paying attention to the local news is an important safety tool. If a controversial major legal verdict is being announced, or if an area's largest employer is shutting its doors, these could be advanced signs of trouble.[11]

Surviving in the midst of a full-fledged riot requires action in three main areas: awareness, behavior, and supplies. If you are aware of your surroundings, behave appropriately given the situation, and have the right materials with you, your chances of survival improve dramatically. In terms of awareness, you need to maintain a sense of where you are. Which way is north? How far are you from some kind of shelter, be it your home or your temporary domicile? Do you have a map or know the area? Do you know how to access public transportation?

In addition to geographic awareness, there is also social awareness. You should be aware of potential threats around you. If there is an ethnic, nationalistic, or racial component to the unrest, are you in one of the potentially targeted groups? In this, social media may be more helpful than the traditional news media. It updates faster and is more attuned with what is going on in local communities. Major media organizations will almost certainly be behind the curve. If there is a Twitter hashtag for whatever unrest is taking place around you, use it to follow tweets on the subject. While doing this, however, you must also maintain awareness of what is going on around you. Do not get caught up in following your iPhone to the exclusion of paying attention to what is happening around you.

Surviving on your own is different than surviving if you have other people with you. While there can be strength in numbers, having others can increase your exposure and decrease your flexibility. Through it all, if you have loved ones with you, especially younger and more vulnerable ones, do not lose sight of them. Do not separate from them voluntarily, either. If you do get separated, make sure you have communicated with them where and how you plan to meet up again.

In addition to being aware, surviving in a riot requires you to act smartly as well. This is the time to survive, not to get involved. Do not interfere with protesters, and do not interfere with the police. At all costs, stay out of any crossfire taking place between the two groups. While you may want to tell those nice young men to stop stealing that television, the middle of a riot is no time to play amateur police officer. The same goes doubly true for your own personal property. If someone in the mob wants to take something you have, let them have it and move on. It would be wise to have some cash on hand to give away as an inducement to convince threatening people to leave you alone.

In general the safest approach is to remain calm and not to draw attention to yourself. Walk, do not run. Do not flash large amounts of cash or try to control the crowd. Stay to the outside of the crowd, and close to walls, if possible. Getting indoors is even better. Do not get involved in the riot, either as an instigator or an objector. Either type of involvement brings dangers, from the police or from the rioters. Stay on your feet at all costs, to avoid being trampled. If you are forced to the ground, curl up into a ball to minimize your exposure.

If you are driving a vehicle, drive with caution. Close the windows and lock the doors, and do not under any circumstances run anyone over. Drive slowly, avoid the most heavily trafficked areas, and focus on getting out of the area. Knowing where public transportation is can be useful, but be wary of it, as it could be out of commission or taken over by the rioters.

In terms of supplies, try to have an extra cell phone in case your primary one gets lost or stolen. Wear thick, comfortable clothing, with shoes you can run in if need be. Make sure that your clothes are as inconspicuous as possible. Do not wear clothes that make you look like a rioter, as that could lead the police to target you improperly. Try to have some food with you, perhaps protein bars that can sustain you and give you bursts of energy when needed. Having a handkerchief to cover your nose, eyes, and mouth can also be helpful. Wetting the handkerchief can help if tear gas is released. If you do encounter tear gas, try not to get hit by and don't pick up the canister. In addition, glasses are better than contact lenses if there is tear gas, although glasses are also more prone to getting lost or broken.

As the list above indicates, riots are dangerous places. If you can avoid it, not being in the middle of a riot is a vastly preferable situation. But even so, civil unrest can have a significant impact on you and your family. To protect yourself you should make sure that your house or apartment can withstand an outside assault. This means having solid locks on the doors, lockable windows, and preferably a room to which you can retreat and lock again should the worst happen. Having some form of home protection, be it a firearm or something else, is important. If not a firearm, mace-like sprays, Tasers, ax handles, and knives can also be useful, but using any of them against a gun is not recommended.[12]

Of course, none of these steps will stop a really determined mob, but everything you do that makes your residence a less inviting target increases your chances of survival. If the mob thinks that breaking down your double-locked door with a battering ram is harder than going through your neighbor's open window, then you will have that much more time to either escape or possibly even call for help. The police are unlikely to provide immediate assistance in these circumstances, but you could always be the lucky one who gets saved when the cavalry arrives.

If you are able to hunker down undisturbed in your home, you must maintain appropriate levels of supplies to wait things out. This includes, of course, food, water, and medications that you and your family may need. Having a backup supply of cash is smart as well, since you probably will not want to go out into a riot with your ATM card and password. Depending on how out of control the unrest gets, the power supply and phone lines could be affected as well. A generator and cell phone will be useful in this scenario.

Another important way to protect yourself in cases of a breakdown of civil order is to maintain close ties to your community. Your neighbors are less likely to loot your belongings if they have shared a meal with you (assuming, of course, that you are a pleasant dining companion). Getting involved in a civic organization or your local church or synagogue can help in this regard as well.

Friendships can potentially deter a mob, but then again they might not. Another advantage to community ties is that you will have established relationships with a group of nearby people who can band together to try to maintain order when the police cannot. There are numerous examples of this happening. In the 1992 Los Angeles riots, for example, a number of Korean store owners saw that the police would be unable to protect them and created their own neighborhood watch to protect their livelihoods. Something similar happened in the 1968 DC riots, in which local businessmen pooled both money and guns and collectively stood watch over their stores, communicating with each other via walkie-talkie.

Local bands of vigilantes, even with the best of intentions and motivations, are not a permanent solution. One would not want to have to rely on these collectives, or any of the strategies described above, for very long. They are short-term measures and not sustainable beyond a few days. But holding off a mob for a few days can very easily be the difference between life and death, and between livelihood and impoverishment.

If civil unrest goes on for more than a few days, then the equation changes. At this point the situation goes beyond unrest, and we start looking at the potential for societal breakdown. Neither the United States nor its Western allies have experienced true societal breakdown—outside of scores of apocalyptic novels, movies, and TV shows—but it can happen. Rwanda in the 1990s and Syria in more recent days have experienced this kind of collapse. In societal breakdown the mechanisms of the state are no longer reliably available. You and your family are on your own. It is perhaps beyond the scope of this book, and it is certainly beyond the scope of any one individual, to come up with ways to cope with such an utter collapse. But we deal in probabilities and risk assessment. Should we experience a societal breakdown, the best thing to do is be prepared to cope in the short term, and to make real-time reassessments if disorder continues for a longer period. The strategies outlined above will help you cope in the short term. If we face a longer-term problem, all of us will have to make those real-time reassessments.

CONCLUSION

ONE GOOD WAY TO GET A SENSE OF THE AMERICAN PEOPLE'S MOOD IS to take a look at the cinematic offerings of Hollywood. Hollywood executives relentlessly follow prevailing trends and the shifting sentiments of the American people in their desperate and increasingly unsuccessful struggle to get people off their sofas and smartphones and into the multiplexes. In addition to believing that the American people have an insatiable hunger for comic book characters and sequels of just about any variety, the taste-followers of Hollywood have apparently concluded that what the American people crave is apocalyptic disaster movies. According to *Entertainment Weekly*, over the last fifteen years, there have been more than eighty-five apocalyptic-themed movies coming out of Hollywood.[1] Given that the average cost of a Hollywood movie is around $100 million, this means that Hollywood has spent over $8.5 billion in bringing visions of the apocalypse to the American people.

As large as this $8.5 billion number is, it pales in comparison to the true cost of disasters. This is true both in terms of the disasters that actually happen—SARS cost $50 billion and did not even strike in the United States—and in terms of preparation as well. FEMA alone spends over $10 billion annually, and the Department of Homeland Security as a whole spends about $60 billion annually. And DHS is far from the only department with prevention and response responsibilities.

The spending itself is not a problem per se. While disaster preparedness is expensive, dealing with catastrophes is a classic example of a public good, something that the nation requires but that individuals are unlikely to procure for themselves. Historically, the paradigmatic example of a public good has been a lighthouse, especially in days when cross-oceanic transport took place exclusively by ship. These days, lighthouses are relatively rare, but the need for public goods continues. According to a recent analysis by Kevin Williamson, author of *The End Is Near and It's Going to Be Awesome*, only about one-third of federal spending today is on public goods.[2]

Our problem today is perhaps not a lack of resources as much as a need to reexamine our priorities. Disaster preparedness is a strategic necessity for the US government. Given that there are many forms of government spending that are not strategic priorities, presidents, working with Congress, need to find ways to trim non-priority spending before reducing government commitment to dealing with catastrophes.

Beyond finding the money to deal with disasters, there is also the question of prioritization. The federal government should not have to deal with every type of possible disaster we could face. Some, particularly weather anomalies and local food or water shortages, should be dealt with at the local level. And even while some disasters clearly require federal involvement—dealing with bioterror, for instance—not every aspect of every disaster requires presidential involvement. Our misguided view of the president as a superman or superwoman of some sort raises unrealistic expectations of what government can do during a disaster. It also threatens to take the president's attention away from areas of needed presidential involvement and direct that attention to less efficient uses of presidential effort. As every White House staff member learns early on, the most precious resource in a White House is the president's time. It is a nonrenewable resource, one that should not be wasted, but one that also must be used in high-leverage situations. A White House that overuses a president misuses its top strategic asset, but so does a White House that underuses the president as well.

In order to best understand how the president should use his time, it is helpful to look at history. As this book has shown, the lessons of the past can and should inform the actions of the future. Woodrow Wilson clearly should have acted more forcefully in response to the 1918 flu. George W. Bush should not have done a mere flyover of the affected areas in Hurricane Katrina. But the lessons of the past (see appendix one) can only take us so far. Presidents and their teams need to develop some kind of algorithm or checklist to determine when to get the federal government involved, and when it pays to involve the president as well (see appendix two for my attempt to develop this checklist).

Assuming a president can resist the political pressure and manage to respond only to the disasters that should be handled at the presidential level, this is still not the end of the story. Some presidents have handled their disasters better than others (see appendix three). Each chapter of this book gave guidance on how presidents should cope with each of the disasters that they could face. It is unlikely that any one president will face all of them, but it is an ironclad certainty that each president will encounter some of them. As disaster chronicler Joshua Cooper Ramo has put it, his ideal candidates to be president of the United States "should have mastered the essential skill of the next fifty years: crisis management."[3]

But just as the governmental response to crisis is important, and clearly—as this book shows—requires more thought and improvement, it is also important to remember how resilient the nation and individuals can be. National resilience, of course, is nothing new. Over two centuries ago, the utilitarian philosopher John Stuart Mill marveled at "the great rapidity with which countries recover from a state of devastation; the disappearance, in a short time, of all traces of the mischiefs done by earthquakes, floods, hurricanes, and the ravages of war." While FEMA and government disaster planners create "Disaster Cities" and try to plan for every possible scenario, the truth of the matter is that the brunt of any disaster, and the bulk of any recovery effort, will fall upon the people.[4]

Fortunately, it is possible that most of the people may be better at this than the pessimists believe. As Jonah Goldberg has written, there is "a strongly held view in Hollywood and DC that says that without the government in Washington American society would descend into anarchy almost instantaneously." Goldberg disagrees. He believes that "if the federal government disappeared tomorrow—and the media didn't report it—it would take days or even weeks for many people to even learn about it."[5] In that time individuals would work in their communities to keep the mechanisms of life going, with or without federal disaster preparedness efforts.

The people writ large may indeed be better than paternalistic government planners think. Unfortunately, that remains a low bar. The level of individual preparedness in this country is far from adequate, and smart Americans need to do more to prepare themselves for realistic future disasters (see appendix four). Part of this preparation is recognizing that the federal government may not be there to bail you out when things are going poorly.

Throughout all of this, what our government must learn, as so many individual Americans already have, is resilience.

Resilience is what keeps things going in the face of challenges. Presidents have a larger job in keeping a massive federal government, with about $4 trillion in spending and two million employees, going. They also have to worry about a populace of over 300 million people. But individuals have a tough job as well. Although many Americans do know what to do in terms of crisis, millions more do not. If disaster strikes, we all will have to keep ourselves, our families, and our loved ones going—without staff, without a massive bureaucracy, without an army—with just ourselves. It is resilience, coupled with smart preparation, that will get us there.

The point of a book like this is not to scare people. Raising anxiety levels does little good on any front. But preparing people is a different matter. Regardless of whether you are running a government or are a lone individual, preparation is essential to the challenges that lie ahead. One way to understand how to prepare is to look at the past, which is the reason for the history lessons in this book. Another way is to understand the best advice of experts, and to recognize the massive logistical challenges that disasters present to our leaders. For this reason, the advice to presidents, based on expert recommendations and insights from within the government apparatus, can help not only presidents but also individuals trying to figure out how to handle the troubles that may lie ahead.

And finally, there is the individual. At its very heart, the story of humankind is one of billions of individual actors trying to survive as best they can in an often difficult and dangerous world. Reading this book will make you better equipped to understand and to overcome whatever disaster the world might throw at us.

Appendix One

Presidential Lessons Learned

1. *Beware the Ratchet Effect:* Any action the president takes increasing the involvement of the federal government will be assumed the next time around. The media and American citizens will expect you to take a greater and greater role in dealing with any sort of disaster.

2. *Consider Moral Hazards:* The more responsibility that American presidents take on for themselves and the federal government, the less responsibility the people will take on for themselves.

3. *Presidents Are Assumed to Be in Charge:* In the case of a disaster, like it or not, the president owns it politically and must recognize that fact.

4. *Show and Tell:* The best preparation and response efforts are useless without effective communication. A successful response can be undone if no one knows you succeeded.

5. *Comfort Is Not Enough:* Americans want more than presidential reassurance in the aftermath of a disaster; they want direction and conviction from their leaders.

6. *TV Alone Is Not Enough:* Presidents need to communicate every way possible with the American public. As new technologies develop, from radio to TV to social media like Twitter, it is important to reach out to the public via the media they are using to get information. Do not assume that just because you gave a speech on TV, the American people watched it.

7. *Say It Again, and Often:* When you communicate is almost as important as how, because the right message at the wrong time will not help. Communicate effectively and communicate frequently; in the midst of a disaster, demonstrating that your attention has not wavered is vital.

8. *Recognize Limits:* Legally presidents cannot do everything they might wish to. Even if sending in the National Guard or military may be tempting, violating the law, even for the best of reasons, is never an option.

9. *Watch Those Vacations:* President James K. Polk had a no vacations policy, and he may have been on to something. When the 1965 Los Angeles riots took place, both President Lyndon Johnson and California governor Pat Brown were slow to react because they were away from their posts—Johnson in Texas and Brown in Greece. In another case, not only was President George W. Bush away on vacation when Katrina hit in 2005, but many of his top staffers were out of the country at communications aide Nicolle Wallace's wedding. And President Obama seemed out of touch when he left to play golf after ISIS terrorists beheaded an American captive.

When Presidents Should Get Involved: A Checklist

In your time as president, there will always be more threats than solutions. Even if you have an inexhaustible supply of time and energy, your resources are limited, and defenses cannot be mounted against every threat the United States faces. For every potential threat that crosses your desk, a judgment must be made on whether to take action, and what action to take. To determine the president's role, a basic set of questions must be asked. Each question is a simple, or not so simple, yes or no question. If most of the questions are answered no, the threat is either not worth addressing, or falls more sensibly within the purview of local government.

1. *Is there widespread consensus among experts that the event will take place?* The core question of disaster preparedness is impossible to answer but vital to ask. The likelihood of a disaster *must* dictate the depth of preparations. If the attack or event is a near certainty, then the maxim of our leaders should be all that we can do, we will do. But when the attack or event is of low probability, going to the maximum is wasteful and will divert resources from other worthy causes.

2. *Is a significant percentage of the population in danger? Will multiple regions be affected?* While it is the responsibility of the government to protect its citizens, spending limited resources to counter a

threat to a small at-risk population limits resources going to protect larger groups who, if harmed, may cause a disproportionately larger harm to the country.

3. *Can the source of the warnings be trusted?* Any information gathered from unreliable sources is inherently unreliable. While utilizing all resources is the best way to keep the United States safe, relying heavily on suspect information can lead us on a wild goose chase, protecting against nonexistent threats and ignoring the looming vulnerabilities in other sectors.

4. *Does the short-term cost of the event exceed the cost of prevention?* If no preparation was taken, what immediate costs would the government face in responding to the attack or event and repairing the damage incurred? Even if the threat level is high, if there is only minor, easily repairable damage, the resources allocated to preventative measures should be lessened.

5. *Does the long-term cost of the disaster exceed the cost of prevention?* Loss of confidence, decades of repairs, large displaced populations are costs that may not be immediately visible after an attack or event but must be taken into account. A relatively minor incident in a city or suburb that causes few fatalities can cause a massive upheaval if large populations are displaced or repairs consume the region's budget for years to come.

6. *Are the needed actions affordable?* If the potential cost of prevention is greater than the cost of responding, the benefits do not outweigh the costs.

7. *Will the preventative measures work?* If the preventative measures are unlikely to succeed, even if they may protect the president from irate citizens, they probably are not worth the time.

8. *Is the threat increasing?* It is illogical to spend large amounts of time and money on a threat that is diminishing every day. Before any large investment, the president must determine if five or ten years down the line the investment will be rational. A long-term

solution to a lessening short-term threat is a foolish allocation of resources.

9. *Are there long-term benefits to the preventative measures?* Threats exploit weaknesses in existing infrastructure and organization. If the solution to a threat is to restructure or repair an existing flaw, it may be worth the money for the positive externalities. Fixing the electrical grid so it is no longer vulnerable to cyber or physical attack will also save money lost to naturally occurring blackouts. Keeping roads and bridges under better repair and inspection saves the country the larger cost of repairing major damage from overlooked problems. Viewing each potential solution as a greater opportunity can cast a positive light over the spending on commonsense reforms that should have been carried out anyway, the threat just providing an impetus to get it right now.

10. *Will the psychological impact on the American people resonate negatively nationwide?* Never forget that an attack or event's damage is not measured only in lives lost or economic response. The loss of hope, optimism, and faith in government can carry the longest and most dangerous result. If two threats present themselves, each with the same probability of occurrence and cost of repair and prevention, the one that threatens that which is assumed safe, or targets children, can carry a disproportionate long-term harm to the psyche of the United States.

Five Best and Five Worst Presidents at Dealing with Disaster

FIVE BEST

1. *Franklin Delano Roosevelt and the Great Depression:* Recognizing that President Hoover had failed to halt the Great Depression, President Roosevelt realized that providing a strong contrast between himself and Hoover would make his ideas, even those that were not unique or new, seem as though they were. By mastering the public relations battle, Roosevelt developed a reputation as the president who ended the Great Depression.

2. *Bill Clinton and the Millennium Bug:* President Clinton faced a defined and date-certain threat. By communicating constantly and making it clear where responsibilities lay, Clinton ensured that Y2K was the "last headache of the twentieth century, not the first crisis of the twenty-first."

3. *George W. Bush and the 9/11 Terrorist Attacks:* At the moment of 9/11, President Bush faced a truly unprecedented event in American history. While Bush's initial response was criticized, he did not spread misinformation and was able to shape the undeniably heartbreaking narrative of 9/11 into one of tragedy, but also heroism. He also effectively reached out to Congress, worked through his agencies with affected industries, and empowered cabinet officials to take actions necessary to deal with the terror threat.

4. *Richard Nixon and Hurricane Camille:* President Nixon not only pledged and provided support to the impacted areas, but he also learned from the disaster what weaknesses the scientific community had in predicting disasters. By having federal officials improve their weather forecasting ability, Hurricane Camille spurred the development of the five-category storm scale used today.

5. *Ronald Reagan and the Tylenol Poisonings:* President Reagan was able to do what many leaders cannot: recognize how to take mediated action. Reagan let Johnson & Johnson take charge of the situation, and the company withdrew their potentially poisoned product from shelves and safely and efficiently managed the fallout.

FIVE WORST

1. *Woodrow Wilson and the Spanish Influenza:* The federal response to the influenza outbreak in 1918 can best be described as neglectful. Hundreds of thousands of Americans died without President Wilson saying anything or mobilizing nonmilitary components of the US government to help the civilian population. Additionally, by choosing to continue troop shipments to the front, Wilson enabled the disease to continue to spread rapidly, even as World War I was winding to a close.

2. *Herbert Hoover and the Great Depression*: President Hoover's handling of the Great Depression is widely considered to be nothing short of disastrous. Even if his actions were not as egregious and harmful as portrayed in textbooks, his inaccurate predictions about the end of the Great Depression and his overall poor communication skills solidified his memory as a poor leader. Hoover and Roosevelt may not have differed much on policy prescriptions, but the wide gap between their abilities as communicators contributed mightily to the differences in their reputations.

3. *Lyndon B. Johnson and Civil Unrest:* President Johnson faced dozens of riots in his tenure as president during the 1960s. While the causes of the riots were varied—poverty, racial strife, and

the assassination of Martin Luther King Jr.—Johnson failed to understand the scope of the civil unrest and to craft a strong and enforceable policy to respond to the riots.

4. *George W. Bush and Hurricane Katrina*: President Bush was severely criticized in the aftermath of Hurricane Katrina. The governmental response was widely characterized as delayed and disorganized. Bush compounded the situation by flying over the affected area, and the disastrous photo of him surveying the damage from above made him seem callous and out of touch.

5. *Jimmy Carter and Power Outages*: President Carter did very little in reaction to the 1977 New York City blackout. Though the blackouts may have been regional, the flaws that allowed them to occur ought to have spurred Carter to take meaningful action to ensure further blackouts did not occur. The disorder caused by the blackout did bring about Carter's famous 1977 trip to the South Bronx, but that trip failed to accomplish much, other than inspire Ronald Reagan's counter trip in 1980 during his successful electoral challenge to Carter.

Individual Lessons Learned

1. *No Man Is an Island:* Knowing your neighbors is vital. If you are not prepared, they might be, plus there is safety in numbers.

2. *Power Is Power:* Backup power is essential. The electrical grid is vulnerable and beyond any individual's reach to fix or protect. Having a generator, or at the very least a store of batteries, can take a situation from dangerous to merely uncomfortable.

3. *Knowledge Is Also Power:* Gather information about the situation. Knowing what risks you and your family are currently facing will allow logical decision making about what action to take without panic or inefficiency.

4. *Everyone Has a Role to Play:* In the aftermath of an attack, remain alert. The government's ability to help everyone is limited; citizens' ability to generate valuable information is far more extensive. Contribute what you know.

5. *Make a Plan Ahead of Time:* Cell towers can go down or become overloaded. Organize with your family where to meet in case of an emergency. It's no good to pick somewhere to meet or prepare a safe room in your house if once cell service goes down they have no way to know where to go or what to do.

6. *Even So, Man Plans and God Laughs:* Disasters follow no schedule; even if hurricane season is over, do not neglect basic safety precautions.

7. *Wash Those Hands:* When disease threatens, basic hygiene goes a long way. Washing hands, covering your nose and mouth to sneeze, and cleaning surfaces can prevent the transmission of disease, thus reducing the likelihood of epidemics or pandemics.

8. *Protect Yourself:* In the case of rioting, police can be overwhelmed. Even if you ordinarily have strong positive relationships with your neighbors, you cannot count on such relationships in times of crisis to protect your home or business. Having the strongest level of home protection you are comfortable with is the best insurance you can provide for your family.

9. *Locks Go a Long Way:* Strong and double locks on doors and windows can deter intruders and ensure they go elsewhere before they come to you. Having a safe room in your house, with a lock on the door, provides an extra measure of safety.

10. *Stock Up:* Maintain a supply of food and water sufficient to feed your family for, at the very least, a long weekend. Keep a section of your pantry stocked with extra food at all times and replace food before it expires.

11. *Be Prepared to Be on Your Own:* Don't expect the government to come running immediately to your aid; in the case of an attack on the homeland or widespread natural disaster, you and your family might not be the government's top priority.

12. *Diversify Food Sources:* Preparation is more than stocking up on food and water. Planting a garden, learning to fish, or researching what plants in your local area are edible will significantly increase your security in an inexpensive and potentially enjoyable way.

13. *Diversify Investments:* Ensure you balance any investments you make. The probability of going through your adult life without an economic downturn is incredibly low, so finding good, reliable financial advice and following it is of utmost importance to you and your family's stability.

Acknowledgments

Starting a book is such a daunting project that each time feels as if it will be the last book one undertakes. Fortunately, I had many friends, family members, and colleagues who helped me through the process. One cannot write a book unless one has a good idea, and in this case I am indebted to my good friend and fellow *Odd Couple* fan Alan Rechtschaffen, who helped me come up with the idea to write about my government experience in preparing for and dealing with disasters. Alan had the insight to make personal preparedness part of the analysis as well, so as to get each individual reader engaged. I am confident that whatever I write about him will not be deemed sufficient, but the fair reader will have to acknowledge that I did my best in this regard.

Another long-standing friend, Don Trigg, gave me the idea of highlighting the link to presidents, kindly adding that I had made presidential studies part of my branding and that I should not neglect that aspect.

From there, I took it to my trusty agent, Gene Brissie. Unfortunately, Gene left the agent game while I was working on this book. Fortunately, when he left agenting, Gene joined Lyons Press and ably shepherded this work to publication. Thanks also to production editor Meredith Dias, copyeditor Ann Seifert, typesetter Rhonda Baker, proofreader Steve Arney, and indexer Kathleen Rocheleau. Thanks also to publicist Jessica Kastner and marketing manager Sara Given. On the agent front, the cool-headed Alex Hoyt stepped in for Gene and did a fantastic job, for which I am greatly appreciative.

Contract in hand, I embarked upon the research and writing. In this, I was fortunate to have help from crack researchers (listed alphabetically) Hannah Brodheim, Eli Greenfield, Kara Jones, Eliyahu

Krakowski, Matthew Niss, Andy Rapoport, Margot Schumann, Ashley Warrum, and Gabriela Weigel. They are all promising young people, and I am grateful for their assistance.

Research is essential and can be a collaborative process. Writing, in contrast, is a solitary activity. That said, I had many fruitful conversations with wise people to sort out the ideas and themes in the book. In this vein I appreciated the insights of disaster experts Anna Abram, Frank Ciluffo, Bruce Gellin, Scott Gottlieb, Michael Herson, Bob Kadlec, Brian Kamoie, Kevin Kosar, Evan Morris, Stewart Simonson, Admiral Craig Vanderwagen, and many others. In addition, the polymathic Jonah Goldberg sat down for a long and fruitful conversation that helped frame my thinking on this issue. First cousin and media adviser Matt Gerson provided excellent cover and title guidance. Rabbi and long-ago camp counselor Micah Halpern gave some excellent advice on a complex issue of Jewish law raised in the manuscript.

My Hudson Institute colleagues—including Rachel Cox, Doug Feith, Lee Lane, Scooter Libby, Bill Luti, uber-Tweeter Chris Sands, Joel Scanlon, Abe Shulsky, Carolyn Stewart, John Walters, John Weicher, and peerless president Ken Weinstein—provided valuable feedback to an early oral presentation of the concept.

I also got good feedback on an early draft from former administration colleagues Tom Bossert and Dan Kaniewski; the great anthropologist Stanley Kurtz; and radio host Seth Leibsohn—please listen to his show.

Jonathan Bronitsky, Alina Czekai, Matt Robinson, Dan Troy, and Gil Troy read an almost final version of this work and provided immensely useful guidance and edits. Improvements are due to them; mistakes are my own.

I am also grateful to my fun and supportive colleagues at the American Health Policy Institute, including sparring partner Rob Andrews; legal eagle Tim Bartl; PR guru Amanda Beck; UCLA softball-loving Shelly Carlin; former board chairman Kevin Cox; health policy maven Alina Czekai; bass-playing Daniel Chasen; founding chair Mike Davis; enforcer Henry Eickelberg; Elise Elliott and Sandy Hughes, who make sure the numbers work; new mom Ani Huang; tech wizard Angelo

Kostopoulos and his team—John Connor, John Cusack, Maria Gupta, Jordan Hayes, Chris Kuhn, Samir Patel, Rhonda Stroman, and Michael Whitted; parkourist Megan Lustig; superior leader Jeff McGuiness; Nats fan Mike McGuiness; insurance expert Colleen McHugh; document master Marie Murphy; history buff Rikki Pelta; current board chairman Marc Reed; Uno shark LaShawn Rozier; outside counsel Vanessa Scott; the always helpful Natalie Stewart; logistics master Price Williams; number cruncher extraordinaire Mark Wilson; and the movie-loving Dan Yager.

A number of editors have allowed me to work out themes and even sections that appeared in this book, including Garrett Graff, Stephen Heuser, Elizabeth Ralph, David Mark, and Blake Hounshell at *Politico*; the *New Atlantis*'s Adam Keiper; Sohrab Ahmari, Michael Judge, Kate Bachelder, Howard Dyckman, David Feith, Paul Gigot, Joe Rago, Nancy deWolf Smith, and Mark Lasswell at the *Wall Street Journal*; Carlos Lozada at the *Washington Post*; Avik Roy and Sarah Hedgecock at *Forbes*; Kathryn Lopez and Rich Lowry at *National Review*; Anneke Green at the *Washington Times*; Moira Bagley and Neil Patel at the *Daily Caller*; Charles Kesler and John Kienker at the *Claremont Review of Books*; and Claudia Anderson, Bill Kristol, and Phil Terzian at the *Weekly Standard*. Also kudos to Ken Kurson, editor of my column at the *New York Observer*.

I could not do any of this without my loving family, including my brothers—Dan and Gil Troy, to whom this book is dedicated—and their great families: Cheryl, Aaron, Leora, and Ariel in Chevy Chase; and Linda, Lia, Yoni, Aviv, and Dina in Jerusalem. I only wish that I could see all of them more often.

My parents, Dov and Elaine Troy, to whom I dedicated my second book, and my in-laws, Drs. Ray and Vita Pliskow, to whom I dedicated my third book, are incredibly supportive, and I appreciate everything that they do. They are also big fans, eager to drop everything to see me on TV or listen to me on the radio.

In my last book I reported that my dear wife, Kami, told me that I am more fun when I am not writing a book. Fortunately, she did not repeat that comment during the writing of this book, which I hope means that I have remained at least somewhat fun. I also hope that this book somehow makes her very funny annual letter to friends and family. As for my children, they are always fun, even on the rare occasions when they get on my nerves. If policymakers listen to the recommendations in this book, Ezra, Ruthie, Rina, and Noey will never have to use the individual preparedness strategies that I lay out.

Endnotes

Introduction

1. Nate Silver, *The Signal and the Noise: Why So Many Predictions Fail—But Some Don't* (New York: Penguin Press, 2012), 454.

2. Carl Bialik, "Statshot: Carl Bialik, 'The Numbers Guy,'" *Wall Street Journal,* June 28, 2013, http://online.wsj.com/article/SB1000142412788732341960457857195149333565 18.html, accessed July 15, 2013.

3. Erwann Michel-Kerjan, "What Is the State of U.S. Disaster-Preparedness? A Freakonomics Quorum," http://freakonomics.com/2007/11/09/what-is-the-state-of -us-disaster-preparedness-a-freakonomics-quorum, accessed November 3, 2013.

4. Mark Halperin and John Heilemann, *Double Down: Game Change 2012* (New York: Penguin Press HC, 2013), 9.

5. Matt A. Mayer, "Congress Should Limit the Presidential Abuse of FEMA," WebMemo #3466 on Homeland Security, The Heritage Foundation, January 24, 2012.

6. Cf. Patrick S. Roberts, *Disasters and the American State: How Politicians, Bureaucrats, and the Public Prepare for the Unexpected* (New York: Cambridge University Press, 2013), 36.

7. David Axelrod, *Believer: My Forty Years in Politics* (New York: Penguin, 2015), 417.

Chapter One: The Pandemic Threat

1. Molly Billings, "The Influenza Pandemic of 1918," June 1997, Stanford University, modified April 7, 2002, www.Stanford.edu/group/virus/uda.

2. John Barry, *The Great Influenza: The Epic Story of the Deadliest Pandemic in History* (New York: Penguin, 2004), 169.

3. Ibid., 300.

4. Billings, "The Influenza Pandemic of 1918."

5. Alfred W. Crosby, *America's Forgotten Pandemic: The Influenza of 1918* (Cambridge: Cambridge University Press, 2003), 24–25.

6. Ibid.

7. Pete Davies, *The Devil's Flu: The World's Deadliest Influenza Epidemic and the Scientific Hunt for the Virus That Caused It* (New York: Holt, 2000), 62.

8. Barry, *The Great Influenza*, 300.

9. Thucydides, *The History of the Peloponnesian War*, translated by Richard Crawley, Chapter VII, www.gutenberg.org/files/7142/7142-h/7142-h.htm, accessed September 11, 2014.

10. Alan Axelrod, *Selling the Great War: The Making of American Propaganda* (New York: Palgrave Macmillan, 2009), 72.

11. H. W. Brands, *Woodrow Wilson: The American Presidents Series: The 28th President, 1913–1921* (New York: Times Books, 2003), 84.

12. Barry, *The Great Influenza*, 144.

13. Berg, A. Scott, *Wilson* (New York: Putnam, 2013), 12.

14. Barry, *The Great Influenza*, 396.

15. John Maynard Keynes, *The Economic Consequences of the Peace* (New York: Harcourt, Brace and Rowe, 1920), 167, 251.

16. H. W. Brands, Woodrow Wilson, 123; John Milton Cooper, *Woodrow Wilson: A Biography* (New York: Knopf, 2011), 487.

17. Barry, *The Great Influenza*, 387.

18. Berg, A. Scott, *Wilson*, 569.

19. Gaia Vince, "Global Transformers: What if a Pandemic Strikes?" BBC, July 11, 2013, www.bbc.com/future/story/20130711-what-if-a-pandemic-strikes, accessed December 31, 2013. Note: Some of the material in this section previously appeared in an article I wrote in the *New Atlantis*. See Tevi Troy, "Heading Off the Next Pandemic," *New Atlantis*, Fall 2010.

20. Figures compiled from a variety of historical and government sources. The worldwide figure for the swine flu pandemic comes from the World Health Organization, while the US range comes from the Centers for Disease Control and Prevention. The discrepancy in the figures for that pandemic—implying that the United States suffered a disproportionately high number of deaths—stems from those entities' different methods for collecting and analyzing data.

21. Lou Lumenick, "Catch It," *New York Post*, September 9, 2011, http://nypost.com/2011/09/09/catch-it, accessed January 1, 2014.

22. Thomas Frieden, Press Briefing Transcript, National Press Club Luncheon, September 10, 2013, www.cdc.gov/media/releases/2013/t0911-National-Press-Club .html, accessed January 10, 2014.

23. Nate Silver, *The Signal and the Noise: Why So Many Predictions Fail—But Some Don't* (New York: Penguin Press, 2012), 229.

24. David Brown, "Bush Outlines $7.1 Billion in Flu Preparations," *Washington Post*, November 2, 2005, www.washingtonpost.com/wp-dyn/content/article/2005/11/01/AR2005110101100.html, accessed January 2, 2014.

25. Donald G. McNeil, "U.S. Issues Guidelines in Case of Flu Pandemic," *New York Times*, February 1, 2007, www.nytimes.com/2007/02/01/health/01cnd-flu.html ?pagewanted=print&_r=0, accessed January 2, 2014.

26. Brown, "Bush Outlines $7.1 Billion in Flu Preparations."

27. Carol E. Lee and Amie Parnes, "Biden Would Avoid Subways, Planes after Swine Flu Outbreak," *Politico*, April 30, 2009, http://dyn.politico.com/printstory.cfm?uuid =F6E30C75-18FE-70B2-A819A1062E1DC69A, accessed January 2, 2014.

28. Andrew Pollack and Donald McNeil Jr., "A Nation Battling Flu, and Short Vaccine Supplies," *New York Times*, October 26, 2009, www.nytimes.com/2009/10/26/health/26flu.html?_r=1&pagewanted=all, accessed January 2, 2014.
29. Ibid.
30. Alex B. Berezow, "Are Liberals or Conservatives More Anti-Vaccine?" *Real Clear Science*, October 20, 2014, www.realclearscience.com/journal_club/2014/10/20/are_liberals_or_conservatives_more_anti-vaccine_108905.html, accessed October 27, 2014.
31. Cynthia G. Whitney, MD, Fangjun Zhou, PhD, James Singleton, PhD, Anne Schuchat, MD, "Benefits from Immunization During the Vaccines for Children Program Era—United States, 1994–2013," Morbidity and Mortality Weekly Report (MMWR) 63(16), April 25, 2014, 352–55, www.cdc.gov/mmwr/preview/mmwrhtml/mm6316a4.htm, accessed October 31, 2014.
32. Tevi Troy, "Enter the Neutral Zone," *Politico*, October 28, 2009, http://dyn.politico.com/printstory.cfm?uuid=972794B1-18FE-70B2-A8A04550DC60E156, accessed October 27, 2014.
33. Michael Fumento, "Why the WHO Faked a Pandemic," *Forbes*, February 5, 2010, http://fumento.com/swineflu/who_faked.html, accessed January 2, 2014.
34. Prepared Statement of Julie L. Gerberding, Director, Centers for Disease Control and Prevention, "The Threat of and Planning for Pandemic Flu," Hearing before the House of Representatives Subcommittee on Health of the Committee on Energy and Commerce, One Hundred Ninth Congress, First Session, May 26, 2005, www.gpo.gov/fdsys/pkg/CHRG-109hhrg21642/html/CHRG-109hhrg21642.htm, accessed January 2, 2014.
35. Eunice Yoon, "Businesses Brace for Pandemic," CNN, November 3, 2005, www.cnn.com/2005/HEALTH/conditions/11/03/birdflu.economics, accessed August 20, 2014.
36. Peter Pitts, "Here Comes the Next Big Healthcare Disaster, Courtesy of HHS," *Washington Examiner*, November 8, 2013, http://washingtonexaminer.com/here-comes-the-next-big-healthcare-disaster-courtesy-of-hhs/article/2538779, accessed January 13, 2014.
37. "Estimating the Future Number of Cases of the Ebola Epidemic—Liberia and Sierra Leone, 2014–2015," Morbidity and Mortality Weekly Report (MMWR), Centers for Disease Control, September 26, 2014, www.cdc.gov/mmwr/preview/mmwrhtml/su6303a1.htm, accessed November 25, 2014.
38. "Ebola 'Overwhelming' Health Services in West Africa," *Business Insider*, September 10, 2014, www.businessinsider.com/afp-ebola-overwhelming-health-services-in-west-africa-2014-9, accessed November 25, 2014.
39. Office of the Inspector General, "DHS Has Not Effectively Managed Pandemic Personal Protective Equipment and Antiviral Medical Countermeasures," Department of Homeland Security, August 26, 2014, www.oig.dhs.gov/assets/Mgmt/2014/OIG_14-129_Aug14.pdf, accessed September 9, 2014.
40. Jennifer Haberkorn, "CDC Chief: U.S. Combating Ebola," Politico, August 7, 2014, www.politico.com/story/2014/08/ebola-cdc-director-tom-frieden-109826.html, accessed August 20, 2014.

CHAPTER TWO: FOOD AND WATER CRISIS

1. Brad Plumer, "Five Big Questions about the Massive Chemical Spill in West Virginia." *Washington Post*, January 21, 2014.

2. Ibid.

3. Pam Ramsey, "Tap Water Still Tainted in West Virginia," Associated Press, January 11, 2014, www.pressherald.com/news/4_hospitalized_in_W_Va__after_chemical_spill_.html.

4. Ian Simpson, "West Virginia AG Vows Probe after Chemical Spill Fouls Water," *Reuters*, January 15, 2014, http://news.yahoo.com/more-west-virginia-customers -cleared-drink-tap-water-142047405--sector.html, accessed January 21, 2014.

5. Roger Runningen and Mark Drajem, "Obama Declares Emergency in West Virginia after Spill," *Bloomberg*, January 10, 2014, www.bloomberg.com/news/2014-01-10/ obama-declares-emergency-in-west-virginia-after-spill.html.

6. Jeff Jenkins, "How Long Will Bottled Water Be Available?" *West Virginia Metro News*, January 21, 2014, http://wvmetronews.com/2014/01/21/how-long-will-bottled -water-be-available, accessed January 22, 2014.

7. Bob King, "West Virginia Declares Some Customers' Water Safe to Drink," *Politico*, January 13, 2014, www.politico.com/story/2014/01/west-virginia-water-102111.html, accessed January 22, 2014.

8. Eugene Robinson, "Washington Is Silent on W.Va.'s Chemical Spill," *Washington Post*, January 20, 2014, www.washingtonpost.com/opinions/eugene-robinson-wash ington-is-silent-on-wvas-chemical-spill/2014/01/20/cd567804-8220-11e3-8099 -9181471f7aaf_print.html.

9. Tom Henry, "Water Crisis Grips Hundreds of Thousands in Toledo Area, State of Emergency Declared," *Toledo Blade*, August 3, 2014, www.toledoblade.com/ local/2014/08/03/Water-crisis-grips-area.html, accessed August 21, 2014.

10. Sara Larimer, "Toledo Mayor Lifts Water Ban in Northwest Ohio," *Washington Post*, August 4, 2014, www.washingtonpost.com/news/post-nation/wp/2014/08/04/toledo- mayor-lifts-ban-declares-drinking-water-safe, accessed August 21, 2014.

11. Kate Bachelder, "Through Hell and Flint Water." *Wall Street Journal*, January 20, 2016. www.wsj.com/articles/through-hell-and-flint-water-1453336838?cb=log ged0.5776705900207162, accessed January 25, 2016.

12. David Frum, "Why 2013 Will Be a Year of Crisis," CNN, September 3, 2012, www .cnn.com/2012/09/03/opinion/frum-food-price-crisis, accessed January 24, 2014.

13. Nanci Hellmich, "People Have Cut Calories and Improved Their Diets," *USA TODAY*, January 16, 2014, www.usatoday.com/story/news/nation/2014/01/16/ americans-cutting-calories/4495401, accessed January 23, 2014.

14. "CDC: US Illness Outbreaks from Imported Food Have Risen," Fox News, March 15, 2012, www.foxnews.com/health/2012/03/15/cdc-us-illness-outbreaks -from-imported-food-have-risen, accessed January 24, 2014.

15. Justin Bachman, "U.S. Food-Safety Inspectors Miss Most Imports. Why Not Outsource It?" *Business Week*, July 29, 2013, www.businessweek.com/articles/2013-07 -29/u-dot-s-dot-food-safety-inspectors-miss-most-imports-dot-why-not-outsource-it.

16. "CDC: US Illness Outbreaks from Imported Food Have Risen."

17. Dan Flynn, "Imports and Exports: Americans Shop the World for Food Every Day of the Week," *Food Safety News*, November 4, 2013, www.foodsafetynews.com/2013/11/americans-dining-on-more-imported-food-than-ever/#.UuGVENIo6M8, accessed January 23, 2014.

18. David Acheson, quoted in Eileen R. Choffnes, David A. Relman, LeighAnne Olsen, Rebekah Hutton, and Alison Mack, *Rapporteurs, Improving Food Safety Through a One Health Approach: Workshop Summary, Institute of Medicine* (Washington, DC: National Academies Press, 2012), http://books.nap.edu/openbook.php?record_id=13423&page=R3, accessed January 27, 2014.

19. Bachman, "U.S. Food-Safety Inspectors Miss Most Imports."

20. Ibid.

21. Paul Rogers, "California Drought: 17 Communities Could Run Out of Water within 60 to 120 Days, State Says," *San Jose Mercury News*, January 28, 2014, www.mercurynews.com/science/ci_25013388/california-drought-17-communities-could-run-out-water, accessed January 30, 2014.

22. Jim Carlton, "California Drought Will Cost $2.2 Billion in Agriculture Losses This Year," *Wall Street Journal*, July 16, 2014, http://online.wsj.com/articles/drought-will-cost-california-2-2-billion-in-losses-costs-this-year-1405452120, accessed July 16, 2014.

23. National Oceanic and Atmospheric Administration. "Drought Annual – 2015," www.ncdc.noaa.gov/sotc/drought/201513, accessed February 2, 2016.

24. Kurtis Alexander, "California Drought: Communities at Risk of Running Dry," *San Francisco Chronicle*, January 30, 2014, www.sfgate.com/news/article/California-drought-communities-at-risk-of-5184906.php, accessed January 30, 2014.

25. Carlton, "California Drought Will Cost $2.2 Billion."

26. Victor Davis Hanson, "California's Two Droughts," *National Review Online*, February 6, 2014, www.nationalreview.com/article/370425/californias-two-droughts-victor-davis-hanson, accessed February 13, 2014.

27. Edward P. Lazear, "Government Dries Up California's Water Supply," *Wall Street Journal*, June 26, 2014, http://online.wsj.com/articles/edward-lazear-government-dries-up-californias-water-supply-1403822789, accessed July 10, 2014.

28. Bryan Walsh, "Hundred Years of Dry: How California's Drought Could Get Much, Much Worse," *Time*, January 23, 2014, http://science.time.com/2014/01/23/hundred-years-of-dry-how-californias-drought-could-get-much-much-worse, accessed February 7, 2014.

29. Bill Tomson, "California Drought Threatens Sushi, Too," *Politico*, September 15, 2014, www.politico.com/story/2014/09/california-drought-sushi-110983.html#ixzz3Da5Woo8O, accessed September 17, 2014.

30. "How the Experts Would Fix the Food Crisis," *Business Week*, January 10, 2013, www.businessweek.com/articles/2013-01-10/how-the-experts-would-fix-the-food-crisis, accessed January 24, 2014.

Chapter Three: Weather: A Growing Federal Role

1. "Disaster Declarations by Year," Federal Emergency Management Agency, www.fema.gov/disasters/grid/year.

2. "Report: Climate Change Already Affecting US." Associated Press, May 7, 2014, www.washingtonpost.com/politics/report-climate-change-already-affecting-us/2014/05/07/6efeb926-d5b6-11e3-8f7d-7786660fff7c_story.html, accessed May 7, 2014.

3. Patrick Roberts, "Our Responder in Chief," *National Affairs*, Fall 2010, www.nationalaffairs.com/publications/detail/our-responder-in-chief, accessed November 3, 2014.

4. Edwin Hutcheson, "Floods of Johnstown: 1889-1936-1977," Johnstown Flood Museum, 1989, www.jaha.org/FloodMuseum/history.html, accessed May 7, 2014.

5. Frank Connelly and George C. Jenks, *Official History of the Johnstown Flood* (Pittsburgh: Journalist Publishing Company, 1889), 152.

6. Ibid., 153. Dr. Carrington was referred to by President Harrison earlier in the telegram as a medical officer stationed in Pittsburgh.

7. Grover Cleveland, "Veto Message," February 16, 1887, www.presidency.ucsb.edu/ws/?pid=71489, accessed July 10, 2014.

8. Connelly and Jenks, *Official History of the Johnstown Flood*, 153.

9. Library of Congress, "Johnstown Local Flood Protection Project," Historical American Engineering Record, HAER No Pa-413, lcweb2.loc.gov/master/pnp/habshaer/pa/pa3500/pa3502/data/pa3502data.pdf, accessed May 8, 2014.

10. David McCullough, *The Johnstown Flood* (New York: Simon and Schuster, 1987), 225, 231.

11. Rick Shenkman, "Interview with Pete Daniel: The Great Flood of 1927," History News Network, http://hnn.us/article/15370, accessed May 8, 2014.

12. Bill Bryson, *One Summer: America, 1927* (New York: Doubleday, 2013), 53.

13. David Greenberg, "Help! Call the White House!" *Slate*, September 5, 2006, www.slate.com/articles/news_and_politics/history_lesson/2006/09/help_call_the_white_house.html, accessed May 9, 2014.

14. Bryson, *One Summer*, 60.

15. John M. Barry, "After the Deluge," *Smithsonian Magazine*, November 2005, www.smithsonianmag.com/history/after-the-deluge-111555373/?no-ist.

16. Greenberg, "Help! Call the White House!"

17. Ibid.

18. Kevin Kosar, "Disaster Response and Appointment of a Recovery Czar: The Executive Branch's Response to the Flood of 1927," Congressional Research Service, reposed as "The Executive Branch's Response to the Flood of 1927," History News Network, http://hnn.us/article/17255, accessed May 8, 2014.

19. Richard Nixon, "Remarks Following Aerial Inspection of Damage Caused by Hurricane Camille in Mississippi," September 8, 1969, The American Presidency Project, UCSB, www.presidency.ucsb.edu/ws/?pid=2228, accessed May 9, 2014.

20. Roger Pielke, Chantal Simonpietri, and Jennifer Oxelson, "Thirty Years after Hurricane Camille: Lessons Learned, Lessons Lost," Center for Science and Technology Policy Research, July 12, 1999, http://sciencepolicy.colorado.edu/about_us/meet_us/roger_pielke/camille/report.html, accessed May 9, 2014.

21. Philip D. Hearn, *Hurricane Camille: Monster Storm of the Gulf Coast* (Jackson: University of Mississippi Press, 2004), 139–40.

22. "Conversation With Bob Hope During the Red Cross Telethon in Mississippi," August 24, 1969, www.presidency.ucsb.edu/ws/?pid=2210, accessed July 10, 2014.

23. "Disaster Relief," *CQ Almanac 1969*, 25th ed., 239–40, Washington, DC: Congressional Quarterly, 1970, http://library.cqpress.com/cqalmanac/document .php?id=cqal69-1248020, accessed May 14, 2014.

24. Willie Drye, "Category Five: How a Hurricane Yardstick Came to Be," *National Geographic News*, December 20, 2005, http://news.nationalgeographic.com/ news/2005/12/1220_051220_saffirsimpson_2.html, accessed May 14, 2014.

25. Ibid.

26. Hearn, *Hurricane Camille*, 139–140.

27. Pielke, Simonpietri, and Oxelson, "Thirty Years after Hurricane Camille."

28. Susan Cutter, Christopher T. Emrich, Jerry T. Mitchell, Walter W. Piegorsch, Mark M. Smith, and Lynn Weber, *Hurricane Katrina and the Forgotten Coast of Mississippi* (New York: Cambridge University Press, 2014), 28.

29. "Historian Remembers Hurricane Camille Recovery," University of South Carolina, October 9, 2010, www.sc.edu/news/newsarticle.php?nid=1223, accessed May 13, 2014.

30. Cutter et al., *Hurricane Katrina and the Forgotten Coast of Mississippi*, 28.

31. "Hurricane Andrew: 20 Facts You May Have Forgotten," Huffington Post, August 24, 2012, www.huffingtonpost.com/2012/08/21/20-facts-hurricane-andrew-anniversary _n_1819405.html, accessed May 15, 2014.

32. David Sutta, "Remembering Hurricane Andrew's Economic Impact," CBS Miami, August 22, 2012, http://miami.cbslocal.com/2012/08/22/remembering-hurricane -andrews-economic-impact, accessed May 15, 2014.

33. Edmund L. Andrews, "Hurricane Andrew; Bush Sending Army to Florida Amid Criticism of Relief Effort," *New York Times*, August 28, 1992, www.nytimes.com/ 1992/08/28/us/hurricane-andrew-bush-sending-army-to-florida-amid-criticism-of -relief-effort.html, accessed May 15, 2014.

34. Bill Adair, "10 Years Ago, Her Angry Plea Got Hurricane Aid Moving," *St. Petersburg Times*, August 20 2002, www.sptimes.com/2002/webspecials02/andrew/ day3/story1.shtml, accessed May 15, 2014.

35. President George H. W. Bush, "The President's News Conference on the Aftermath of Hurricane Andrew," August 28, 1992, The American Presidency Project, UCSB, www.presidency.ucsb.edu/ws/?pid=21388, accessed May 15, 2014.

36. Andrews, "Hurricane Andrew."

37. Tom Curry, "In Election Year, Hurricanes, Too, Are Political," NBC News, August 15, 2004, www.nbcnews.com/id/5716031, accessed May 16, 2014.

38. Andy Newman, "Hurricane Sandy vs. Hurricane Katrina." *New York Times*, November 28, 2012, A28.

39. Editorial, "Nine Years Post-Katrina, a Recovery Still in Progress," *New Orleans Time-Picayune*, August 29, 2014, www.nola.com/opinions/index.ssf/2014/08/nine _years_post-katrina_a_reco.html#incart_maj-story-1, accessed November 25, 2014.

40. George W. Bush, *Decision Points* (New York: Crown, 2010), 330.

41. Ibid., 331.

42. Michael Eric Dyson, *Come Hell or High Water: Hurricane Katrina and the Color of Disaster* (New York: Basic Civitas, 2006), 27, 88, 100, 109.

43. Peter Baker, *Days of Fire: Bush and Cheney in the White House* (New York: Doubleday, 2013), 409.

44. Roberts, "Our Responder in Chief."

45. Bob Williams, "Blame Amid the Tragedy," *Wall Street Journal*, September 6, 2005, http://online.wsj.com/news/articles/SB112596602138332256, accessed July 9, 2014.

46. Roy S. Popkin, "The History and Politics of Disaster Management in the United States," in Andrew Kirby, ed., *Nothing to Fear: Risks and Hazards in American Society* (Tucson: University of Arizona Press, 1990), 101.

47. Jennifer Loven and Tom Raum, "Obama Oil Spill Press Conference: Government in Charge of Oil Disaster Response," AP/Huffington Post, May 27, 2010, www.huffington post.com/2010/05/27/obama-oil-spill-press-con_n_592149.html, accessed May 16, 2014.

48. One person who did have this "Superman" approach was Donald Trump, who called White House aide David Axelrod during the spill and made the following offer: "That Admiral you have down there running this leak operation seems like a nice guy, but he doesn't know what he's doing. I know how to run big projects. Put me in charge of this thing, and I'll get that leak shut down and the damage repaired." David Axelrod, *Believer: My Forty Years in Politics* (New York: Penguin, 2015), 419.

49. George W. Bush, "Remarks on Labor Day in Richfield, Ohio," September 1, 2003, The American Presidency Project, UCSB, www.presidency.ucsb.edu/ws/?pid=63752, accessed May 20, 2014.

50. Bruce Bartlett, "How Bush Bankrupted America," CATO Policy Report, January/February 2006, www.cato.org/policy-report/januaryfebruary-2006/how-bush-bank rupted-america, accessed May 20, 2014.

51. Jonah Goldberg, "Goodbye to All That," *National Review Online*, September 23, 2005, www.nationalreview.com/articles/215507/goodbye-all/jonah-goldberg, accessed May 20, 2014.

52. Joel Gehrke, "Obama: 'Somewhere, Somehow, Somebody in the Federal Government Is Screwing Up,'" *Washington Examiner*, January 28, 2013, http://washingtonexaminer.com/obama-somewhere-somehow-somebody-in-the-federal -government-is-screwing-up/article/2519856, accessed May 20, 2014.

53. Daniel J. Weiss and Jackie Weidman, "Disastrous Spending: Federal Disaster-Relief Expenditures Rise amid More Extreme Weather," The Center for American Progress, April 29, 2013, www.americanprogress.org/issues/green/report/2013/04/29/61633/ disastrous-spending-federal-disaster-relief-expenditures-rise-amid-more-extreme -weather, accessed May 22, 2014.

54. Ibid.

55. David Rogers, "Wildland Fires Pose New Budget Challenge," *Politico*, May 20, 2014, www.politico.com/story/2014/05/wildfires-budget-challenge-106904.html?hp=l8, accessed May 21, 2014.

56. James W. Fossett, "Let's Stop Improvising Disaster Recovery," Observations, The Rockefeller Institute, July 9, 2013, www.rockinst.org/observations/fossettj/2013-07-09 -Improvising_Disaster_Recovery.aspx, accessed May 22, 2014.

57. Newman, "Hurricane Sandy vs. Hurricane Katrina."

58. Dan Friedman and Erin Durkin, "Sandy Victims See Almost None of Promised $60 Billion in Aid a Year after Storm," *New York Daily News*, October 28, 2013, www .nydailynews.com/new-york/hurricane-sandy/sandy-vics-60-billion-aid-article-1 .1499613, accessed November 3, 2014.

59. "Sandy Relief Spending Too Liberal and Costly, Says U.S. Sen. Kelly Ayotte," *Politifact*, February 8, 2013, www.politifact.com/new-hampshire/statements/2013/ feb/08/kelly-ayotte/sandy-relief-spending-too-liberal-and-costly-says-, accessed May 23, 2014.

60. Nia-Malika Henderson and Ed O'Keefe, "Christie, Republicans Slam Boehner for Delay on Hurricane Sandy Relief Measure," *Washington Post*, January 2, 2013, www .washingtonpost.com/politics/christie-republicans-slam-boehner-for-delay-on-hurri cane-sandy-relief-measure/2013/01/02/5d22454c-54f7-11e2-8b9e-dd8773594efc _story.html, accessed May 23, 2014.

61. Justin Grieser, "Report: 243 Million Americans Affected by Weather Disasters Since 2007," *Washington Post*, April 9, 2013, www.washingtonpost.com/blogs/capital -weather-gang/wp/2013/04/09/report-243-million-americans-affected-by-weather -disasters-since-2007, accessed May 23, 2014.

Chapter Four: Economic Collapse

1. George Nash, "Herbert Hoover's Crusade against Collectivism," *Defining Ideas*, December 18, 2013, www.hoover.org/publications/defining-ideas/article/163861, accessed February 14, 2014.

2. David Nasaw, *The Patriarch: The Remarkable Life and Turbulent Times of Joseph P. Kennedy* (New York: Penguin, 2012), 167.

3. Jonah Goldberg, "Hoover-Era Ghost Stories No Longer Apply," *National Review Online*, October 3, 2008, www.nationalreview.com/articles/225860/hoover-era-ghost -stories-no-longer-apply/jonah-goldberg, accessed February 24, 2014.

4. Amity Shlaes, "It Wasn't Hoover's Austerity That Made the Depression 'Great'." *Bloomberg*, September 11, 2012, www.bloomberg.com/news/2012-09-11/herbert -hoover-may-haunt-romney-but-not-ryan.html, accessed February 24, 2014.

5. Nasaw, *The Patriarch*, 167.

6. Robert M. Eisinger, *The Evolution of Presidential Polling* (New York: Cambridge University Press, 2003), 107.

7. Giuliana Muscio, *Hollywood's New Deal* (Philadelphia: Temple University Press, 1997), 19.

8. Glen Jeansonne, *The Life of Herbert Hoover: Fighting Quaker, 1928–1933* (New York: Palgrave Macmillan, 2012), 395.

9. Betty Houchin Winfield, *FDR and the News Media* (New York: Columbia University Press, 1994), 17.

10. Tevi Troy, *What Jefferson Read, Ike Watched, and Obama Tweeted: 200 Years of Popular Culture in the White House* (Washington, DC: Regnery History, 2013), 79–80.

11. John Sayle Watterson, *The Games Presidents Play: Sports and the Presidency*, op. cit. (Baltimore: Johns Hopkins, 2009), 135.

12. Geoffrey C. Ward and Ken Burns, *Baseball: An Illustrated History* (New York: Knopf, 1996), 210; Alan Howard Levy, *Joe McCarthy: Architect of the Yankee Dynasty* (Jefferson: McFarland & Company, 2005), 178.

13. Davis W. Houck, *Rhetoric As Currency: Hoover, Roosevelt and the Great Depression* (College Station: Texas A&M Press, 2001), 9.

14. Nash, "Herbert Hoover's Crusade against Collectivism."

15. Liaquat Ahamed, "Transition Lessons from FDR," Reuters, November 14, 2008, http://blogs.reuters.com/great-debate/2008/11/14/transition-lessons-from-fdr, accessed February 26, 2014.

16. Conrad Black, *Franklin Delano Roosevelt: Champion of Freedom* (New York: Public Affairs, 2003), 271.

17. Amity Shlaes, *The Forgotten Man: A New History of the Great Depression* (New York: Harper, 2007), 9.

18. George W. Bush, *Decision Points* (New York: Crown, 2010), 440.

19. Eliza Barclay, "U.S. Lets 141 Trillion Calories of Food Go to Waste Each Year," National Public Radio, February 27, 2014, www.npr.org/blogs/thesalt/2014/02/27/283071610/u-s-lets-141-trillion-calories-of-food-go-to-waste-each-year?ft=1&f=1007, accessed March 3, 2014.

20. U.S. Department of Energy, Residential Energy Consumption Survey, 2005.

21. As U.S. government spending patterns over this period indicate, when forced to confront the choice between A and B, Congress has consistently chosen both.

22. Daniel Henninger, "The Growth Revolutions Erupt," *Wall Street Journal*, February 26, 2014, http://online.wsj.com/news/articles/SB10001424052702304255604579407270835417610?mg=reno64-wsj&url=http%3A%2F%2Fonline.wsj.com%2Farticle%2FSB10001424052702304255604579407270835417610.html, accessed February 26, 2014.

23. "The Budget and Economic Outlook, 2015–2025," The Congressional Budget Office, January 2016, www.cbo.gov/sites/default/files/114th-congress-2015-2016/reports/49892-Outlook2015.pdf, accessed February 2, 2016.

24. Derek Thompson, "Is Our Debt Burden Really $100 Trillion?" *The Atlantic*, November 28, 2012, www.theatlantic.com/business/archive/2012/11/is-our-debt-burden-really-100-trillion/265644, accessed March 3, 2014.

25. Peter Schiff, quoted in "Schiff: ⅔ of America to Lose Everything Because of This Crisis," Money Morning, http://moneymorning.com/ob-article/schiff-us-will-win-currency-war.php, accessed March 4, 2014.

26. Summers quoted in Joshua Cooper Ramo, *The Age of the Unthinkable: Why the New World Disorder Constantly Surprises Us and What We Can Do About It* (New York: Little Brown, 2009), 57–58.

27. Ibid.

28. Martin Feldstein, "America's Challenge," AEI Annual Dinner Address 2011, May 03, 2011, www.aei.org/speech/foreign-and-defense-policy/regional/asia/americas-challenge-speech, accessed March 4, 2014.

29. David Frum, "Three Seeds for America's Future Economic Boom," CNN, June 18, 2012, www.cnn.com/2012/06/18/opinion/frum-three-leaps-ahead, accessed March 4, 2014.

CHAPTER FIVE: HOW TO PREPARE FOR ACTS OF GOD

1. Jeanne E. Abrams, *Revolutionary Medicine: The Founding Fathers and Mothers in Sickness and in Health* (New York: NYU Press, 2013), 23.

2. "CDC Says 'Take 3' Actions to Fight the Flu," Centers for Disease Control, www .cdc.gov/flu/protect/preventing.htm, accessed January 17, 2014.

3. Allison Aubrey, "Where Germs Lurk in Grade School," NPR, October 05, 2005, www.npr.org/templates/story/story.php?storyId=4945960, accessed January 17, 2014.

4. Richard Knox, "Shots for Kids May Be Best Flu Defense," NPR, October 05, 2005, www.npr.org/templates/story/story.php?storyId=4945957, accessed January 17, 2014.

5. Sam Sheridan, *The Disaster Diaries: How I Learned to Stop Worrying and Love the Apocalypse* (New York: Penguin, 2013), 45–46.

6. Carolyn Nicolaysen, "How Does the California Drought Affect You?" *Meridian Magazine*, January 30, 2014, http://ldsmag.com/article/1/13874, accessed February 7, 2014.

7. Sheridan, *The Disaster Diaries*, 319.

8. Lara Salahi, "Disaster Preparedness: Could the U.S. Hold Water?" *Good Morning America*, March 14, 2011, http://abcnews.go.com/Health/Wellness/disaster-prepared ness-us-hold-water/story?id=13135457, accessed May 23, 2014.

9. Ibid.

10. Ibid.

11. Angela Chen, "Smarter Hurricane Preparation," *Wall Street Journal*, July 30, 2013, http://online.wsj.com/article/SB10001424127887324170004578638150415983978 .html, accessed May 23, 2014.

12. Amanda Ripley, entry in "What Is the State of U.S. Disaster-Preparedness? A Freakonomics Quorum," November 9, 2007, http://freakonomics.com/2007/11/09/ what-is-the-state-of-us-disaster-preparedness-a-freakonomics-quorum, accessed May 23, 2014.

13. Lee Clarke, entry in "What Is the State of U.S. Disaster-Preparedness? A Freakonomics Quorum," November 9, 2007, http://freakonomics.com/2007/11/09/ what-is-the-state-of-us-disaster-preparedness-a-freakonomics-quorum, accessed May 23, 2014.

14. Ripley, "What Is the State of U.S. Disaster-Preparedness?"

15. "FEMA: The Citizen's Role in Disaster Preparedness," http://training.fema.gov/ emiweb/downloads/is7unit_5.pdf, accessed May 23, 2014.

16. Given increasingly long life expectancies, some feel that this method is too conservative. Consult a financial professional for the exact mix that works for you, but be sure to adjust your asset mix as you age.

17. Kevin Freeman, *Game Plan: How to Protect Yourself from the Coming Cyber-Economic Attack* (Washington, DC: Regnery, 2014), 160.

18. Victor Davis Hanson, *Carnage and Culture: Landmark Battles in the Rise to Western Power* (New York: Anchor Books, 2001), 233–78.

19. Warren E. Buffett, "Buy American. I Am," *New York Times*, October 16, 2008, www.nytimes.com/2008/10/17/opinion/17buffett.html?pagewanted=print, accessed November 25, 2014.

CHAPTER SIX: TERROR ATTACKS

1. The book was not called "My Pet Goat," one of many common misconceptions about that day.

2. Peter Baker, *Days of Fire: Bush and Cheney in the White House* (New York: Doubleday, 2013), 120.

3. Ibid., 12.

4. George W. Bush, *Decision Points* (New York: Crown, 2010), 139.

5. Ibid., 132.

6. David Frum, *The Right Man: An Inside Account of the Bush White House* (New York: Random House, 2005), 137–40.

7. George Packer, *The Unwinding: An Inner History of the New America* (New York: Farrar, Straus, and Giroux, 2013), 352.

8. Garrett M. Graff, *The Threat Matrix: The FBI at War in the Age of Global Terror* (New York: Little, Brown, 2011), 18.

9. Ibid., 388.

10. Matt Apuzzo and Adam Goldman, *Enemies Within: Inside the NYPD's Secret Spying Unit and Bin Laden's Final Plot Against America* (New York: Touchstone, 2013), 203.

11. Ibid., 204.

12. Advisory Panel on Department of Defense Capabilities for Support of Civil Authorities after Certain Incidents, "Before Disaster Strikes: Imperatives for Enhancing Defense Support of Civil Authorities," September 15, 2010, 29, www.rand.org/content/dam/rand/www/external/nsrd/DoD-CBRNE-Panel/Report-Advisory-Panel.pdf, accessed December 29, 2012.

13. Apuzzo and Goldman, *Enemies Within*, 113.

14. Edward H. Kaplan, "How Dangerous Is America?" *Boston Globe*, July 28, 2013, www.bostonglobe.com/magazine/2013/07/27/how-dangerous-america/TrzB0skxcsJH8yjAlslZCL/story.html.

15. Lara Logan, "Where America Stands: Terrorism," CBS News, January 26, 2010, www.cbsnews.com/8301-18563_162-6143576.html.

16. Graff, *The Threat Matrix*, 547.

17. L. Gordon Crovitz, "Mr. Obama, Tear Down Your Wall," *Wall Street Journal*, January 27, 2014, A11.

18. Michael Allen, *Blinking Red: Crisis and Compromise in American Intelligence after 9/11* (Washington, DC: Potomac, 2013), 48.

19. Christopher Dickey, *Securing the City: Inside America's Best Counterterror Force— The NYPD* (New York: Simon & Schuster, 2009), 167.

20. Apuzzo and Goldman, *Enemies Within*, 169.

21. Ibid., 269.

22. Tal Kopan, "Poll: Big Government Is Big Threat," *Politico*, December 18, 2013, www.politico.com/story/2013/12/poll-big-government-is-big-threat-101292.html #ixzz2nxdDd1ni.

23. Anita Kumar, "Obama on Spying: I Am Not Big Brother," McClatchy Washington Bureau, June 7, 2013, www.mcclatchydc.com/2013/06/07/193340/obama-on-spying-i-am-not-big-brother.html#storylink=cpy, accessed December 23, 2013.

24. Fox News Insider, "Hot Exchange: Ed Henry Lasers in on President Obama," Fox News, December 20, 2013, http://nation.foxnews.com/2013/12/22/hot-exchange-ed -henry-lasers-president-obama, accessed December 23, 2013.

25. Bret Baier, "Terrorism Is a 'Man-Caused' Disaster?" FoxNews.com, March 17, 2009, www.foxnews.com/story/2009/03/17/terrorism-is-man-caused-disaster.

26. Victor Davis Hanson, "The Obama Borg: How 'Man-Caused Disasters' Replaced Islamist Terrorism in the Obama Lexicon, *National Review Online*, April 30, 2013, www.nationalreview.com/article/346930/obama-borg.

27. Michael Ramirez, "Man-Caused Disasters," editorial cartoon, *Weekly Standard*, October 8, 2012, vol. 18, no. 04, www.weeklystandard.com/articles/man-caused -disasters_653248.html.

28. Peter Berger, "A War by Another Name: The Geography of Horror," *American Interest*, August 6, 2014, www.the-american-interest.com/berger/2014/08/06/the -geography-of-horror, accessed August 7, 2014.

29. Peter Juul, "Moving Beyond 9/11: The United States Needs a Broader-Based and Sustainable Counterterrorism Policy," The Center for American Progress, February 6, 2013.

30. Ibid.

31. Jessica Zuckerman, "Forty-Fifth Attempted Terrorist Plot: U.S. Must Resist Complacency," The Heritage Foundation, Issue Brief #3512, February 7, 2012, www .heritage.org/research/reports/2012/02/terrorist-attack-45th-attempted-terrorist-plot -against-united-states.

32. "Candidate Briefing: Terrorism," The Heritage Foundation, www.candidatebriefing .com/terrorism.

33. Apuzzo and Goldman, *Enemies Within*, 259.

34. Tom Kean and Lee Hamilton, "Terror Threat Enters Danger Zone," *USA Today*, July 22, 2014, www.usatoday.com/story/opinion/2014/07/22/kean-hamilton-terror -threat-terrorism-cyber-intelligence-column/12967963, accessed August 7, 2014.

35. Baker, *Days of Fire*, 131.

36. Meir Elran, "Lessons in Resiliency from the Civilian Front in Israel: Operation Protective Edge," lecture, Homeland Security Policy Institute, Washington, DC, September 5, 2014.

37. Ibid.

38. Quoted in Ariel Ben Solomon, "Analysis: Does Terrorism Work?" *Jerusalem Post*, December 23, 2013, www.jpost.com/Diplomacy-and-Politics/Does-terrorism- work-335858, accessed December 23, 2013.

39. Ibid.

CHAPTER SEVEN: THE BIOTERROR THREAT

1. Garrett M. Graff, *The Threat Matrix: The FBI at War in the Age of Global Terror* (New York: Little, Brown, 2011), 327; George Stephanopoulos, "Condoleezza Rice on the Moment She Thought President Bush Could Have Been Poisoned," ABC News, November 1, 2011, http://abcnews.go.com/blogs/politics/2011/11/condoleezza-rice

-on-the-moment-she-thought-president-bush-could-have-been-poisoned, accessed September 11, 2014.

2. Rachael Bell, "The Tylenol Terrorist Crime Library: Criminal Minds and Methods," www.crimelibrary.com/terrorists_spies/terrorists/tylenol_murders/index.html, accessed March 8, 2014; Lisa Fielding, "Tylenol Poisonings Remain Unsolved 30 Years Later," CBS Chicago, September 25, 2012, http://chicago.cbslocal.com/2012/09/25/tylenol -poisnonings-remain-unsolved-30-years-later, accessed September 11, 2014.

3. Congressional Quarterly, "Reagan Vetoes Package of Anti-Crime Bills," *CQ Almanac 1982*, 38th ed., 419–21, Washington, DC: Congressional Quarterly, 1983; Ronald Reagan, "Memorandum Returning without Approval a Bill concerning Contract Services for Drug Dependent Federal Offenders," January 14, 1983, Ronald Reagan Archives, University of Texas, www.reagan.utexas.edu/archives/speeches/1983/11483c. htm, accessed March 18, 2014.

4. Reagan, "Memorandum Returning without Approval."

5. Ronald Reagan. "Statement on Signing the Federal Anti-Tampering Act," October 14, 1983, Ronald Reagan Archives, University of Texas, www.reagan.utexas.edu/ archives/speeches/1983/101483e.htm, accessed March 18, 2014.

6. Irvin Molotsky, "Tylenol Maker Hopeful on Solving Poisoning Case," *New York Times*, February 20, 1986, www.nytimes.com/1986/02/20/nyregion/tylenol-maker -hopeful-on-solving-poisoning-case.html, accessed March 8, 2014.

7. Associated Press, "President Praises J&J Chairman in Tylenol Scare," February 19, 1986.

8. Philip Elmer-DeWitt, "America's First Bioterrorism Attack," *Time*, September 30, 2001, http://content.time.com/time/magazine/article/0,9171,176937,00.html, accessed March 16, 2014.

9. Ibid.

10. Dylan Thuras, "The Secret's in the Sauce: Bioterror at the Salsa Bar," *Slate*, January 9, 2014, www.slate.com/blogs/atlas_obscura/2014/01/09/the_largest_bioterror_attack _in_us_history_began_at_taco_time_in_the_dalles.html, accessed March 16, 2014.

11. Federal Bureau of Investigation, Portland Division, www.fbi.gov/portland/about-us/ history-1/history, accessed March 16, 2014.

12. Dan Flynn, "Salmonella Bioterrorism: 25 Years Later," *Food Safety News*, October 7, 2009, www.foodsafetynews.com/2009/10/For-The-First-12/#.Uymmuj9dxhk.

13. Ibid.

14. Nate Silver, *The Signal and the Noise: Why So Many Predictions Fail—but Some Don't* (New York: Penguin Press, 2012), 438.

15. Ted Thornhill, "Is ISIS Trying to Develop Biological Weapons?" *Daily Mail*, August 29, 2014, www.dailymail.co.uk/news/article-2737639/ISIS-laptop-reveals-terror-group -working-biological-weapon-spread-bubonic-plague.html, accessed September 11, 2014.

16. "A National Blueprint for Biodefense: Leadership and Major Reform Needed to Optimize Efforts. Bipartisan Report of the Blue Ribbon Study Panel on Biodefense," Joe Lieberman and Tom Ridge, co-chairs, October 2015, www.biodefensestudy.org/ SiteAssets/Pages/default/1425-2139_BRSP_Report_100815b[1][6].pdf, accessed February 3, 2016.

17. Sarah Lister and Dana Shea, "The BioWatch Program: Detection of Bioterrorism," Congressional Research Service Report, No. RL 32152, November 19, 2003.

18. Richard Hoffman, "Preparing for a Bioterrorist Attack: Legal and Administrative Strategies," *Emerging Infectious Diseases*, vol. 9, no. 2, February 2003, wwwnc.cdc.gov/eid/article/9/2/02-0538_article.htm, accessed March 21, 2014.

19. "CDC–PHPR–Strategic National Stockpile," Centers for Disease Control and Prevention, www.cdc.gov/phpr/stockpile/stockpile.htm, accessed July 15, 2013.

20. U.S. Department of Health and Human Services, Chemical Hazards Emergency Medical Management, "Strategic National Stockpile–SNS," http://chemm.nlm.nih.gov/sns.htm, accessed July 15, 2013.

21. Congressional Research Service, "Medical Countermeasures to Chemical, Biological, Radiological, and Nuclear Terrorism," Issues in Homeland Security Policy for the 113th Congress, fpc.state.gov/documents/organization/206134.pdf, accessed July 15, 2013.

22. U.S. Department of Health and Human Services, "Strengthening Health and Opportunity for All Americans," Fiscal Year 2013 Budget in Brief, www.hhs.gov/budget/budget-brief-fy2013.pdf, accessed July 15, 2013; and US Department of Health and Human Services, Fiscal Year 2016 Budget in Brief, www.hhs.gov/about/budget/budget-in-brief/phssef/index.html, accessed February 2, 2016.

23. Stacy A. Robarge-Silkiner, "Introduction to the Strategic National Stockpile," KDHE Center for Public Health Preparedness, www.kdheks.gov/cphp/download/Intro_SNS.pdf, accessed September 13, 2013.

24. "Strategic National Stockpile Fact Sheet," Association of State and Territorial Health Officials, www.astho.org/Programs/Preparedness/Public-Health-Emergency-Law/Emergency-Use-Authorization-Toolkit/Strategic-National-Stockpile-Fact-Sheet, accessed July 17, 2013.

25. Wil S. Hylton, "How Ready Are We for Bioterrorism?" *New York Times*, October 26, 2011, www.nytimes.com/2011/10/30/magazine/how-ready-are-we-for-bioterrorism.html?pagewanted=all&_r=0, accessed July 17, 2013.

26. Col. Jim A. Davis and Dr. Anna Johnson-Winegar, "The Anthrax Terror: DOD's Number-One Biological Threat," *Air and Space Power Journal* (Winter 2000), 15–29, www.au.af.mil/au/awc/awcgate/cpc-pubs/biostorm/winegar.pdf, accessed July 17, 2013.

27. U.S. Department of Health and Human Services, "2009 H1N1 Influenza Improvement Plan," www.phe.gov/Preparedness/mcm/h1n1-retrospective/Documents/2009-h1n1-improvementplan.pdf, accessed July 17, 2013.

28. Lawrence M. Wein, "Neither Snow, Nor Rain, Nor Anthrax . . ." *New York Times*, October 13, 2008, www.nytimes.com/2008/10/13/opinion/13wein.html?pagewanted=print&_r=0, accessed July 17, 2013.

29. Kevin Johnson, "Katrina Made Police Choose between Duty and Loved Ones," *USA Today*, February 20, 2006, http://usatoday30.usatoday.com/news/nation/2006-02-20-neworleanspolice_x.htm?csp=34, accessed July 18, 2013.

30. National Association of County and City Health Officials, "Alternative Methods of Dispensing: Model Highlights," www.naccho.org/topics/emergency/SNS/upload/POD-Article-4_polling-places.pdf, accessed July 18, 2013.

31. Tevi Troy, "Preparing for Bioterrorism," *Weekly Standard*, February 23, 2010, www
.weeklystandard.com/blogs/preparing-bioterrorism?page=1, accessed July 18, 2013.
32. Onora Lien, Crystal Franco, Gigi KwikGronvall, and Beth Maldin, "Getting
Medicine to Millions: New Strategies for Mass Distribution," UPMC Center for
Health Security, Biosecurity and Bioterrorism 4, no. 2, 2006, www.upmchealthsecurity
.org/website/resources/publications/2006/2006-06-15-medicinetomillions.html,
accessed July 18, 2013.
33. Volunteer Protection Act of 1997, U.S. Government Printing Office, www.gpo.gov/
fdsys/pkg/PLAW-105publ19/pdf/PLAW-105publ19.pdf, accessed July 18, 2013.
34. Erika Check Hayden, "Budget Forces Tough Look at Biodefense," *Nature*, April
10, 2013, www.nature.com/news/budget-forces-tough-look-at-biodefence-1.12766#/
stockpile, accessed July 18, 2013.
35. Marta Wosinska, "Drug Shortages: Why a Government Stockpile Falls Short as a
Solution," Health Affairs Blog, May 2, 2012, http://healthaffairs.org/blog/2012/05/02/
drug-shortages-why-a-government-stockpile-falls-short-as-a-solution, accessed July
18, 2013.

CHAPTER EIGHT: LOSS OF THE POWER GRID

1. Wendell Jamieson, "Pay Day the Blackout, 1977," *New York Daily News*, November 4,
1998, www.nydailynews.com/archives/news/pay-day-blackout-1977-article-1.816190
#ixzz3CAtORjsM, accessed September 2, 2014.
2. Ibid.
3. Tony Long, "July 13, 1977: Massive Blackout Plunges New York into Rioting,"
Wired, July 13, 2010, www.wired.com/2010/07/0713massive-blackout-hits-new-york,
accessed September 2, 2014.
4. Tom Foty, "New York Blackout II," UPI Audio, 1977, www.upi.com/Archives/Audio/
Events-of-1977/New-York-Blackout-II/#ixzz3CAvJKZLO, accessed September 2, 2014.
5. Jamieson, "Pay Day the Blackout, 1977."
6. George Will, "Shock of Recognition," *Newsweek*, July 25, 1977, 80.
7. David E. Nye, *When the Lights Went Out: A History of Blackouts in America*
(Cambridge: MIT Press, 2010), 253.
8. Foty, "New York Blackout II."
9. Jimmy Carter, "Interview with the National Black Network, July 18, 1977," Public
Papers of the Presidents of the United States, Jimmy Carter: 1977–, Washington, DC:
US Government Printing Office, 1977.
10. Ibid.
11. James Goodman and Jonathan Mahler, "The '77 Blackout: Authors Take Questions,
Part 3," *New York Times*, City Room Blog, July 14, 2007, http://cityroom.blogs.nytimes
.com/2007/07/14/the-77-blackout-authors-take-questions-part-3/?_php=true&_type
=blogs&_r=0, accessed October 21, 2014.
12. Ibid.
13. Joe Mathews, "A Waste Landmark in the Bronx Recycling," *Baltimore Sun Journal*,
March 30, 1998, http://articles.baltimoresun.com/1998-03-30/news/1998089067_1
_south-bronx-bronx-community-paper-mill, accessed October 21, 2014.

14. Will, "Shock of Recognition."

15. Mindi Gile, "Preparing for the Millennium Bug's Bite: Legislators, Lawyers and Potential Litigants Race to Define Duty and Limit Liability," Lawtechjournal.com, November 16, 1999, www.lawtechjournal.com/archives/blt/i6-y2k.html#I, accessed April 1, 2014.

16. Steven Levy, "The Day the World Shuts Down," *Newsweek*, June 1, 1997. www .newsweek.com/day-world-shuts-down-173474, accessed April 1, 2014.

17. B. A. Marbue Brown, *The Clinton Economic Boom* (Xulon Press, 2008), 30, 31.

18. Scott Kirsner, "What's the Government Up to Now?" *CIO Magazine*, Special Issue, Winter/Spring 1999, 54.

19. Robert Bennett et al., *Senate Special Report on Y2K* (New York: Thomas Nelson, 1999).

20. Brown, *The Clinton Economic Boom*, 31–32.

21. Bill Clinton, "Remarks by the President Concerning the Year 2000 Conversion," Techlawjournal.com, July 14, 1998.

22. Stephen Barr, "Smiling in the Face of Millennial Madness," *Washington Post*, December 16, 1999, G01.

23. Clinton, "Remarks by the President Concerning the Year 2000 Conversion."

24. Stephen Barr, "President: Social Security Killed Y2K Bug," *Washington Post*, December 29, 1998, www.washingtonpost.com/wp-srv/politics/special/security/stories/ clinton122998.htm, accessed April 4, 2014.

25. "Clinton Administration to Develop Y2K Contingency Plans," *FCW*, March 7, 1999, http://fcw.com/articles/1999/03/07/clinton-administration-to-develop-y2k -contingency-plans.aspx, accessed April 4, 2014.

26. "White House Voices Y2K Fears Over Nuclear Plants," *Chicago Tribune*, April 22, 1999, http://articles.chicagotribune.com/1999-04-22/news/9904220173_1_nuclear -plants-date-rollover-white-house, accessed April 4, 2014.

27. "Clinton Y2K Concerns," CBS News, November 10, 1999, www.cbsnews.com/ news/clinton-y2k-concerns, accessed April 4, 2014.

28. "Clinton Signs Y2K Legislation," *New York Times*, October 20, 1998, http://part ners.nytimes.com/library/tech/98/10/biztech/articles/20millennium.html, accessed April 4, 2014.

29. Bill Clinton, "Statement on Signing the Y2K Act," The American Presidency Project, UCSB, July 20, 1999, www.presidency.ucsb.edu/ws/?pid=57923, accessed April 4, 2014.

30. "Clinton: Y2K Will Not Bug US," BBC News, November 10, 1999, http://news.bbc .co.uk/2/hi/americas/514673.stm, accessed April 4, 2014.

31. Jim Puzzanghera, "President Clinton Predicts No Major National Y2K Problems," *Philadelphia Inquirer*, November 11, 1999, http://articles.philly.com/1999-11-11/news/ 25496847_1_social-security-payment-systems-computer-problem-contingency-plan, accessed April 4, 2014.

32. "Clinton Y2K Concerns." CBS News.

33. "Clinton Upbeat in His Final Y2K Report," *Chicago Tribune*, December 15, 1999, http://articles.chicagotribune.com/1999-12-15/news/9912150099_1_y2k-rollover-date-change-ready, accessed April 4, 2014.

34. Barr, "Smiling in the Face of Millennial Madness."

35. "We Killed Y2K Bug, Claims the Clinton Administration," *Chicago Tribune*, February 18, 2000, http://articles.chicagotribune.com/2000-02-18/news/000219 0006_1_y2k-john-koskinen-press-secretary-joe-lockhart.

36. Peggy Noonan, "America's Power Is Under Threat," *Wall Street Journal*, February 6, 2014, http://online.wsj.com/news/articles/SB100014240527023046809045793654124 79185116, accessed April 11, 2014.

37. Joseph Kramek, "The Critical Infrastructure Gap: U.S. Port Facilities and Cyber Vulnerabilities." Brookings Institution, July 3, 2013. www.brookings.edu/research/papers/2013/07/03-cyber-ports-security-kramek, accessed April 11, 2014.

38. John Steele Gordon, "The Little Miracle Spurring Inequality," *Wall Street Journal*, June 3, 2014, A13.

39. "Electromagnetic pulse in fiction and popular culture," Wikipedia, http://en.wikipedia.org/wiki/Electromagnetic_pulse_in_fiction_and_popular_culture, accessed April 9, 2014.

40. Rebecca Smith, "Nation's Power Grid Vulnerable to Sabotage," *Wall Street Journal*, March 12, 2014, A1.

41. L. Gordon Crovitz, "The Power Grid: Our Achilles' Hill," *Wall Street Journal*, February 10, 2014, A11.

42. Ellen Nakashima and Andrea Peterson, "Report: Cybercrime and Espionage Costs $445 Billion Annually," *Washington Post*, June 9, 2014, www.washingtonpost.com/world/national-security/report-cybercrime-and-espionage-costs-445-billion-annually/2014/06/08/8995291c-ecce-11e3-9f5c-9075d5508f0a_story.html, accessed July 9, 2014.

43. Tal Kopan, "Cybercrime Costs $575 Billion a Year, $100 Billion to US," *Politico*, June 9, 2014, www.politico.com/story/2014/06/cybercrime-yearly-costs-107601.html, accessed June 11, 2014.

44. Peter Baker, *Days of Fire: Bush and Cheney in the White House* (New York: Doubleday, 2013), 619.

45. "The Attack against Israel You Haven't Heard About," IDF Blog, August 22, 2014, www.idfblog.com/blog/2014/08/22/attack-israel-havent-heard, accessed October 24, 2014.

46. Peter Suciu, "Why Israel Dominates in Cyber Security," *Fortune*, September 1, 2015, http://fortune.com/2015/09/01/why-israel-dominates-in-cyber-security, accessed October 14, 2015.

47. Robert Gates, *Duty: Memoirs of a Secretary at War* (New York: Knopf, 2014), 449–51.

48. Ibid., 450–51.

49. Jerry Brito and Tate Watkins, "Loving the Cyber Bomb? The Dangers of Threat Inflation in Cybersecurity Policy," Mercatus Institute Working Papers, April 26, 2011.

50. Danny Vinik, "America's Secret Arsenal." *Politico*, December 9, 2015, www.politico.com/agenda/story/2015/12/defense-department-cyber-offense-strategy-000331#ixzz3z2mq2LrM, accessed February 2, 2016.

51. Brandon Valeriano and Ryan Maness, "The Fog of Cyberwar: Why the Threat Doesn't Live Up to the Hype," *Foreign Affairs*, November 21, 2012, www.foreignaffairs.com/articles/138443/brandon-valeriano-and-ryan-maness/the-fog-of-cyberwar, accessed April 24, 2014.

52. "War in the Fifth Domain," *Economist*, July 1, 2010, www.economist.com/node/16478792, accessed April 24, 2014.

53. David Perera, "U.S. Grid Safe from Large-Scale Attack, Experts Say," *Politico*, September 10, 2014, www.politico.com/story/2014/09/power-grid-safety-110815.html#ixzz3Da3nLnHz, accessed September 17, 2014.

54. James Andrew Lewis, "Low-Level Cyberattacks Are Common but Truly Damaging Ones Are Rare," *Washington Post*, October 10, 2013, www.washingtonpost.com/post live/truly-damaging-cyberattacks-are-rare/2013/10/09/ae628656-2d00-11e3-b139 -029811dbb57f_story.html, accessed April 24, 2014.

55. Valeriano and Maness, "The Fog of Cyberwar."

56. Lewis, "Low-Level Cyberattacks Are Common but Truly Damaging Ones Are Rare."

57. Gates, *Duty*, 144.

58. Perera, "U.S. Grid Safe from Large-Scale Attack."

CHAPTER NINE: CIVIL UNREST

1. Daniel Patrick Moynihan, *The Politics of a Guaranteed Income: The Nixon Administration and the Family Assistance Plan* (New York: Random House, 1973), 488.

2. Clay Risen, *A Nation on Fire: America in the Wake of the King Assassination* (Hoboken: John Wiley & Sons, 2009), 6.

3. Abigail Thernstrom and Stephan Thernstrom, *America in Black and White: One Nation, Indivisible* (New York: Touchstone, 1997), 159.

4. Fred Siegel, *The Revolt Against the Masses: How Liberalism Has Undermined the Middle Class* (New York: Encounter, 2013), 135.

5. Joseph A. Califano, *The Triumph and Tragedy of Lyndon Johnson: The White House Years* (New York: Simon & Schuster, 1991), 59–64.

6. Ethan Rarick, *California Rising: The Life and Times of Pat Brown* (Berkeley: University of California Press, 2005), 314, 325, 335.

7. Califano, *The Triumph and Tragedy of Lyndon Johnson*, 59–64.

8. Over the course of six pages, Califano notes his inability to reach Johnson six separate times: "He didn't return my calls"; "Johnson continued to refuse to take my calls"; "Still unable to get the President on the phone"; "I called the ranch again, but did not reach the President"; "I repeated, not wanting to reveal that I couldn't get the President to take a phone call"; "the President called me from the ranch as soon as he'd read the note. It was 9:09 P.M. Eastern time, my first conversation with him since the disturbance had begun three nights earlier."

9. Califano, *The Triumph and Tragedy of Lyndon Johnson*, 64.

10. Nick Kotz, *Judgment Days: Lyndon Baines Johnson, Martin Luther King Jr., and the Laws That Changed America* (Boston: Houghton Mifflin, 2005), 340–41.

11. Califano, *The Triumph and Tragedy of Lyndon Johnson*, 63–64.

12. Kotz, *Judgment Days*, 340–41.

13. Recording, "President Johnson and Martin Luther King Jr. on the Watts Riots," Miller Center, 2013, http://millercenter.org/presidentialclassroom/exhibits/president -johnson-and-martin-luther-king-jr-on-the-watts-riots, accessed June 19, 2014.

14. Risen, *A Nation on Fire*, 13.

15. Recording, "President Johnson and Martin Luther King Jr. on the Watts Riots."

16. Robert Dallek, *Flawed Giant: Lyndon Johnson and His Times, 1961–1973* (New York: Oxford University Press, 1998), 224.

17. Ibid.

18. Risen, *A Nation on Fire*, 32–34.

19. Ibid., 69–70.

20. Ibid., 165.

21. Karen Tumulty, "On D.C. Home Rule, LBJ Didn't Make It All the Way," *Washington Post*, May 21, 2014, www.washingtonpost.com/local/dc-politics/2014/ 05/21/0e93e430-e0ec-11e3-9743-bb9b59cde7b9_story.html, accessed July 1, 2014; Lyndon B. Johnson, "Remarks at the Signing of the Public Works and Economic Development Act," August 26, 1965, The American Presidency Project, UCSB, www .presidency.ucsb.edu/ws/?pid=27188, accessed July 1, 2014.

22. Johnson is supposed to have said either that "Ford is so dumb that he cannot walk and chew gum at the same time," or that "Ford is so dumb that he cannot fart and chew gum at the same time." The latter, more earthier, quote is the more likely one, but the "walk" comment became better known.

23. *Violence in the City—An End or a Beginning?* Report by the Governor's Commission on the Los Angeles Riots, 1965, www.usc.edu/libraries/archives/cityinstress/mccone/ part1.html, accessed June 20, 2014.

24. Michael W. Flamm, *Law and Order: Street Crime, Civil Unrest, and the Crisis of Liberalism in the 1960s* (New York: Columbia University Press, 2005), 110.

25. Ben J. Wattenberg, *The First Universal Nation: Leading Indicators and Ideas About the Surge of America in the 1990s* (New York: Free Press, 1991), 61–63.

26. David C. Carter, *The Music Has Gone Out of the Movement: Civil Rights and the Johnson Administration, 1965–1968* (Chapel Hill: University of North Carolina Press, 2009), 229–30.

27. Clay Risen, "The Unmaking of the President," *Smithsonian*, April 2008, www.smith sonianmag.com/history-archaeology/president-lbj.html#ixzz2nHRrjlqu, accessed June 23, 2014.

28. Ibid.

29. Ben A. Franklin, "Army Troops in Capital as Negroes Riot," *New York Times*, April 6, 1968, http://partners.nytimes.com/library/national/race/040668race-ra.html, accessed June 23, 2014.

30. Michael Yockel, "100 Years: The Riots of 1968," *Baltimore Magazine*, May 2007, www.baltimoremagazine.net/2007/5/100-years-the-riots-of-1968, accessed June 23, 2014.

31. Johnson photo, from the LBJ library, appears at the top of the sixth page of the photo inserts in Risen, *A Nation on Fire*.

32. Ibid., 122–23.

33. Califano, *The Triumph and Tragedy of Lyndon Johnson*, 279.

34. CNN Library, "Los Angeles Riots Fast Facts," CNN, May 3, 2014, www.cnn.com/ 2013/09/18/us/los-angeles-riots-fast-facts, accessed June 25, 2014.

35. Jim Kuhnhenn, "Obama: Time to Review Local Police Militarization," ABC News, August 18, 2014, http://abcnews.go.com/Politics/wireStory/obama-back-washington -rare-vacation-break-25017934?singlePage=true, accessed August 25, 2014.

36. Nick Hanauer, "The Pitchforks Are Coming . . . For Us Plutocrats," *Politico Magazine*, July/August, 2014, www.politico.com/magazine/story/2014/06/the-pitch forks-are-coming-for-us-plutocrats-108014_full.html#.U7G9h5RdUhY, accessed June 30, 2014.

37. Aaron C. Davis, "Kevin McCarthy's Fast Rise in Politics Fueled by People Skills He Honed as Calif. Lawmaker," *Washington Post*, June 21, 2014, www.washingtonpost .com/politics/kevin-mccarthys-fast-rise-in-politics-fueled-by-people-skills-he-honed -as-calif-lawmaker/2014/06/21/7085d700-f8c7-11e3-a606-946fd632f9f1_story.html, accessed June 27, 2014.

38. Forrest McDonald, "Foreword" to *Addison's Cato: A Tragedy and Selected Essays*, by Joseph Addison (Indianapolis: Liberty Fund, 2004).

39. Vincent J. Cannato, *The Ungovernable City: John Lindsay and His Struggle to Save New York* (New York: Basic Books, 2001), 210–12.

40. "RetroIndy: Bobby Kennedy on the Day Martin Luther King Died," *Indianapolis Star*, January 9, 2013, http://archive.indystar.com/article/99999999/NEWS06/80822071/ RetroIndy-Bobby-Kennedy-day-Martin-Luther-King-died, accessed June 25, 2014.

Chapter Ten: How to Prepare for Acts of Man

1. Adam Kredo, "Watchdog Group Says Federal Government Has Offered Little Guidance to Major Cities," *Washington Free Beacon*, October 1, 2013, http://free beacon.com/u-s-cities-unprepared-to-deal-with-large-scale-nuclear-radiological-attack.

2. Edward H. Kaplan, "How Dangerous Is America?" *Boston Globe*, July 28, 2013, www .bostonglobe.com/magazine/2013/07/27/how-dangerous-america/TrzB0skxcs JH8yjAlslZCL/story.html.

3. "Candidate Briefing: Terrorism," The Heritage Foundation, www.candidatebriefing .com/terrorism.

4. Ibid.

5. Kaplan, "How Dangerous Is America?"

6. "CDC's Division of Strategic National Stockpile Emergency MedKit Evaluation Study Summary: Background, Key Results, and Next Steps," Centers for Disease Control and Prevention, www.bt.cdc.gov/agent/anthrax/prep/pdf/medkit-evaluation -summary-2007.pdf, accessed July 18, 2013.

7. There are a number of websites that provide this kind of advice. See, for example, "Advice for Safeguarding Buildings Against Chemical or Biological Attack," http:// securebuildings.lbl.gov/secure.html, accessed March 31, 2014.

8. "Emergency Preparedness and You," Centers for Disease Control and Prevention, www.bt.cdc.gov/bioterrorism/overview.asp, accessed March 31, 2014.

9. "Blackouts," www.ready.gov/blackouts, accessed April 30, 2014.

10. David Shenk, "How to Survive an EMP or Superworm Attack," *Slate*, September 8, 2006, www.slate.com/articles/news_and_politics/the_survivalist/features/2006/the_survivalist/how_to_survive_an_emp_or_superworm_attack.html, accessed April 30, 2014.

11. For many of the tips in this section and more, see "How to Survive a Riot: Additional Precautions for High-Risk Areas," www.wikihow.com/Survive-a-Riot, accessed July 1, 2014.

12. The one exception to this rule is James Coburn's character Britt in the 1960 film *The Magnificent Seven*. Bet on him with a knife in a gunfight every time. See www .youtube.com/watch?v=KctqZVYgmO4.

CONCLUSION

1. "A Brief History of the Cinematic Apocalypse," *Entertainment Weekly*, June 27, 2014, www.ew.com/article/2014/06/27/brief-history-cinematic-apocalypse, accessed July 17, 2014.

2. Kevin D. Williamson, *The End Is Near and It's Going to Be Awesome: How Going Broke Will Leave America Richer, Happier, and More Secure* (New York: Broadside Books, 2013).

3. Joshua Cooper Ramo, *The Age of the Unthinkable: Why the New World Disorder Constantly Surprises Us and What We Can Do About It* (New York: Little Brown, 2009), 198.

4. John Stuart Mill, *Principles of Political Economy with Some of Their Applications to Social Philosophy* (London: Longmans, Green and Co., 1848), Book 1, Chapter 5, Paragraph I.5.19.

5. Jonah Goldberg, "A Return to Hidden Law," "The Goldberg File," *National Review Online*, February 28, 2014.

Index

bird-borne viruses, 10
Black, Conrad, 70
blackouts, 135–37, 180–81. *See also* power
  grid, loss of
Blanco, Kathleen, 58
Boehner, John, 63
Boko Haram, 106
border security, xv
Borg, Scott, 150–51
Boston Marathon bombings, 175–76
botulism, 12, 115
Bowman, Jerry, 81
Brands, H.W., 7
Brennan, John, 100–101
Brito, Jerry, 149
Brown, Jerry, 39–40, 158, 161
Brown, Joe, 136–37
Brown, Mike, 170
Brown, Pat, 156–57
bubonic plague, 121
budget, government, 51–62
Buffett, Warren, 91
Burke, Edmund, xvi, 119
Burke, James, 118
Bush, George H.W., 117
  and Hurricane Andrew, 55–56
  and Hurricane Charley, 56–57
  and LA riots, 165
Bush, George W.
  and bioterrorism, 122, 125
  and disaster management, 56–57, 59–60
  and financial crisis of 2007-2008, xii,
    70–71
  and flu pandemics, 10–11
  and Homeland Security Act, 125
  and Hurricane Katrina, xii, 57–58, 169,
    170, 188
  and national security state, 167
  and 9/11 attacks, xi, 95–98, 109
  and terrorism, 100, 108–9
Byrne, Jane, 116

Califano, Joseph, 156–57, 158, 159, 161,
  164, 169
California drought, 39–42
Camille, Hurricane, 46, 52–53

Cannato, Vincent, 168
Carafano, James, 105
Card, Andrew, 26, 57, 95
Carmichael, Stokely, 164
Carnage and Culture (Hanson), 90
Carter, Jimmy, 136–38, 144
cash reserves, 90
CDC (Centers for Disease Control and
    Prevention), 13
  and bioterrorism, 122, 123
  and Elk River chemical spill, 31
  and National Pharmaceutical Stockpile,
    125
CDC.gov, 81
Champion, Hale, 156
Chan, Margaret, 18
Charley, Hurricane, 56–57
chemical leak, 29–31
Chertoff, Michael, 26
Chicago, 162
China, 17–19, 24, 148–49, 166
Chinese People's Liberation Army, 148–49
Christie, Chris, 63
Christopher, Warren, 161, 163, 170–71
CIA, 102
citizens, American
  expectations regarding disaster
    mitigation, 63
  judging mood of, 187
  support of anti-terror efforts, 107–8
  trust in government, 6, 11, 14, 23–24
civil liberties, 148, 167
Civil Rights Act of 1964, 53–54
civil rights movement, 158
civil unrest, 135–36, 155–71
  defusing, 164–71
  and Obama, xii
  and poverty, 76–77
  self-protection, 181–86
Clark, Guy, 53–54
Clark, Ramsay, 161
Clarke, Lee, 87
Cleveland, Grover, 48–49, 51
Cleveland, OH, 159
climate catastrophes, xiii
climate change, 39, 46